Previous works

Clive Caldwell Air Ace

'Thoroughly researched, well written and insightful account that will stand the test of time as the definitive Caldwell biography' *Wartime*

'Comprehensive biography written by an expert researcher' *Aircrew Book Review*

'When [Clive Caldwell] died in Sydney in August 1994, the tributes poured in, but only now do we have one worthy of the man' *The Australian*

Jack Davenport Beaufighter Leader

'Blending sound research and enlightening anecdotes, the author explores the personal qualities that underpinned Davenport's leadership' *Chief of Air Force's 2010 Reading List*

'[Kristen Alexander] writes with empathy and understanding, in crisp prose, building a sense of awe for her subject. She also has real understanding for the technical details ... A considerable achievement' *The Canberra Times*

'A fascinating story ... A terrific read' *Launceston Examiner*

Australian Eagles: Australians in the Battle of Britain

'Moving tribute ... Alexander has ... brought out the human tragedy of a wasted youth ... not only well written and a great read, it is a must' *Australian Defence Force Journal*

'To the boyish faces staring out from the photographs upon the page, Kristen's words have breathed new life' *Flightpath*

'Kristen Alexander's research, her understanding and presentation of the strategic issues embedded in the battle [of Britain] and the sensitivity in presenting the personal stories of the pilots make the book an engrossing and ... very easy read. It has left a lasting impression on me' *Journal of the Royal Australian Historical Society*

Australia's Few and the Battle of Britain

'full of genuine empathy ... a truly excellent read ... masterful ... a fascinating and worthy account' Andy Saunders, *Britain at War Magazine*

'Outstanding book' *1940: The Magazine of the Friends of the Few*

'The author has an exceptional ability to set specific material, such as quotations from original documents, into a broader familial, social and political context, and in this way inform the reader at several levels at once ... incomparable writing style' *2015 ACT Writing and Publishing Awards (non-fiction, Winner)*

Taking Flight: Lores Bonney's Extraordinary Flying Career

'Vividly-written biography ... A valuable contribution to aviation history' *2017 ACT Writing and Publishing Awards (non-fiction, Highly Commended)*

'An excellent and well-rounded biography of one of Australia's important early aviators' *The Aviation Historian*

'An insightful and revealing book' *Aircrew Book Review*

Kristen Alexander has been writing about Australian aviators since 2002. Published in Australia, the United Kingdom, and Japan, her works include *Clive Caldwell Air Ace*, *Jack Davenport Beaufighter Leader*, and *Australia's Few and the Battle of Britain*. Two of her books have been included on the Chief of Air Force's reading list. She is the 2021 winner of the Australian War Memorial's Bryan Gandevia Prize for Australian military–medical history. Her sixth book, *Kriegies: The Australian Airmen of Stalag Luft III*, is based on that award-winning PhD thesis.

http://www.kristenalexander.com.au
https://www.facebook.com/KristenAlexanderAuthor
Twitter: Kristen Alexander @kristenauthor

KRIEGIES

The Australian Airmen of Stalag Luft III

KRISTEN ALEXANDER

Kriegies
The Australian Airmen of Stalag Luft III
Kristen Alexander

First published 2023
Copyright Kristen Alexander 2023

Published by
Ad Astra Press
PO Box 746
Mawson ACT 2607

ISBN: 978-0-6457925-0-8 (hard cover)
ISBN: 978-0-6457925-1-5 (paper back)
ISBN: 978-0-6457925-2-2 (ebook)

A catalogue record for this book is available from the National Library of Australia

Book design, including map and cover, by Diane Bricknell, Diartist Graphic Design

This book is copyright. Apart from any fair dealing for the purpose of private study, research, criticism or review, as permitted under the Copyright Act, no part of this book may be reproduced by any process without written permission. Inquiries should be addressed to the publisher. alexfax@alexanderfaxbooks.com.au.

Cover image: 'Everlasting Vigil – The Goon in His Box'. Watercolour, Tim Mayo 1944. Courtesy of Peter Mayo.

Rear cover image: Australians in North Compound, Stalag Luft III, 25 April 1943 (Anzac Day). Courtesy of Ian Fraser.

All reasonable efforts were taken to obtain permission to use copyright material reproduced in this book.

Professor Peter Stanley, FAHA

Kriegies is a rich and powerful work of historical research. This insightful book takes us behind the barbed wire, physically but also emotionally, going beyond wartime bravado to reveal the profound effects of captivity on individual airmen and their families.

Dr Karl James FRHistS, Head, Military History Section, Australian War Memorial

An impressive piece of work. Meticulously researched, Kristen Alexander skilfully blends the experiences of Australian airmen held as prisoners of the Germans with those they left behind in Australia. These are powerful personal stories of shame, fear, boredom, humour, defiance, love and loss. This is the most significant work published on the RAAF in the Second World War in some time.

Dr Kate Ariotti, author, *Captive Anzacs* and winner, 2015 CEW Bean Prize for Military History

Kriegies is a fascinating take on the lives of Australia's POW airmen of the Second World War that is not afraid to tackle sensitive topics like selfishness, suicide, and sex. Alexander's meticulous research and engaging prose combine to offer a profound new contribution to our understanding of wartime captivity. *Kriegies* is a must-read.

Peter Rees, author, *Lancaster Men*

Kristen Alexander reveals the existential challenges 351 Australian POWs faced at Stalag Luft III in their battle to survive the brutal Nazi war machine. *Kriegies* is insightful, compelling and sensitive; a very human story of war.

Andy Saunders, aviation historian and author

This is the most powerful read I have ever encountered on the Kriegie experience of the Second World War. At times almost shockingly visceral, *Kriegies* is an emotional and thought provokingly honest account of what it meant to be a POW in German hands. Another truly masterful offering from Kristen Alexander.

For David

CONTENTS

Foreword XIII
Author's Word XV
Introduction 1

Part One: In the Bag
Chapter One: Capture 8
Chapter Two: Interrogation 15

Part Two: Kriegie Life
Chapter Three: Kriegies 23
Chapter Four: Brotherhood 33
Chapter Five: Kriegie Ingenuity 43

Part Three: Bridging the Divide
Chapter Six: Not Forgotten 51
Chapter Seven: Romantic Lives 62
Chapter Eight: Sex 75

Part Four: Escape
Chapter Nine: Duty to Escape 86
Chapter Ten: The Escape Myth 96
Chapter Eleven: The Great Escape 102
Chapter Twelve: Murder Squads 111
Chapter Thirteen: Deep Personal Loss 121
Chapter Fourteen: Bereavement 130
Chapter Fifteen: Retribution 143

Part Five: The Strains of Captivity
Chapter Sixteen: Faith 148
Chapter Seventeen: Round the Bend 156
Chapter Eighteen: Keeping Mentally Strong 164
Chapter Nineteen: Barbed-wire Suicide 175

Part Six: War's End
Chapter Twenty: Forced Marches 181
Chapter Twenty-one: Homecoming 189
Afterword 197
Acknowledgements 199
Bibliography 203
Index 214

FOREWORD

Military service and aviation are deeply embedded in my cultural and genetic DNA. My paternal grandfather served as an aircraft technician in the Second World War, and my father also did a short stint in the Royal Australian Air Force. Steeped in their pride of service, I devoured military-themed comics as a child, but it was Biggles who really caught my imagination. As I got older, I moved on from fiction to the stories of the aviation pioneers such as the Wright Brothers, Charles Lindbergh, Amelia Earhart, Amy Johnson, and the Australian icons – Ross and Keith Smith, Charles Kingsford Smith, Bert Hinkler, Nancy Bird Walton, and Lawrence Wackett. I joined the RAAF straight from high school. One of my brothers, a sister, and my wife have also served. As a family, we understand the high calling of military duty and service. Like the Australian airmen of Stalag Luft III, I am a proud member of the Air Force family. I cannot imagine myself ever pursuing a different career or enjoying it even half as much. That belonging, the sense of camaraderie based on duty and an affinity with the air, means much to me. As it did to them.

Like many, I have watched the classic POW films such as *Colditz* and *The Bridge on the River Kwai* many times – *The Great Escape* is one of my favourites! Whether the protagonists were prisoners of the Germans or the Japanese, the key message for me as a teenager was that though captivity was hard, it could be survived with the help of collective innovation, ingenuity, and mateship. *The Great Escape*, especially, showed that military men, although captured, could still participate in the war effort by escaping and tying up enemy resources. The war wasn't over for them.

Those films – and the books on which they are based – have been viewed and read by millions. But they cover little of the Australian experience of captivity. Three hundred and fifty-one Australian officers and non-commissioned officers were imprisoned in Stalag Luft III at various times, but we know little of their lives or how they coped with wartime imprisonment. In many ways they – and other aviator prisoners of war – are forgotten members of the RAAF. How the Australian airmen of Stalag Luft III maintained their Air Force identities and commitment to duty during captivity has been an untold story. Until now.

Two of Kristen Alexander's previous books have featured in The Chief of Air Force's reading lists. *Kriegies: The Australian Airmen of Stalag Luft III* is another fine work. In it, Kristen draws extensively on private, official, and medical records to portray how our airmen responded to incarceration. Kristen presents their very personal journeys in their own words, highlighting how their fraternity and inherent resilience helped them bear their internment. Families then – as now – were also important members of the Air Force community. Kristen describes their reaction to long term separation and their efforts to ensure that their men were supported and remembered.

This unapologetically raw account sensitively and empathetically addresses difficult subjects such as selfishness, sex, homosexuality, depression, anxiety, and suicide. The darker side of life in Stalag Luft III is countered by stories of altruism, fraternity, great humour, and resilience. As well as depicting the full experience of captivity and its effects in one of Germany's most notorious POW camps, Kristen reveals the tragic story of the five Australian 'Great Escapers' who, in a heart-breaking and disgraceful breach of the Geneva Convention, were shot by the Germans.

The Australian airmen of Stalag Luft III are not forgotten. Kristen Alexander provides a new perspective of their captivity which showcases the human element of RAAF experience in a challenging environment. She demonstrates that the Australians did not succumb to the trials of captivity. They continued to uphold their Air Force duty. They were determined to resist the Germans and, in whatever way they could, wage war from behind the barbed wire. *Kriegies: The Australian Airmen of Stalag Luft III* is a powerful book. It is a significant work of aviation history. I commend it to all readers as a worthy contribution to Air Force's story.

Robert Lawson OAM
Air Commodore
Director-General of History and Heritage – Air Force
May 2023

AUTHOR'S WORD

I've lived with Australian pilots for two decades. I flew across continents with a 1930's aviatrix, through the Battle of Britain, the Western Desert, Darwin's skies, the Southwest Pacific Area, and the fjords of Norway. Those men and women were imbued with the sheer joy of flying. Their adventures fuelled my imagination, dreams, and writing.

When researching my biography of Jack Davenport, I came across the story of James Catanach – Jimmy to his friends. His Hampden was shot down en route to Russia in 1942. Jack then stepped into Jimmy's shoes as a flight commander. He proved himself and enjoyed a sterling aviation career and post-war business success. But what happened to 20-year-old Jimmy? He eventually found his way to Stalag Luft III and death as one of the recaptured participants in the Great Escape. I started a small collection of clippings relating to Jimmy and frequently 'talked' (via email) about him with Alan Righetti, a former pilot with 3 Squadron RAAF. Downed in the Middle East, and a one-time prisoner of the Italians, Alan was cattle-trucked to Stalag Luft III by the Germans after Italy surrendered. Our conversations prompted me to wonder how airmen coped if they could not fly – if they had been grounded not through illness, death, or choice, but because of captivity. Later, I met Alec Arnel, a former fighter pilot of 451 Squadron RAAF who had also been confined in Stalag Luft III. He told me precisely what it felt like to be knocked out of the air and taken into captivity.

Stalag Luft III was an interesting camp. Located in the German province of Lower Silesia, Australian airmen had been imprisoned in the *Luftwaffe* facility at all times after it opened in April 1942 until January 1945 when it was evacuated ahead of the Red Army's advance from the east. Approximately a quarter of all Australian airmen prisoners of war (POWs) in Europe were incarcerated there at some point. But what makes Stalag Luft III most interesting – and infamous – is, of course, the Great Escape. Incidentally, the 'Great Escape' is an anachronistic, yet convenient term. It was coined in the early 1950s by the publishers of Paul Brickhill, the Australian journalist and former Stalag Luft III POW, who penned *The Great Escape* and has been universally adopted to describe the camp's March 1944 mass escape.

Who hasn't read Brickhill's book? Who hasn't seen the 1963 film? Who can forget Steve McQueen and his (historically inaccurate) motorbike and the film's iconic theme music? Who hasn't shed tears as brave men fell to German bullets?

The book is still in print, and the film, released in the year of my birth, has had almost annual cinema or television reruns ever since; it is also available on DVD and streaming services. It is a great film – I still weep whenever I watch it – but, coming from Hollywood, it presents a more American perspective; it focuses on the adventure underpinning the enterprise. Stalag Luft III was 'home' to many nationalities but, other than James Coburn's portrayal of the fictional Louis Sedgwick (complete with an appalling Australian accent), Australians are virtually absent from our cultural memory of Stalag Luft III and the Great Escape. I was surprised to discover that Jimmy Catanach was not the only Australian killed in the post-escape reprisals. Albert Hake, Reginald Kierath, Thomas Leigh, and John Williams were also murdered on Hitler's order. West Australian Paul Royle, too, escaped from behind barbed wire. He was captured but survived. I wanted to know more about these men.

In mid-2013, I started delving head-long into the history of the Great Escape, concentrating on the Australian perspective. But fascinating evidence from family archives not connected to the Escape also came my way. The more I researched, the more I realised the Great Escape was not representative of Stalag Luft III's captivity experience. Rather than focusing just on the mass exit of March 1944, I decided to explore the broader Australian experience in Stalag Luft III. After all, that was as little acknowledged as Australian participation in the Great Escape. But I wanted to do more than just describe what POWs did in captivity: the sports they played; the theatrical productions they mounted; the escape tunnels they dug. I wanted to know what they felt about being POWs. I wanted to understand how incarceration affected them and their loved ones; why they dubbed themselves kriegies, derived from the first syllable of *Kriegsgefangener* – war prisoner. I wanted to tell the story of what captivity meant. That, however, was easier said than done. I simply did not have the skills to do it. I was in despair.

I attended a friend's book launch in October 2014. So too, did historian Michael McKernan. After the usual pleasantries, he asked how the book was going. I'd known Michael for many years so blurted to him that I had stalled, and explained why. 'Have you ever considered doing a PhD?', he asked. I had not. But by the time I'd walked back to the bus stop after the function, I had. Before the day was out, I had contacted Peter Stanley for advice. Recently installed as a professor at UNSW Canberra, he encouraged me to embark on a PhD program. Six months later, with Peter as my principal supervisor and Michael my co-supervisor, I began my candidature at UNSW Canberra. I submitted my thesis in June 2020 and, in March 2022, the Australian War Memorial awarded it the 2021 Bryan Gandevia Prize for Australian military–medical history. At the risk of sounding immodest, I can't resist sharing some of the panel's comments: 'Rated outstanding by examiners, this work demonstrates a masterful command of the Australian and international literature related to captivity and prisoners of war. Richly researched and well written, its descriptions of life in captivity and its impact is wide-ranging and comprehensive'.

Intellectual detour out of the way, with a new set of skills, a lot more knowledge, and a deep appreciation of what it meant to be a prisoner of war, it was time to write a book. And ten years after my first forays into life in Stalag Luft III, here it is: *Kriegies: The Australian Airmen of Stalag Luft III*.

*****

The research I conducted during my PhD candidature underpins *Kriegies*. Readers will notice that some names are in italics. *Kriegies* draws on the confidential medical records held by the Department of Veterans' Affairs that I consulted as part of that research. One of DVA's access conditions is that I do not identify individuals. As such, other than where I have obtained family permission or if documents are publicly available, I have used pseudonyms in italics (for example *Simon McGrath*). Scholars and other interested readers can follow the academic thread through footnotes and bibliography, or, particularly if they want to know more about my methodology, can go straight to the thesis: it is unembargoed and 'out there'. I have listed books, chapters, articles, and web-based references by author's surname and short title only in the footnotes. Full details, including explanations of sources/archives, are included in the bibliography.

Three hundred and fifty-one Australian airmen were interned in Stalag Luft III at various times. I could not hope to acquire documents or oral history accounts relating to all of them. Many did not record their stories: they left a silence in their life history which still deeply unsettles family members. Those men and women who did speak or write of their experiences, however, shed light on the collective experience of captivity in Stalag Luft III. They speak for themselves, *and* their fellows. *Kriegies*, then, is written for those who want to gain an insight into captivity, either from curiosity or because they need to gain a sense of what 'their' prisoner of war went through.

Kriegies is not a history of Stalag Luft III. Rather, it explores how that camp's Australian airmen and their family members responded to captivity. This book delves into the kriegies' emotional worlds as it describes how they coped with the trials of wartime incarceration, ameliorated and mitigated the monotony, separation from loved ones, absence of sex, threats to communal living including self-interest and homosexuality, and assaults on their mental health.

Kriegies also considers those on the home front who provided love and support to their captured menfolk, and particularly highlights the reactions to captivity of mothers, wives, fiancées, and girlfriends. It features the events of the Great Escape, the tragic fate of five young Australians, and the grief expressed by their comrades and families.

Inner lives of airmen and their loved ones are at the heart of this book: their emotions and motivations. So too is agency – the ability to act, make choices, and even exert power (or a semblance of power) in seemingly powerless situations. Altruism, duty, community, loving relationships, faith, death, and resilience are also examined. *Kriegies* reveals the human story of captivity. It makes clear that there was more to life in Stalag Luft III than the Great Escape.

INTRODUCTION

'We were going down fast.' *Simon McGrath* could see 'the flames coming back'. He felt 'the heat searing'. The 'slip-stream, being so strong, was frightening'. The gunner threw himself backwards to get out of the 'burning hulk'. 'Caught up by my right leg … I clawed at the sides of the turret.' *McGrath* was trapped.¹ Fighter pilot Alexander 'Alec' Arnel, felt 'stark staring fear' at the 'smoke and the fire' when his Spitfire was hit by flak and its engine seized.²

Captivity, for airmen, occurred after a traumatic event. Fighter pilots had been engaged in battle, other airmen were attacked before, during or after bombing sorties. Like *McGrath* and Arnel, they baled out of burning, plummeting aircraft, landing in water or on ground; they crawled from crashed wrecks. Often wounded, and despite their terror, some men retained a sense of the ridiculous. More than half a century after baling out, gunner Hector 'Hec' Henry could still hear one of his crew members shouting to him, '"The Fockers are shooting at us." And he was not yelling about German Aircraft.'³ Others faced their mortality. *McGrath* thought he would die. So too, did Arnel, who was engulfed by the 'horror of ending it' by incineration.⁴ They, and 'pretty well every one of these boys have looked death in the face', recalled Henry 'Harry' Train.⁵ Having survived battle, the airmen faced an uncertain future. Even so, as they later perceived it, they were fortunate. 'I think you will admit that I am amazingly lucky to be alive', a seriously wounded Charles Lark – the sole survivor of his crew – wrote within weeks of losing his liberty. 'I myself often wonder why I am not dead.'⁶

German and Italian forces captured about 13,000 British and Commonwealth airmen, including 1,476 Australians serving in both Royal Air Force (RAF) and Royal Australian Air Force (RAAF) squadrons.⁷ Of those, 351 Australians were confined in Stalag Luft III between its opening in April 1942 and evacuation in January 1945.⁸ The earliest were held in *Wehrmacht* (German army) camps until

---

1   DVA NMX280688-01: personal statement, [undated, received 6 August 1993].
2   AR: Arnel, interview, 29 October 2015.
3   Henry FA Henry, 'BEING SHOT DOWN OVER GERMANY', September 1996.
4   AR: Arnel, interview, 29 October 2015.
5   Arnel archive: Train, 'A Barbed-Wire World', 15 May 1942, 8.
6   Lark FA: Charles Lark to Dear Folks, 22 August 1942.
7   Gilbert, POW, 28; Beaumont et al., *The Australian Centenary History of Defence Volume VI*, 338.
8   Alexander, 'Emotions of Captivity: Australian Airmen Prisoners of Stalag Luft III and their Families', nominal roll, 599–601.

the *Luftwaffe* (German air force) established its own. Many experienced brutal treatment at the hands of the Gestapo in France's Fresnes prison including the nine Australian airmen who were later illegally incarcerated in Buchenwald concentration camp.

The Italian system was overwhelmed in 1941 by prisoners from Greece, Crete, and North Africa. Italy did not segregate members of different services so smaller numbers of air force and naval personnel mixed with the tens of thousands of soldiers – including thirty Australian airmen who were later transported to Stalag Luft III. Officers and non-commissioned officers (NCOs) were housed in different compounds or camps. A perception developed that captivity under the Italians was a relatively benign experience.[9] The reality was that some were treated badly.[10] Prisoners were often neglected during lengthy, unpleasant stays in transit camps. Italy's main collection centre at Benghazi, Libya was squalid. The 'existence [there] was unutterably depressing,' recalled John 'Jock' Bryce, who had suffered hunger, septic sores, and dysentery. 'Hundreds of the men were walking skeletons after five months of under-nourishment.'[11] It was perhaps worse at *Prigione di Guerra* – prisoner of war – camp No. 75 (PG 75) at Bari, a transit camp on the Italian mainland, where many were mistreated or endured substandard conditions.

Accommodation improved once the airmen reached Italy's permanent camps. Some existing structures such as the monastery at Padula were commandeered but, more usually, new barbed-wire camps were constructed. Life, however, were still far from comfortable. Horace 'Bill' Fordyce and Kenneth 'Ken' Carson recollected that PG 78, Sulmona was riddled with bed bugs.[12] Rations in some places were little better than in transit camps. Alan Righetti recalled they were 'absolutely basic' at PG 57, Gruppignano, a camp for NCOs. There, supplementation by the Red Cross was essential and a parcel shared between four men was an 'absolute treat.'[13] Fordyce later claimed he would have starved without those sustaining packages.[14] Some prisoners improved their diet through unofficial trading over the fence with civilians. Others cultivated vegetable gardens. Despite predominating memories of poor rations, captivity in Italian camps was not a uniform experience. While Jock Bryce acknowledged that he first felt real hunger at Bari, he enjoyed decent conditions and better food at PG 35, Padula. There, he and his fellows revelled in the monthly tradition

---

9   Spark, 'Australian Prisoners of War of Italy in World War II', in Beaumont et al. (eds), *Beyond Surrender*, 135–152; Gilbert, *POW*, 69; Herington, *Air Power Over Europe, 1944–1945*, 474; Absalom, '"Another crack at Jerry"?', 24–25.
10 Spark, 'Australian Prisoners of War of Italy in World War II', in Beaumont et al. (eds), *Beyond Surrender*, 135.
11 Bryce FA: 'Jock Bryce's POW Diary 1942–1945', 45.
12 AAWFA: Fordyce 0523, 19 June 2003; Carson, 'Brisbane's Ken Carson: Prisoner of the Axis. Part Four', 26.
13 AAWFA: Righetti 0984, 16 September 2003.
14 AAWFA: Fordyce 0523, 19 June 2003.

of RAF dinners. Similar in spirit to dining-in nights in pre-war messes, these were 'splendid affairs' with 'a good deal of wine and enough to eat'.[15] After Italy's armistice with the Allies in September 1943, several hundred POWs made their way to allied lines, neutral Switzerland, or France, or linked up with local resistance forces. The majority, however, were taken into German custody.

The *Luftwaffe* opened its first POW facility in July 1940. Located at Barth in western Pomerania, about 170 kilometres north-west of Berlin, aircrew prisoners who had been housed in army camps joined the recently captured in a purpose-built facility which featured huts surrounded by barbed wire. This provided the architectural template for later *Luftwaffe* camps. Officially, the complex at Barth was referred to as *Kriegsgefangenenslager der Luftwaffe* – the *Luftwaffe*'s prisoner of war camp – but was soon known as Stalag Luft. After more holding facilities were opened, it was designated Stalag Luft I. By mid-1941 it was obvious that the camp would not accommodate all air force prisoners and so the *Luftwaffe* expanded its prison infrastructure. The new camp had to be larger and more secure than Stalag Luft I which had already seen several escape attempts, including by Australians. It would be escape proof.

Located in the province of Lower Silesia, Stalag Luft III opened in April 1942. It was a considerable distance from major population centres as well as neutral or friendly territory; Switzerland was approximately 690 kilometres away in a direct line. Bordered by the Sudeten mountain range, the camp was fringed to the east, south and south-west by a dense coniferous forest, extending 30–48 kilometres towards the Czech border. It was about 200 kilometres south-east of Berlin, about 177 kilometres north-east of Dresden, and less than 2 kilometres from the centre of Sagan, (now Żagań, west Poland). The camp was tantalisingly close (from a prisoner's perspective) to what its first *kommandant*, Friedrich Wilhelm von Lindeiner gennant von Wildau (referred to throughout as von Lindeiner), termed a 'lively railway junction' of six lines connecting the town to most of Germany and Eastern Europe.[16] If any prisoner managed to break out, Sagan's population of 24,000 and the *Wehrmacht* guards of nearby Stalag VIII-C would provide plenty of searchers.

Discipline and security were strict, and compounds were intentionally threatening environments. Each was ringed by two barbed-wire fences, three metres high. Their tops sloped inwards, making climbing out difficult. The two-metre gap between was filled with thick coils of barbed wire about a metre high. The wire was a 'persistent nightmare', John 'Jack' Morschel recalled.[17] Nine

---
15 Bryce FA: 'Jock Bryce's POW Diary 1942–1945', 90.
16 Walton and Eberhardt, *From Commandant to Captive*, 55.
17 Morschel, *A Lancaster's Participation in Normandy Invasion 1944*, 64.

or so metres from the inside fence was a wooden rail which prisoners were forbidden to cross. If they did, they were given two alerts. The guards were ordered to shoot prisoners who did not step back. Those seen outside at night were also fired upon. On each corner of the fence, and every 90 metres around the perimeter, watch towers overlooked the huts. Armed guards surveyed the airmen below. Sentries patrolled the wire and inside compounds, warded the gates, and escorted all vehicles and visitors into camp. Searchlights swept the compounds from nightfall until dawn. *Hündführers* and their Alsatian guard dogs ceaselessly circuited the grounds. Following a successful daylight escape in September 1942, patrols roved outside the fence into the nearby woods.

As signatories to the 1929 Geneva Convention, Germany and Italy were obliged to adhere to humanitarian governance and oversight. Everyday life was made bearable through the Convention's welfare provisions and regular reporting by Red Cross and Protecting Powers representatives; the latter were from neutral countries – originally the United States before it entered the war, and then Switzerland. Along with Red Cross personnel, they regularly inspected POW camps, spoke privately with prisoners, and reported on concerns relating to health, well-being, and the conditions of confinement. Stalag Luft III met the Geneva Convention's basic stipulation that prisoners were to be treated similarly to the detaining power's garrison troops. There were, however, many times when parity of rations was not possible and Red Cross food parcels were vital for sustaining health.[18] Australians were considered British. As such, they, as well as Canadians and other members of Empire, Commonwealth, and Dominion forces, were housed together. As the Convention provided for different treatment of different ranks, two compounds were built, one for officers (East) and the other for NCOs (Centre). After Stalag Luft III's non-commissioned and warrant officers were sent to Stalag Luft VI, Heydekrug in mid-1943, Centre became an American officers' compound.

While the *Luftwaffe* generally treated NCOs and officers similarly, officer camps were more congenial than those for non-commissioned personnel. Accordingly, some airmen lied about their rank, including Albert Hake and Ross Breheny.[19] Officer compounds were serviced by NCO orderlies, usually soldiers – including a few Australians – who performed 'household' duties and personal services, much as batmen did on RAF stations. While Stalag Luft III ostensibly remained an officers-only camp after the NCO exit, orderlies were not the only exceptions to the officer/NCO mix. The camp accommodated more NCOs after

---

18 NAUK AIR 40/269: Stalag Luft III reports and nominal roll.
19 Preen FA: Albert Hake, letter to Noela Hake, 23 November 1942; Harrison RC: Warrant Officer Ross Thomas Breheny, 404957, 145 Squadron RAF, [2008].

the allied invasion of June 1944 when Germany's captivity infrastructure became stretched. In addition, all airmen extracted from Buchenwald concentration camp, regardless of rank, were sent to Stalag Luft III.

By August 1942, Stalag Luft III was full. Some of its prisoners were despatched to army camps until a new compound was built. Over time, more compounds were constructed. The third was referred to as West Compound when it opened on 27 March 1943 but became known as North Compound from September 1943 when South Compound opened. (To avoid confusion, I refer to the third compound throughout as North Compound.) The nearby satellite at Belaria began operating in early 1944 and West Compound followed in July 1944. Australians were held in East, Centre, and North compounds and Belaria.

Dubbed variously huts, blocks, or barracks, the prisoners' single-story wooden quarters were built about 30 centimetres off the ground to enable personnel from the *Abwehr*, the German anti-escape organisation, to crawl underneath searching for tunnel traps, fresh sand, and other signs of digging. Called 'ferrets' by the prisoners, they also raided the huts without warning, and ranged through roof cavities looking for contraband and evidence of escape work. These 'blitz' searches were inconvenient and threatening. 'At any time', recalled Justin O'Byrne, 'dozens of Germans would rush into the barracks with bayonets fixed and kick us out. They would then proceed to upset beds, tear up linings of clothes, rip up floors and walls and pry into every minute corner of our belongings.'[20]

Huts were positioned at least 35 metres from the perimeter. They were, for Jock Bryce, 'drab' and 'in keeping with the general cheerlessness of our surroundings.'[21] Depending on when a man arrived, living quarters were just comfortable or hopelessly beyond capacity. When the camp population increased as the war progressed, some rooms, originally designed to hold six or eight men, held 'ten bods', such as in Paul Royle's and Ken Carson's immediately before the camp's evacuation.[22] When Bruce Lumsden, Cyril 'Cy' Borsht, and Irwin John Dack (known as John) arrived at Belaria in November 1944, they had to share a six metre square room with fifteen others.[23] An official report for North Compound notes that apart from overcrowding, 'living conditions were at all times tolerable.'[24] Most of the Australians who commented on their living arrangements immediately after the war concurred with this assessment.[25] Of course, it all depended on personal definitions of 'tolerable', and many were affected by the lack of privacy.

---

20 O'Byrne FA: O'Byrne, '*Mercury* Radio Roundsman'.
21 Bryce FA: 'Jock Bryce's POW Diary 1942–1945', 147.
22 Royle archive: Royle, wartime log, 'Ten bods', 13; Carson FA: Ken Carson to mother and sister, 10 May 1945 (first letter).
23 Dack, *So you Wanted Wings, Hey!*, 85.
24 NAUK AIR 40/269: Stalag Luft III reports and nominal roll.
25 Or at least considered them 'fair'. AWM 54 779/3/129: 11 PDRC post-liberation debriefs, Melin and Harold Roberts.

In the wake of the Great War, many of the Australian airmen or their families had experienced adversity on the land and during the Depression. One of the legacies of that hardship was a resilience which stood them in good stead during their childhoods, early manhood, air force training, operational careers, and in captivity. 'There was a maturity in that sense; the people did seem to cope with the rough and tumble' of life, Alec Arnel reflected.[26] That ability to adapt to new and threatening situations is central to successfully adjusting to captivity.[27] It enabled the airmen to overcome the shock of capture and to adjust to the challenges they faced as prisoners of war.

Despite a crippled aircraft, Warrant Officer Albert Hake of 72 Squadron RAF continued to fight, managing to strike one of his attackers. His Spitfire was too damaged to cross the Channel homeward so he was forced to bale. His rank insignia were burnt off and he didn't disillusion his captors who assumed he was an officer, and thus entitled to better quarters than non-commissioned officers. Courtesy of the Preen family.

---

26 AR: Arnel, interview 2 March 2017.
27 Ursano and Rundell, 'The Prisoner of War', in Jones et al., *War Psychiatry*, 435.

PART ONE: IN THE BAG

Chapter One:

CAPTURE

'Suddenly hell broke loose.' Charles Lark stood in the middle of the Wellington bomber, tracer streaming all around. Shells exploded. Incendiaries set the fabric on fire. The 24-year-old 'felt myself hit in several places'. He fell to the floor, 'wondering when the bullets would stop ... the plane seemed out of control'. Assisted by a crew member, Lark jumped.[1]

From the moment they baled out of or crawled from burning, crashed or sinking aircraft, many airmen suffered intense shock. Their disorientation was often compounded by physical debility. Lark, who splashed into a Dutch lake, 'felt quite helpless and cold' as he bobbed in the water, growing weaker. The pain was intense, his right arm was numb. The young man was appalled to realise that the thing flopping about on his cheek was his right eye. He made it to shore, then collapsed, exhausted.[2] Pilot John Dack's response to the accumulated shock of flying through flak, holding a burning heavy bomber steady while his crew baled out, searching for his parachute, half drowning before he remembered to inflate his Mae West, spending hours in the water before rescue, followed by being told that his captors had shot his crew, was, 'for some inexplicable reason', to laugh. 'I laughed, and laughed, and laughed myself into hysterical oblivion.'[3]

Despite any personal fear, sense of helplessness, or shock, an airman's first duty was to his fellow crew members. This was particularly the case for captains of bomber aircraft who, like Dack, stayed at the controls until everyone who could had parachuted out; some lost their own lives by doing so. Other crew looked to the safety of their comrades. The able-bodied tried to help the wounded, such as Lark, to abandon out-of-control aircraft, pulled comrades from flames, or hauled them into dinghies. When duty to crew had been satisfied, the airmen fulfilled their obligations to King and service. They destroyed papers, secret devices, and intact aircraft to ensure they did not fall into enemy hands. Sometimes it worked, but, not in Jimmy Catanach's case. Rapidly losing fuel, he took the first opportunity to land rather than risk the engines cutting out. He touched down safely on a strip of heather adjoining a beach near Vardo, in northern Norway. Jimmy, his navigator George 'Bob' Anderson, wireless operator/upper gunner Cecil Cameron, lower rear gunner John Hayes and their passenger John

---

1 Lark FA: Charles Lark to Dear Folks, 25 August 1942.
2 Lark, *A Lark on the Wing*, 62–63.
3 Dack, *So you Wanted Wings, Hey!*, 74–75.

Davidson, a ground crew fitter, attempted to destroy the Hampden, but they were fired on by soldiers from one direction and a patrol boat from the coast. The five were taken prisoner.[4]

Parachutists disposed of silken canopies. The injured hid escape kits. The hale tried to evade so they could return to Britain and active duty. Paul Royle's responsibility to his crew overrode any thought of evasion, however. After force-landing in a field at Fontaine-au-Pire, southeast of Cambrai, France, Royle and his gunner carried their observer (navigator), who had broken his leg, to a nearby village, leaving him in the care of a local priest. Despite being injured himself, Royle returned to his Blenheim to destroy it. He hiked back to the village then passed out from his wounds. When he regained consciousness about two hours later, the gunner, who was unscathed, went in search of an ambulance. Royle stayed with the injured man. Before their gunner returned, the Germans arrived; the priest had informed on his unwelcome guests.[5]

Most evaders seldom remained at liberty for long. *Cedric Brandon* was free for three days but became 'blinded by burns and captured.'[6] Reginald 'Reg' Giddey dodged the enemy for weeks, established contact with operatives who could get him to Spain, but was then betrayed.[7] Often wearing civilian clothes, evaders were treated as spies or saboteurs. Without the protections of the Geneva Convention they were more vulnerable than the majority of airmen entering German custody, often receiving harsh treatment in civilian prisons. Many betrayed on the escape lines were tortured by Gestapo. Nine Australian airmen were brutally abused in Buchenwald concentration camp.

Most downed airmen fell directly into enemy hands, or 'in the bag.'[8] Many others, like Royle, were turned over shortly afterwards. Capture, Alec Arnel recalled, was 'a knockout blow'. The loss of freedom was almost too difficult to articulate; he could barely acknowledge his new status as a POW because it was 'too crushing.'[9] Emotions were still raw four months later when, writing to his sweetheart's mother, he asked her to imagine a fighter pilot's 'thoughts when his free, vital life is suddenly exchanged for that of a prisoner of war.'[10] The burning shame at being removed from the air war flared in interview over 70 years later as Arnel relived the experience. He remembered feeling 'very low emotionally', so overwhelmed by 'the awfulness' of the end of his flying career

---
4 Alexander, *Jack Davenport Beaufighter Leader*, 83.
5 NAUK WO 208/3334/1574: MI9/SPG/LIB Liberation reports, Royle; Royle archive: Royle, 'Stalag Luft III', 1985, 1.
6 NAA B503 POW Trust Fund application: R528, 2 April 1973.
7 AWM 54 81/4/135: MI9 reports: Giddey.
8 Ward-Jackson, *'It's a Piece of Cake'*, 11. For example of use, refer Baines FA: Baines, 19.
9 AR: Arnel, interview 29 October 2015.
10 Arnel archive: Arnel to Mrs M. Gray 30 October 1944.

– the utter humiliation of it – that he hardly noticed his wounds.[11] The 24-year old's depression worsened when he was paraded through the streets in front of jeering civilians. He laughed maniacally during his preliminary interrogation.[12]

Arnel was just one of many captured servicemen throughout the history of war who was struck by shame. It was still apparent decades later as they recalled their 'downfall', 'that regrettable day', or their 'fateful day'.[13] Still bewildered by it, some queried their competency. 'Why didn't I fly lower? Could I have weaved more? If only …'[14] Others were miserable at what they saw as their failure or dreaded that loved ones would be disappointed in them. Mixing his tenses suggests that Rex Austin stepped from the present and, like Arnel, returned to that emotional moment: 'what's Mum and Dad going to say about this? I had a girlfriend in England, what's she going to say?'[15] Shame, however, often mingled with an almost embarrassing relief. 'I think I was pleased to be alive to be honest', recalled Cy Borsht.[16] Even despite his deep mortification, an unsettling 'sense of relief at having my feet on the ground' washed over Arnel.[17]

Capture was a turning point. Justin O'Byrne recalled the 'horrible thought' that 'passed through my mind, My God, I am a prisoner of war!'[18] 'It was at this time that my career as a prisoner of war began', Thomas 'Tom' Wood acknowledged.[19] They also recognised their powerlessness. 'You no longer have any control over your life. You are at the mercy of your captors', Wesley Betts realised.[20] Others vividly remembered hearing in either English, German, or French 'the usual taunt' offered to POWs, 'For you the war is over.'[21] Geoffrey 'Geoff' Cornish, also known as 'Cherub' because of his baby face, recalled with wry humour that the words were uttered while a loaded, fully cocked pistol was pointed at his head.[22]

Even as they grappled with the thought that their flying careers were over, some pondered their immediate future. Still dazed from being under fire and a crash landing, Ronald Baines watched the disappearing African coast through the window of a German transport aircraft. He 'fell into a dark black hole of the deepest misery as the reality of the situation sunk in'. Baines turned his thoughts

---

11 AR: Arnel, interview 2 March 2017.
12 Arnel in Rolland (ed.), *Airmen I have Met*, 173.
13 'my downfall': Baines FA: Baines, 'Shock 1942', 16; 'that regrettable day': Bryce FA: 'Jock Bryce's POW Diary 1942–1945', 5; 'fateful day': Carson, 'Brisbane's Ken Carson: Prisoner of the Axis. Part Two', 22.
14 Baines FA: Baines, 'Shock 1942', 18.
15 AAWFA: Austin 0382, 5 June 2003.
16 AR: Borsht, interview 28 January 2016.
17 AR: Arnel, interview 2 March 2017.
18 O'Byrne, 'Nine o'clock above!'
19 3 Squadron RAAFA: 'Tom Wood Diary', 26.
20 SLSA SRG 869 Series 14: Wesley H. Betts, item 92, 23 January 2002.
21 'Usual taunt', Lumsden FA: Bradbeer and Lumsden, 'The Complete Tour', Lumsden, letter 24 June 1986.
22 AAWFA: Cornish 1388, 2 July 2004.

towards his bride of only a few weeks. 'I could no longer contact my beautiful wife. Would I ever see her again?' He tried to contemplate his fate but it was useless. 'My future [was] a complete blank.'[23]

Rapid removal from the scene of their downing resulted in a strong sense of dislocation. *Marcus Myatt* was 'shocked and confused'; time had little meaning.[24] Jock Bryce and his fellow captives 'felt ourselves at the start to be strangers in a queer world'.[25] Everything was totally alien to their normal environment of well-apportioned and -provisioned British-based RAF stations or the dirty but convivial tented accommodation on desert landing grounds. Their dislocation was not just geographical. It also emanated from disbelief. While they accepted that they might die in action and had been briefed about the possibility, the idea of surviving as prisoners of war had never occurred to them.

Disorientation and disbelief robbed some of the physically able of the desire to escape before transferring to permanent POW camps. Jock Bryce admitted the 'sad truth' that his failure was because he had 'suffered from what the R.A.F. calls lack of moral fibre'.[26] 'Lack of moral fibre' (LMF) was a disciplinary term which was applied to aircrew of both the RAF and RAAF who refused to carry out operations without a justifiable medical reason.[27] LMF was not a psychiatric diagnosis: it reflected diminished operational effectiveness and efficiency.[28] There is also an affective dimension to LMF because of its connection to service duty and efficient crew relationships such as in bomber and coastal commands: those who baulked at operations strained a crew's close ties even as they imperilled their fellows' lives. Fighter pilots could also put other squadron members at risk by not playing their part in attack or defensive sorties. While a compassionate commanding officer might quietly organise a non-operational posting, the guidelines were clear: airmen deemed to have LMF were to be sent to a disposal centre 'in disgrace', where they were subject to 'unsympathetic treatment'. The unfortunates 'had their rank and flying brevets taken from them and were given ground jobs', recalled Alexander 'Alex' Kerr.[29] As well as public acknowledgement that they had let down their comrades, airmen dreaded the taint of cowardice, the perception of character flaw, and the 'absolutely terrible' consequences.[30] Even in 1995, LMF remained 'a sensitive subject' for Jack

---

23 Baines FA: Baines, 'Shock 1942', 16.
24 DVA NCPX25587-01: supplementary letter of explanation to injuries, 18 July 1970 [1978].
25 Bryce FA: 'Jock Bryce's POW Diary 1942–1945', 86.
26 Bryce FA: 'Jock Bryce's POW Diary 1942–1945', 39.
27 McCarthy, 'Aircrew and "Lack of Moral Fibre"', 87–101.
28 Jones, '"LMF": The use of Psychiatric Stigma in the Royal Air Force during the Second World War', 439–458.
29 Quotes: Kerr, *Shot Down*, 37.
30 Jones, '"LMF"', 439–458. Character flaw: Allport: *Demobbed*, 195. Cowardice: McCarthy, 'Aircrew and "Lack of Moral Fibre"', 87–101. Quote: AAWFA: Kerr 1489, 3 March 2004.

Morschel.³¹ It was 'a stigma you feared you'd have to live with forever', Cy Borsht admitted.³² Accordingly, operational airmen wrestled with genuine flying fatigue and stress in order not to be designated LMF. Jock Bryce explained that, while he had at first tried to gauge his chances of escape, he soon realised 'I had not the will to make the attempt'. The 'shock of being taken prisoner of war had robbed me of sufficient initiative to escape alone'.³³ Bryce – who had barely passed his 21st birthday – was wrong in his self-diagnosis. He did not have LMF. Lassitude, arising from disorientation or perhaps linked to depression, was a common 'symptom' of early captivity. Many airmen experienced it, including those whose final operational sortie and aftermath had been particularly harrowing.

*****

While the Geneva Convention provided that captives were to be handled humanely and with respect, this was not always the case; Australians received a disparity of medical treatment. German troops applied first aid to Ken Carson after his Kittyhawk crashed in flames. Later, treatment was less than adequate with shortages of drugs and bandages during his seven month convalescence for gunshot wounds in Italian hospitals.³⁴ Alan Righetti, however, received good care. The Neapolitan hospital 'wasn't badly set up. The plumbing of course being Italian, didn't work but at the same time we were quite well looked after … the staff of nuns were very kind'.³⁵ The quality of German medical attention also varied. Frankfurt's Hohemark clinic was often so full that those suffering shock and minor wounds were neglected. As in Italian facilities, drugs were often in short supply.³⁶ *Sean Hanrahan*, who had been trapped in the wreck of his aircraft for five hours with wounds to his leg that resulted in numbness for nine months, 'had no medical attention at all'.³⁷

After August 1943, *Volksjustiz* (peoples' justice) was an officially sanctioned form of civil vengeance throughout German-held territories. '*Luftgangster*' 'gangster commandos', 'terror bandits' and other derogatory terms used to describe allied airmen and soldiers often featured in German propaganda, including in a circular addressed 'To all Prisoners of War!' which was distributed in September 1944.³⁸ 'Air Gangsters, the Terror Fliers, or the Murderers, as the air force was called were not very popular', Ken Carson recalled,³⁹ and many airmen

---
31 Morschel, *A Lancaster's Participation in Normandy Invasion 1944*, 16. Originally published in 1995.
32 Borsht Archive: Borsht, 'A Life Well Lived', 16.
33 Bryce FA: 'Jock Bryce's POW Diary 1942–1945', 39.
34 AWM 54 779/3/129: 11 PDRC post-liberation debrief, Carson.
35 AAWFA: Righetti 0984, 16 September 2003.
36 AWM 54 779/3/129: 11 PDRC post-liberation debrief, Collings.
37 DVA NCX065122-02: personal statement, 17 January 1980.
38 Hall, 'Luftgangster over Germany', 277–312; Gordon FA: 'To All Prisoners of War' poster.
39 Carson FA: Ken Carson to mother and sister, 10 May 1945 (second letter).

experienced the full gamut of fear-inducing violence. An injured Carson tried to stop his captors stealing his watch, but a German soldier put his boot on his face. He surrendered the timepiece then passed out.[40] Before he was transferred to hospital, a wounded Geoffrey Coombes was taken to a guard house. There, a German, 'who looked like a bloody gorilla', threw him and the camp bed on which he was reclining against the cell wall.[41] *Lynchjustiz* – lynching of downed airmen and summary execution in some instances – was also a condoned form of *Volksjustiz*.[42] Alan McInnes was accosted by civilians shortly after landing. They beat him so badly a rib was broken. His attackers 'had just brought in a coil of rope when police arrived and took charge of us.'[43]

Some airmen were able to look back on their mistreatment with sardonic humour. Ronald 'Ron' Mackenzie, who was 'scared stiff' when threatened with torture at a local gaol, 'lost the working part of one tooth to a rifle butt'.[44] When describing his capture by the Gestapo, Kevin Light noted they were a 'nice set of boys who are very handy with their feet'.[45] Light may have been able to retrospectively joke about his kicking, but few found interrogation a laughing matter.

---

40 Carson, 'Brisbane's Ken Carson: Prisoner of the Axis. Part Two', 21.
41 AWM S00551 KMSA: Coombes, Geoffrey Bernard, 23 March 1989.
42 Hall, 'Luftgangster over Germany', 277–312.
43 NAA A9300 McInns [sic] A F, war crimes questionnaire.
44 Mackenzie, *An Ordinary War 1940–1945*, 36.
45 AWM 54 779/3/129: 11 PDRC post-liberation debrief, Light.

Albert Comber, 'somewhere in England', waiting to take off on a shipping strike, February 1942. Six months later, Comber, an observer with 39 Squadron RAF, was shot down while attacking a convoy. Their Beaufort crashed into the sea off the Italian coast. The crew were 'all safe – taken POW', Comber later stated. Courtesy of the Comber family.

Alec Arnel of 451 Squadron RAAF felt 'stark staring fear' when his Spitfire was hit by flak. Courtesy of Alec Arnel.

Chapter Two:

INTERROGATION

Shortly after arriving at the *Luftwaffe*'s interrogation facility, a German officer asked Justin O'Byrne if he had eaten. O'Byrne was hungry, but realised courtesy had little to do with the enquiry. 'He asked me to answer a few questions and he would see that food was sent into me immediately.' The German's 'manner was gushingly polite' at first. After about two hours of O'Byrne's stonewalling, though, the interrogator began to threaten him: 'I would never see any of my friends and relations again if I did not give him the information he wanted. I told him that was just too bad, and he stormed out and slammed the door.'[1]

Within weeks of war's outbreak, the Germans had recognised that allied personnel captured within Germany and German-held territories were important assets who might provide intelligence about British morale, war-readiness, military strength, and matériel. Believing the disorientated would more easily succumb to the pressure of interrogation, new POWs were rushed to preliminary detention for questioning by local military personnel.

They, like O'Byrne, were then transferred to *Durchgangslager der Luftwaffe*, known to POWs as Dulag Luft. Located at Oberursel, just north-west of Frankfurt, one part of Dulag Luft served as the *Luftwaffe*'s main transit camp. The other half contained a professional intelligence-gathering centre. By intensively questioning new arrivals, scrutinising documents and equipment still carried by the airmen, and examining crashed aircraft, intelligence staff developed a detailed knowledge of allied air operations. (Despite a number of name changes over the years, it continued to be referred to as Dulag Luft. The intelligence and transit sections were separated in September 1943; the intelligence staff remained at Oberursel but the transit camp was relocated to Frankfurt. That was destroyed in a raid in March 1944 and a camp was constructed at Wetzlar. Interrogations continued to be carried out at Oberursel.)

It was a disturbing time. Richard Winn's emotions at Dulag Luft oscillated between despondency, near panic, and hope. 'These mood swings were very frequent.'[2] Ronald Baines was mortified when he had to pull a lever signalling that he needed to go to the toilet, then 'ignominiously [wait] for the guard to

---

1 O'Byrne FA: O'Byrne, 'Nine o'clock above!'
2 Winn, *A Fighter Pilot's Diary of World War 2*, 44.

answer the call'.[3] The airmen were stripped of belts, boots, tunic or battledress, and trousers. They were x-rayed, and subjected to 'embarrassing' body searches.[4] Personal possessions were also confiscated, including Bruce Lumsden's New Testament.[5] While this was later returned, uniforms usually were not. In their stead, the airmen received an assortment of mismatched clothing. Loss of uniform was a blow. It heralded the start of Dulag Luft's humiliating 'demoralisation process', as Baines referred to it.[6]

The Australian airmen were prepared for interrogation. They had been given clear instructions on 'how best to serve our, and our country's, interests'.[7] First issued in 1936, *Air Publication 1548* was into its third edition by April 1944.[8] All British-based personnel had been required to read the booklet which emphasised that, even if captured, airmen were still members of the air force and, as such, had to adhere to the *Air Force Act*. It clearly placed on all ranks a 'duty not to give … any information' during interrogation in order to protect air force security.[9] Many airmen had also viewed *Enemy Interrogation of Prisoners*, a 1940 training film which detailed the tricks the enemy might deploy to gain intelligence; indicated how the newly captured should conduct themselves; revealed the consequences of disobeying RAF orders and procedure when in enemy hands; and stressed that they were still duty bound to follow RAF protocol. It also reinforced the onus of air force discipline and continuing service.[10] Errol Green and others trained in Canada were briefed on how to behave in the event of capture by their station intelligence officer.[11] In addition, the rumour mill worked overtime and many heard that they might be threatened, beaten, or tortured to extract vital military details.

Justin O'Byrne was not the only one who found polite, seemingly friendly and courteous German examiners who attempted to build a rapport by cajoling with cigarettes and bonhomie. Interrogators tried to unsettle the airmen, showing them dossiers of press clippings, photographs, and maps, as well as squadron histories and comprehensive lists of personnel. Torres Ferres recalled the 'shock of seeing your face in a photo' in a German intelligence file.[12]

The airmen were aware of their entitlements and protections under the Geneva Convention, particularly the requirement to provide only name, rank, and service

---

3   Baines FA: Baines, 'Shock 1942', 17.
4   Baines FA: Baines, wartime log book, 9.
5   Lumsden FA: Bradbeer and Lumsden, 'The Complete Tour', Lumsden, letter 5 March 1987.
6   Baines FA: Baines, 'Shock 1942', 17.
7   AWM PR90/035: Ferres, 'A POW in Germany'.
8   Each edition had slightly different titles and different content.
9   Quote from Arnel archive: Harvey, 'Over, Down and Out', 8.
10 *Enemy Interrogation of Prisoners*, 1940.
11 Green FA: Errol Green, MI9 'General Questionnaire' 23574, 18 May 1945.
12 AWM PR90/035: Ferres, 'A POW in Germany'.

number. Beyond that, *Air Publication 1548* exhorted them to give 'no further information whatsoever.'[13] Accordingly, they tried to resist German trickery. Rex Austin was unfailingly polite to his interrogators. 'I'm sorry sir, I'm not permitted to say.'[14] When the soft touch and displays of intelligence already gathered failed to overcome the airmen's commitment to reticence, the demeanour of Dulag Luft's personnel changed. Lorraine 'Laurie' Simpson's interrogator 'quite often became coldly stern and raving later on.'[15] Some underwent as many as four or five separate sessions where questioners played to the airmen's emotions. They lied to Douglas McLeod to weaken his defence, telling him that 'three members of my crew had been killed.'[16] When O'Byrne, like many others, refused to fill in bogus Red Cross forms, he was warned 'that unless I completed it my next-of-kin would not be advised of the fact that I was still alive.'[17]

Graham Berry believed the Germans abided by the Geneva Convention and, indeed, despite its catalogue of acknowledged war crimes, including the murders of the Great Escape participants, Germany is generally credited with adhering to the Convention's provisions, at least for non-Soviet prisoners.[18] There were many breaches of the Convention's articles at Dulag Luft, however, including, as in Justin O'Byrne's case, denial of food. The Germans tried to take advantage of the airmen's post-capture vulnerability. As *Cedric Brandon* realised, it was 'to condition one for the interrogation.'[19] Every aspect of confinement was designed to increase mental distress, thus breaking down resistance to interrogation. Dulag Luft's staff erratically varied cell temperatures. Torres Ferres was in a 'constant state of heavy perspiration' from the 'soul-destroying treatment.'[20] Experienced English-speaking interrogators had considerable success in extracting 'gen' (information). Their techniques included 'softening up', repetitive questioning, wheedling apparent irrelevancies from the still shocked airmen, and alternately adopting friendly or menacing styles. They also deployed deliberate physical, psychological and emotional threats, and violence. According to one of Dulag Luft's *kommandants*, 'no amount of solitary confinement, privation and psychological blackmail was considered excessive.'[21]

Cy Borsht's interrogator hit him on the back of the head, lightly at first and then increasingly harder. Finally, in the face of Borsht's continued defiance, he

---

13 *Air Publication 1548*, 2nd Edition, June 1941 and 3rd Edition, April 1944.
14 AAWFA: Austin 0382, 5 June 2003.
15 AWM 54 779/3/126 part 1: Simpson, POW statement, 31 July 1945.
16 AWM 54 779/3/129: 11 PDRC post-liberation debrief, Douglas McLeod.
17 O'Byrne FA: O'Byrne, 'Nine o'clock above!'
18 AR: Berry, interview 7 June 2016; Oppenheimer, '"Our Number One Priority": The Australian Red Cross and prisoners of war in the world wars', in Joan Beaumont, Lachlan Grant, and Aaron Pegram (eds), *Beyond Surrender: Australian Prisoners of War in the Twentieth Century*, 82.
19 NAA B503 POW Trust Fund application: R528, 2 April 1973.
20 AWM PR90/035: Ferres, 'A POW in Germany'.
21 Mason, *Official History of New Zealand in the Second World War 1939–45*, 139.

'played the Jew card', threatening to hand the Jewish airman over to the Gestapo.²² Some were tortured or deliberately neglected. Douglas 'Doug' Hutchinson, who had already received preliminary medical attention on Crete, was sent to Hohemark clinic where he was questioned every day and denied treatment for three weeks.²³ He was on his back during interrogation. 'I couldn't move very much, I had a leg that was aching like hell. … I had bits and pieces off all over me, and I was starting to feel sore.'²⁴

Prisoners drew on their inner strengths and sense of duty to resist divulging sensitive details and to mitigate the worst of the debilitating effects of sensory deprivation, psychological pressure, and bodily harm. Justin O'Byrne ignored the emotional threats and 'evaded every leading question' to gain the upper hand.²⁵ When silence failed, Doug Hutchinson's interrogator aggravated his foot wound.²⁶ Despite pain and discomfort, Hutchinson continued to resist. It became a battle of the wits where he 'tried to be smarter all the time'.²⁷ So too did Cy Borsht. It 'was just simply a matter of repeating what you've already told him'.²⁸

The airmen fought against German attempts to demoralise them, even in their cells. Some prayed or recited psalms. Rather than 'make any conscious effort' to psychologically 'remove myself from that space', Rex Austin confronted his situation by focusing his anger on the 'mongrel fleas' attacking him, and refused to be humiliated by both solitary confinement and the insanitary conditions of his cell.²⁹ Richard Winn composed rhyming poetry in his head. He also carried out some self-serving sabotage. Instead of putting up with the 'unbearably hot' room, he disconnected one of the heater's electrical wires with his 'dog tag', now returned to him, and manipulated his fountain pen barrel to turn the heater on and off.³⁰ In physically alleviating the worst effects of the heat torture by rubbing his handkerchief on the early morning condensation in his cell and later urinating into it to 'just wet the lips', Kenneth Gaulton also waged a psychological defence. 'That was the way I beat the system in my mind.'³¹

Not all airmen resisted, however. Many revealed more than air force protocol allowed. Borsht recalled that one of his crew members disclosed much that was 'not very secret or special' while being wined and dined by his cross-

---

22 Borsht Archive: Borsht, 'A Life Well Lived', 20; AR: Borsht, interview 28 January 2016. Quote: Veitch, *Heroes of the Skies*, 55.
23 NAA A9300, Hutchinson D F, war crimes questionnaire.
24 AAWFA: Hutchinson 0540, 17 June 2003.
25 O'Byrne FA: O'Byrne, 'Nine o'clock above!'
26 AR: Robert Douglas Hutchinson, interview 19 December 2016.
27 AAWFA: Hutchinson 0540, 17 June 2003.
28 Veitch, *Heroes of the Skies*, 55; Borsht Archive: Borsht, 'A Life Well Lived', 20; AR: Borsht, interview 28 January 2016.
29 AAWFA: Austin 0382, 5 June 2003.
30 Winn, *A Fighter Pilot's Diary*, 44.
31 AAWFA: Gaulton 1276, 3 February 2004.

examiners.[32] In some cases, slips may have been unintentional. One man believed he was obliged to give 'only those details as required by the Geneva Convention i.e. Name, Rank, Nationality, Address, Next-of-Kin'.[33] In the face of emotional pressure, others made conscious decisions after weighing potential consequences.

While Bruce Lumsden had viewed the training film *Enemy Interrogation of Prisoners*, its script ill-prepared him for the shock, anxiety, and emotional fug of capture and interrogation. He turned to his religious background. 'I sought comfort and strength in prayer and in softly singing a hymn'. Even with the solace of faith, Lumsden 'found the process' of interrogation and solitary confinement 'horribly demeaning … powerless even to protest'. He was so demoralised that, when his interrogator told him that withholding his address and other details would result in a lengthy delay in advising the British authorities of his capture, 'my most urgent concern was that my mother, widowed earlier that year, and my two sisters 12,000 miles away, should be spared the distress of a long waiting to know whether I was alive or dead'. Deciding that his family's needs 'outweighed all other considerations', Lumsden succumbed to emotional pressure and his inherent sense of compassion to reveal his Australian address and other minor details.[34]

Lumsden was not the only airman swayed by affective concerns. Torres Ferres understood his duty. However, when taken to the wreckage of his Lancaster and faced with the bodies of two dead friends, he put aside his security obligations and identified them. 'I preferred to know that their families would hear of their fate much sooner than if I had refused to identify them'. In 'associating myself with the aircraft' which bore its squadron markings, Ferres was fully aware that his altruistic 'deliberate disobedience' would 'probably present some difficulties, at future interrogations, concerning my Pathfinder Force duties'.[35]

Those who placed compassion above duty may have breached protocol, but making that choice was important. It gave them a measure of power. Yet, for many years, Bruce Lumsden saw only his failure to fulfil air force duty and 'felt I had compromised myself and yielded ground'. Acceptance of what was in essence an empathetic action came decades later after deep reflection and rationalisation. 'If the war [was] lost because I gave the Germans my address in Australia, it would be just too bad'.[36]

*****

---

32 Borsht Archive: Borsht, 'A Life Well Lived', 20.
33 AWM 54 779/3/129: 11 PDRC post-liberation debrief, Crump.
34 Lumsden FA: Bradbeer and Lumsden, 'The Complete Tour', Lumsden, letter 5 March 1987.
35 AWM PR90/035: Ferres, 'A POW in Germany'.
36 Lumsden FA: Bradbeer and Lumsden, 'The Complete Tour', Lumsden, letter 5 March 1987.

Interrogation over, the POWs were taken to Dulag Luft's transit camp. Shortly after the *Luftwaffe* assumed control of captured airmen, some British and French prisoners of war had been transferred there as a cadre of permanent staff to help alleviate the shock of captivity and accustom new arrivals to the 'facts of life'.[37] In doing so, they cooperated with the Germans to the extent that many POWs erroneously believed they were collaborating.[38] With the permanent staff's help, the horrors of final combat, the shock and shame of captivity, and any lingering effects of ill-treatment and 'such depravity' at the hands of German intelligence officers were pushed to the back of the airmen's minds.[39] Ordeal over – for the time being – the new prisoners enjoyed 'wizard' food provided courtesy of the Red Cross and an energetic social life which included sport, films, concerts, and a steady stream of new arrivals.[40] 'What a relief it was to mix with our own crowd again!' recalled Charles Lark.[41] Despite the solace of friends, at no point could the airmen totally relax into captivity. As Ronald Baines noted, 'we were prisoners and the Germans did not let you forget that fact'.[42] Even so, by taking control as much as possible to resist sophisticated interrogation techniques, and by maintaining morale and self-discipline in challenging, painful, and often distressing circumstances, the airmen demonstrated emotional strength as well as an ability to act for their own benefit and, altruistically, for comrades and loved ones. They were not entirely powerless. In doing so, they had defied the German taunt. They may have been behind barbed wire, but the war, for them, was not over.

---

37 Dack, *So you Wanted Wings, Hey!*, 81.
38 MacKenzie, *The Colditz Myth*, 137–138; AWM PR90/035: Ferres, 'A POW in Germany'.
39 Arnel archive: Train, 'A Barbed-Wire World', 20–26 May 1942, 8–9; 'such depravity': Baines FA: Baines, 'Shock 1942', 18.
40 'wizard' food: Archer FA: Archer, 1942 Diary, 28 July–2 August 1942.
41 Lark, *A Lark on the Wing*, 65.
42 Baines FA: Baines, '1939 Experiences'.

Justin O'Byrne, a 452 Squadron RAAF Spitfire pilot, was one of many kriegies who, during interrogation at Dulag Luft, 'evaded every leading question'. Such an attitude set the precedent for continued resistance – including escape attempts – during captivity. Courtesy of Anne O'Byrne.

PART TWO: KRIEGIE LIFE

Chapter Three:

KRIEGIES

'The place was grey sand,' Ronald Baines recalled of his first glimpse of Stalag Luft III after transferring there from Dulag Luft. 'All the trees had been cut down and you were surrounded by barbed wire and that's all you saw, barbed wire and guards, German guards, were stomping around the place.' At that 'most depressing place', Baines and his fellow POWs had to adjust to incarceration for an indefinite period.[1]

The new arrivals were searched then taken to the *Kommandantur* – the staff block. Family and personal details were recorded and they were photographed for their identification cards. Their captors took finger prints and issued identity discs stamped with the camp's name and the prisoner's identification number. The airmen could not avoid that number: they had to include it on every letter home; their loved ones wrote it on each envelope and parcel they posted to Germany. So ingrained were the digits that Ian Fraser recalled his father, Donald, reeling them off decades after the war.[2] For John Dack, the number signified a loss of identity. 'From henceforth, I became "Kriegsgefangene Nummer achttausend siebenhundert und vier"; – Prisoner of War number 8704.'[3] Despite the humiliation of numerical identification and POW discs, Robert Mills, one of the nine Australian airmen who had spent two months in Buchenwald concentration camp before transferring to *Luftwaffe* custody, was grateful to be 'officially recognised as POW'. Not only would he and his fellows enjoy for the first time since capture the protections of the Geneva Convention, but he could now communicate with his friends and relatives.[4]

After an initial period of vetting to ensure they were not 'stool pigeons' – Germans pretending to be allied personnel to gain intelligence – newcomers, still suffering the after-effects of injury, capture, and interrogation, were warmly embraced into the camp community.[5] Jimmy Catanach, with his friendly, welcoming face, was one who extended a cheery hallo to a still-shocked Ronald Baines.[6] As well as an opportunity to reunite with friends from home, training, or squadrons, fresh faces were a source of gen, gossip and news. While many heard

---

1   Baines FA: Ronald Baines, interview with Brooke Carrigan, [undated].
2   AR: Ian Fraser, interview, 25 May 2016.
3   Dack, *So, You Wanted Wings, Hey!*, 81. Quote as written by Dack.
4   Burgess RC: Robert Mills, wartime log book, 1.
5   'stool pigeons': Carson, 'Brisbane's Ken Carson: Prisoner of the Axis. Part Nine', 23.
6   AR: Stuart Baines, interview 9 July 2015.

that service friends had died, Harry Train seemed to take it with equanimity; news of deaths reinforced his good fortune in surviving.[7] Alec Arnel took strength from the presence of 'old cobbers' and a shared predicament. He saw that he was 'just one of many who found themselves in the same situation'.[8] More than that, they made 'my initiation' to life in captivity 'much easier'.[9]

Permanent camps were closely scrutinised by Protecting Powers observers to ensure prisoners were treated in accordance with the Geneva Convention. As such, contrary to earlier experiences where prisoners had been refused medical treatment, those who required attention received it promptly and efficiently in the camp's sick quarters. Mervyn Bradford who had endured scabies for over three months was given a punishing regime of scalding baths, painful scrubbing, and yellow sulphur ointment plastered all over.[10] Douglas Keith Carmody, known as Keith, received special rations and Vitamin B injections.[11] Doug Hutchinson was treated for an abscess on his foot.[12]

The airmen may have been out of the war but their safety was not assured. Many recorded in war crimes statements that they had been exposed 'to danger of gunfire, bombing' and 'other hazards of war' during confinement in camps. Some attested to physical and verbal threats. For Jock Bryce, there was a prevailing undercurrent of that 'German influence, fear'.[13] The anxiety of being fired upon by their captors was always with them. Shortly after Harry Train arrived, three cricket balls were hit outside the warning wire 'and one of the Goons [guards] took a shot at one of our chaps … who attempted to retrieve one'.[14] When reports of the D-Day invasion came through, the men 'over-reacted to the extent that some of the guards took exception and fired some shots, luckily over our heads', recalled Torres Ferres. 'We cooled down rather quickly and rapidly dispersed.'[15] Some prisoners were seriously wounded and died. The situation was so grim that Stalag Luft III's senior British officers frequently complained to Protecting Powers' visitors about orders 'which are endangering the life of entirely innocent prisoners'.[16]

*****

The stark reality that the airmen were hors de combat struck to the core of their identity as members of the air force. That involuntary disconnection from their

---

7   Arnel archive: Train, 'A Barbed-Wire World', 11 September 1942, 26.
8   AR: Arnel, interview 27 November 2014.
9   Arnel archive: Arnel to Margery Gray, [undated].
10 SLSA SRG 869 Series 16: Mervyn Bradford, item 2, 30 November 1989.
11 Barker, *Keith Carmody*, 52.
12 AWM 54 779/3/129: 11 PDRC post-liberation debrief, Hutchinson; NAA A9300 Hutchinson, D F, war crimes questionnaire.
13 Bryce FA: 'Jock Bryce's POW Diary 1942–1945', 86.
14 Arnel archive: Train, 'A Barbed-Wire World, 17 June 1942, 12.
15 AWM PR90/035: Ferres, 'A POW in Germany'.
16 NAUK WO 224/63A: Red Cross and Protecting Powers reports, 22–24 February 1944, Complaints, 7.

service rationale and the contemporary perception that they were something less than fighting men was summed up for some by the term 'wingless'.[17] Accordingly, it was essential that they throw off any residual sense of humiliation and depression and reclaim their 'wings'. They had to find a way to wage battle against the enemy within the confines of Stalag Luft III.

Service morale encompasses a sense of duty, military resilience, motivation to fight, comradeship, and firm leadership. 'We were kept together by our senior officers and the maxim "unity in strength" certainly applies' to prisoners of war, Laurie Simpson reported.[18] Morale was traditionally high in RAF and RAAF squadrons and, despite captivity, most airmen prisoners remained mentally positive. Assurance of allied victory sustained their belief in ultimate release and homecoming. 'Four months nearer victory', wrote James Anthony 'Tony' Gordon to his Aunt Mag. 'Everyone here very confident.'[19] 'I think that in any prison camp I've been in morale was high always. They never gave up', recalled Bill Fordyce.[20] Agency and sense of control are important for morale. So, too, is humour.

Airmen of all musterings were particularly adept at finding the funny side of any situation and many soon discovered they could lift morale by poking fun at their plight. As Calton Younger, a skilled cartoonist, noted, 'behind barbed wire in Germany, where despondency was the enemy, there was always something incongruous, something to provoke laughter'.[21]

How else could you cope with potatoes mixed into porridge to make it go round, if not by laughing at it, as Norman Maxwell 'Max' Dunne did?[22]

A meeting's called – a flap is imminent

And all the Great Brains gather to the fray: …

Our quantity of spuds exceeds demand

Yet calls for porridge far outweigh supplies; …

'The answer's easy for a well-trained brain;

Supply, Demand, are both now equalised,

Just mix the spuds and the porridge, with some grain'.

Many ironically likened Stalag Luft III to a 'holiday camp'.[23] Some claimed they were on 'vacation'.[24] 'Life here is like a camping holiday', Digby Young told

---

17 Thompson, *Captives to Freedom*, 156.
18 AWM 54 779/3/126 part 1: Simpson, POW statement, 31 July 1945.
19 Gordon FA: Gordon to Aunt Mag, [undated: c. April 1942].
20 AAWFA: Fordyce 0523, 19 June 2003.
21 Younger, *Get a Load of this*, [4].
22 Dunn, *Poems of Norman Maxwell Dunn*, 'The Kitchen Kings', 12–13.
23 'Prison Like Holiday Camp', *Daily News* (Perth), 22 March 1943, 6.
24 NLA FERG/4550: *P.O.W.*, No. 24, 15 January 1944, unattributed letter, 10 June 1943, 11.

a friend. 'After years of practice at doing nothing, I am getting a chance to put it into full use.'[25] Mock travel posters depicted the delights of their 'super-duper salubrious' quarters.[26] Even sanitary arrangements, which were far from hygienic, provoked sardonic humour. Commenting on the proximity of the 50-hole latrine above a 'huge pit' with no partitions, Rex Austin wryly recalled that, 'you had to be a bit careful that it was your own bum that you were wiping.'[27]

The airmen turned to their wartime log books to reframe their ignominious exits from battle into amusingly self-deprecating caricatures. Provided by the British, American and Canadian Young Men's Christian Associations, wartime log books are similar to commonplace books and, as such, are different from the log books in which airmen recorded operational sorties and training flights. The airmen's comic drawings appropriated icons from air force and popular culture. In one image, James McCleery parodied himself plummeting to the ground declaring, 'Germany here I come!' In another, he took on the guise of a disconsolate Percy Prune wearing prison garb of patched uniform and wooden clogs.[28] 'Pilot Officer Percy Prune', an awkward and hapless character who featured in RAF and RAAF training manuals representing what *not* to do, was a much loved and laughed-at caricatured airman.[29] He was a particularly apt doppelgänger in the circumstances and McCleery was only one of many to identify with Prune's humorously salutary escapades.

'Donald Duck' also proved an appropriate alter ego. He had recently been 'drafted' into the American army, appearing in propaganda films including November 1942's *Sky Trooper* in which he desperately wanted to fly. After a series of misadventures he had his chance as part of a parachute troop. During a fight, he fell out of an aeroplane. The comedic icon with military connections had become a downed airman. Although he was never captured, British, Canadian, American, and Australian airmen alike related to Donald angrily bemoaning the ironic outcome of his (their) great desire for 'wings' – aircrew flying badges – 'I wanted wings!' Many images of the irate duck appeared in wartime log books. Lest anyone think the men were simply copying American prisoner Emmet Cook's rendition of Walt Disney's creation, some versions of 'Downed Donald' bore the artist's prisoner of war number and aircrew insignia.[30]

Even as they laughed at themselves as failed, fallen airmen, the Australians asserted their strong, professional service identity. Those lacking uniforms

---

25 'Prisoner of War. Frankston Footballer-Pilot', *Standard* (Frankston, VIC), 21 March 1941, 1.
26 Borsht Archive: Borsht, wartime log book, 5.
27 AAWFA: Austin 0382, 5 June 2003.
28 AWM PR88/160: McCleery, wartime log book, unpaginated particulars page and 1.
29 Gunderson, 'Pilot Officer Prune, Royal Air Force: "Dutiful but Dumb"', 23–29.
30 The US Militaria Forum, 'Stalag Luft III "I Wanted Wings"'.

through damage or confiscation attempted to replace them. Miscellaneous and not necessarily well-fitting army or air force jackets, trousers, and shirts, were issued on arrival. They were not good enough for some. Tony Gordon asked his Aunt Mag to send 'shirts and collars service and khaki ... Uniforms two <u>old</u> blue (airmen's issue ie without patch pockets).'[31] John Osborne wrote to Cairo for his 'uniform and coat.'[32] Those who were eligible applied to the Irving Air Chute Company for membership of the Caterpillar Club which celebrated successful bale-outs, or the Goldfish Club, an exclusive association of airmen who were saved from drowning by lifejacket or dinghy. They claimed their caterpillar and goldfish emblems as badges of honour. Others reinforced their sense of self as successful operational airmen. They made models of aircraft, representing a continuing affinity with their tools of trade. Perhaps hoping to soften the blow of their own downings, fighter pilots told loved ones they had scored an enemy 'kill' during their last action. Some pasted into their wartime log books news clippings of British and American operations. Others in the later stages of the war culled from German newspapers images of allied airmen labelled *terrorflieger*, *luftgangster*, and *terrorbomber*. A particular favourite, captioned 'Der Mordverein', was a photograph of two American airmen, one of whom had been allowed to fly over Germany with 'Murder Inc.' emblazoned on his jacket.[33]

While some airmen were initially bemused by the derisory terms deployed by the German press, they soon put away their uncomfortable recollections, ignored the intended insults, and even – in some cases – welcomed their membership of 'Der Mord Verein', 'the murder club'. Looking far from clean-cut when he was captured, Richard Winn recalled speculating that the Germans might use his photograph to depict 'a typical terror bomber' and seemed disappointed when 'nothing happened about that.'[34] Cy Borsht told me it was 'a great feeling' being dubbed a member of the 'Murder Inc.' fraternity.[35] Ken Carson and his roommates proudly appropriated the name, '*luftgangsters*'; Carson sent home a group photo with the designation written on the back.[36]

Humorous depictions of ill-starred parachutists, crashed pilots, and downed-duck-airman, along with the sober identification with 'the murder club', demonstrated that the newly-captured still considered themselves operational airmen. Reappropriating names such as '*luftgangster*' perhaps alleviated the humiliation and terror of *lynchjustiz*. Deeply religious Bruce Lumsden, however, did not approve of the designation. Nor did he want membership of 'Der Mord

---

31 Gordon FA: Gordon to Aunt Mag, [undated: c. April 1942]. Original emphasis.
32 NAM JOC: John Osborne to family, 20 October 1942.
33 As captioned. *Der Mord Verein*: 'the murder club'. Borsht Archive: Borsht, wartime log book, 55.
34 AAWFA: Winn 1508, 4 March 2004.
35 AR: Borsht, interview 28 January 2016.
36 Carson, 'Brisbane's Ken Carson: Prisoner of the Axis. Part Eleven', 16.

Verein'. 'I remember feeling justly offended when, as a POW, I came to know that the common German term for allied aircrew was "terreur-fliegers". I saw this as base propaganda.'[37]

Most may have willingly appropriated derogatory terms as tribute to their military prowess, but none were keen to be known as *Kriegsgefangener* – war prisoner – because of the negative and shameful connotations surrounding the word 'prisoner'. Like many others in different services and theatres, captured airmen abhorred the sense of emasculation, powerlessness, and passivity emanating from their forced removal from operations. As such, they spurned the phrase, 'prisoner of war' and adopted the easier-to-pronounce abbreviation of 'kriegie'. They even called themselves 'kriegies' in letters home. Derived from the first syllable – the German word for 'war' – it indicated that they were still military men. By seizing linguistic power and changing '*Kriegsgefangener*' into 'kriegie', airmen drew on a long air force tradition of using language to distance themselves from circumstances which engendered difficult emotions, such as death in service. The result was that they effectively detached themselves from the sense of disgrace implied by the word 'prisoner'. The more robust 'kriegie' reflected the airmen's fighting spirit and, rather than an insulting label, became, Alec Arnel recalled, 'a fun word'[38]. Their ensuing self-confidence and elevated morale enabled them to confidently negotiate captivity as individuals and collectively as an air force group. They may have been 'wingless' but the German taunt that for them the war was over was meaningless. As the RAAF's historian John Herington noted retrospectively, 'they remained combatants even as prisoners'.[39] They were still men of war.

*****

Dulag Luft's permanent staff of longer-term British POWs implemented an effective administration system. They also devised ways to continue waging the war despite captivity. They covertly sent coded letters to the British Directorate of Military Intelligence (more commonly known as MI9) and coordinated escape efforts.[40] That system (including its dedicated escape organisation) was later installed at Stalag Luft I, Barth. The captured airmen then transplanted their culture of air force discipline, strong leadership, and modified self-rule into Stalag Luft III where it was condoned by the camp's *kommandant*.[41] Discipline became

a way for the airmen to 'pull together as a unit', Geoff Cornish recalled, and to

---

37 Lumsden FA: Bradbeer and Lumsden, 'The Complete Tour', Lumsden, letter 23 September 1986.
38 AR: Arnel, interview 29 January 2015.
39 Herington, *Air Power Over Europe, 1944–1945*, 485.
40 Gould, 'Those Icarian Rustics: Reminiscence of an "Old Boy" A.H. Gould', 11.
41 Walton and Eberhardt, *From Commandant to Captive*, 62.

continue the fight against the Germans.⁴² It also underpinned later escape efforts.

Following RAF tradition, the senior airman for all commissioned prisoners was automatically the Senior British Officer. Personal qualities rather than rank determined the Man of Confidence, who was elected by the NCOs. The senior British officers (in officer compounds) and Man of Confidence (in the NCO compound) liaised with the *Luftwaffe* staff to represent the kriegies' interests. They also ensured a degree of military control within their ranks. Stalag Luft III's inspiring senior men included Senior British Officer Group Captain Herbert Martin Massey, (known as Martin), morale-minded Wing Commander Harry 'Wings' Day; NCO James 'Dixie' Deans; and Roger Bushell, leader of the North Compound's escape organisation.⁴³ Australians were incorporated into the prisoners' administration at many levels, including Group Captain Douglas Wilson, the Australian ranking officer who relieved as Senior British Officer during October–November 1943 while Massey was in hospital and, when Massey was medically repatriated, took the post permanently from May 1944 until January 1945.

Stalag Luft III 'was organised as far as possible on RAF station lines.'⁴⁴ It became in effect, 'RAF Station Sagan'. Ronald Baines insisted the prisoners' hierarchy 'did their best under the circumstances, [the] camp ran without friction and provided the best for the community'.⁴⁵ Robert Roy Nightingale, known as Roy, considered that they 'maintained a high degree of morale and discipline' which engendered a vital *esprit de corps*.⁴⁶ Camp and compound command structures were implemented. Accommodation blocks were run like squadrons, with their own commanding officers known as 'block heads'. 'Prisoner committees' coordinated non-administrative departments such as entertainment, education, sports, and leisure pursuits. As at any training station, men were encouraged to participate; it was all part of keeping mentally and physically fit and building group morale.⁴⁷ Those who could were also expected to work in escape-related departments.⁴⁸

Strong discipline underpinned security.⁴⁹ 'I became attached to the security side of the escape organisation and did at least a one hour shift each day', recalled Tom Wood. 'We arrived in Sagan in November 1943 and the big escape from the hut next door occurred the following March … none of we ex-Italian POWs were aware of what was going on until a week or so before.'⁵⁰ Alan Righetti,

---

42 Quote: AAWFA: Cornish 1388, 2 July 2004.
43 Meale, 'Leadership of Australian POWs in the Second World War', PhD thesis.
44 NAUK AIR 40/269: Stalag Luft III reports and nominal roll. Quote: AWM 54 779/3/129: 11 PDRC post-liberation debrief, Baines.
45 AWM 54 779/3/129: 11 PDRC post-liberation debrief, Baines.
46 AWM 54 779/3/129: 11 PDRC post-liberation debrief, Nightingale.
47 NAUK AIR 40/269: Stalag Luft III reports and nominal roll.
48 Brickhill and Norton, *Escape to Danger*, 236–237.
49 NAUK AIR 40/285: 'X' report.
50 3 Squadron RAAFA: 'Tom Wood Diary', 34.

another ex-'Italian', was let in on the secret after he joined the look-out crew – the stooges – who logged the movements of German staff in and around the huts. He recalled that 'we were all on honour never to discuss anything to do with it, and your mates [were] on honour to report you if you did.' 'To mention the word "escape" was prohibited.' Righetti, who spent much time 'on the circuit' with Jimmy Catanach, never once discussed the planned escape with him as they walked around the compound boundary; neither knew of the other's involvement.[51] 'As a matter of fact', Ross Breheny recalled, one of his roommates 'didn't know I was working on the tunnel, and I didn't know [he] was working on the tunnel' until sometime later. 'That's how good the security was.'[52]

The allied airmen never forgot that they were in the thrall of their enemy. Accordingly, communication with the Germans was prohibited. The only German-speaking kriegies allowed to converse with them were those required to as part of their duties like Kenneth Gaulton and Justin O'Byrne who liaised with their guard 'contacts', or when carrying out official escape or intelligence related work.[53] Paul Royle only used his linguistic talents to translate German newspapers so they could pin extracts on the noticeboard.[54] If you did have to speak to 'these bastards', Bill Fordyce recalled, 'you got up close to them and you shouted in English.'[55] Some kriegies tried to learn German – usually to enhance their chances if they managed to escape – but it was either too hard, or, with the strictures against contact with guards, there was little opportunity to practise. When guards challenged the communal disinclination to speak with them in German, adamant English-speakers undermined their captors' confidence in Axis victory and 'just said, "Oh German's a dead language." They didn't like that', recalled Richard Winn.[56] Those small but morale-raising triumphs in their battle behind barbed wire were important. The kriegies not only bolstered their martial identities, they strengthened their close bonds of air force fraternity.

---

51 AR: Alan Righetti, emails 4 January 2012; 17 October 2013; 7 February 2014.
52 Harrison RC: Warrant Officer Ross Thomas Breheny, 404957, 145 Squadron RAF, [2008].
53 AAWFA: Gaulton 1276, 3 February 2004; O'Byrne FA: O'Byrne, '*Mercury* Radio Roundsman'.
54 SLWA: Royle, 4 March 2014.
55 AAWFA: Fordyce 0523, 19 June 2003.
56 AAWFA: Winn 1508, 4 March 2004.

KRIEGIES

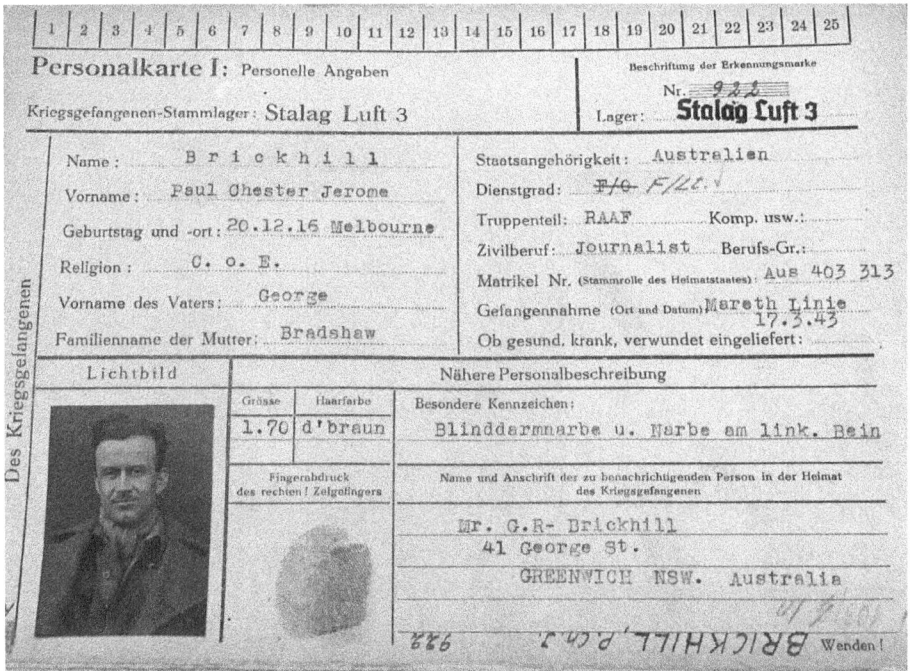

A Personalkarte was completed for every British and allied serviceman entering permanent German custody. Like Paul Brickhill, who eighteen days earlier had been flying his Spitfire into battle with 92 Squadron RAF, new arrivals were usually tired, hungry, dirty, and disoriented. NAA A13950.

'We were prisoners and the Germans did not let you forget that fact.' Ronald Baines found the early stages of captivity humiliating but his POW identification photo – like many – shows a hint of defiance. NAA A13950.

Many of the kriegies copied this image of Donald Duck into their wartime log books, including Ronald Baines, a Hurricane pilot of 213 Squadron RAF. It sums up their frustration at being captured and highlights the irony of their situation: they wanted to fly, and look what happened! Courtesy of the Baines family.

Chapter Four:

BROTHERHOOD

'We valued each other so much. We got to know each other better than you'd know your own brother.'[1] Alan Righetti had developed such a close bond with his fellow pilots during operational training that he dubbed them 'my particular little band of brothers'. Novices like Righetti had experienced many perils even in training; 'we were very, very close together' because flying in British skies during winter 'was a very dangerous thing'. Righetti and his fellow trainees were not the only airmen to recognise strong fraternal ties. From the earliest days of flight and warfare, flyers claimed de facto membership of an international 'brotherhood of the air', or 'brotherhood of airmen'.[2] That fraternity was carefully cultivated by Air Marshal Sir Hugh Trenchard as 'Air Force spirit' in RAF ethos, training, and on squadrons. Trenchard spoke of squadrons as 'homes' in his proposals to establish a peacetime RAF.[3] His construct was also embraced by men of the RAAF, like Righetti. For many airmen, the strong air force comradeship, based on crew, squadron, and service bonds, was all. 'Fate can never rob me, / Of the friendship of my friends', wrote Max Dunn.[4] Those sustaining brotherly relationships in camp were recognised as a surrogate family. 'We are a growing family', Group Captain Douglas Wilson, North Compound's acting Senior British Officer, stated in October 1943.[5]

Air force fraternity and solidarity underpinned every facet of captive lives. Frederick Seamer, the Australian representative in Centre Compound and later in Stalag Luft VI, Heydekrug, met all arrivals in his compound and immediately made them feel at home.[6] Seamer and his counterparts in other compounds introduced newcomers to their fellow Australians who generally helped with their welfare and supplied them with necessities, often donated by the longer-term prisoners or purchased from the profits of Foodacco, a points-based trading mart for food, cigarettes, and other luxury items.[7] The Australians in Belaria Compound formed the Boomerang Club.[8] As well as looking after the

---

1 AAWFA: Righetti 0984, 16 September 2003.
2 Alexander, 'Australian Knights of the Air and their Little Touches of Chivalry', 5.
3 Mahoney, 'Trenchard's Doctrine', 152, 153, 155–162; 'homes', 154.
4 Dunn, *Poems of Norman Maxwell Dunn*, 'To My Friends', 10.
5 NAUK WO 224/63A: Red Cross and Protecting Powers reports, 25–26 October 1943.
6 AAWFA: Kerr 1489, 3 March 2004.
7 AWM 54 779/3/126 part 1: Seamer, POW statement, [undated, c. June 1945].
8 Cousens (ed.), *The Log*, 68.

sporting, educational, and social activities of Belaria's resident Australians, club members provided new arrivals with a cheery reception.[9]

Some airmen clung to existing relationships with crew members imprisoned with them or reestablished bonds with schoolboy friends or comrades from training schools. Others looked out for those who hailed from their home town. When Peter Armytage arrived, so the story goes, he yelled out, 'is there any other bastard here from Melbourne?', and Rupert Steele replied.[10] Many new kriegies, however, accepted the reality that they were isolated indefinitely from the close companionship of existing squadron and civilian friendships. Accordingly, they turned to their fellow prisoners. Forging new connections was relatively easy, as Reginald Spear found. 'The spirit here of friendliness is excellent, and the chaps help each other magnificently.'[11] New boys soon discovered the benefits of mixing with old hands who had adapted to kriegie life and, as a consequence, were well-organised. 'I am settled down with some very nice lads who are quite ingenious old-timers', one airman told his parents.[12] Another was 'lucky to be with old prisoners who know all the angles.'[13]

Those who could not slot into former friendship groups because of overcrowding, existing alliances, or because friends were in other compounds, were directed to spare bunks by the senior British officers or Man of Confidence. Others were invited to join a room because the long-term members were 'looking for somebody who would fit in', Alec Arnel recalled.[14] Such randomness was similar to the peculiarly informal, haphazard method of forming crews – known as 'crewing up' – that occurred on bomber squadrons. Generally speaking, pilots, navigators and aircrew had congregated in a large room, hall, or hangar, and were then 'left to it'. A pilot might approach a navigator, a wireless operator would start chatting with a bomb aimer. There were no rules, and more often than not it worked. The banding together of roommates from different operational commands, squadrons and musterings, nationalities, and social backgrounds proved in many instances just as successful in co-mingling dissimilar personalities.

The close comradeships within rooms – variously called messes or combines – ensured conviviality and solidarity against the Germans. The airmen gossiped, confided fears, and discussed plans for the future; they exchanged the most personal of secrets. Their fraternal bonds also determined how well a man managed what Jock Bryce termed, the 'struggle for existence'. He joined a room

---

9   NLA FERG/4550: *P.O.W.*, No. 27, 15 April 1944, unattributed letter, 9 November 1943, 1.
10 'A thoroughbred in every sense', *The Age* (Melbourne), 19 June 2010.
11 Reginald Spear, 'Letter from R.A.A.F. Prisoner of War', *Horsham Times*, 3 March 1944, 2.
12 NLA FERG/4550: *P.O.W.*, No. 16, 15 May 1943, unattributed letter, 10 December 1942, 14.
13 NLA FERG/4550: *P.O.W.*, No. 16, 15 May 1943, unattributed letter, 26 January 1943, 14.
14 AR: Arnel, interview 23 June 2016.

of fellow prisoners newly arrived from Italian camps. Their common experience was 'helpful in that we preserved a unity of purpose'.[15]

Despite their obviously strong connections, some former prisoners rarely mentioned their friends by name in memoirs or late-life interviews. Jennifer Walsh, who worked with her father, Charles Lark, on his memoir was constantly frustrated because he spoke of 'we', rather than 'I'. The account was his, but Lark told of the collective experience.[16] Over the course of ten interviews, Alec Arnel consistently used 'I' when offering an opinion or speaking about his present emotions, but when recalling captivity used 'we'. Wartime imprisonment was 'not about me', he explained, emphatically stating that, '"I" wasn't just "me", "I" was "us"'. For Arnel, and others, there was no sense that captivity was an individual experience because 'it was happening to all of us. We were all in this together'.[17] Once established, the affective bonds of 'we' alleviated the inherent strains of captivity. Bolstering those ties, as Rex Austin indicated, was the fraternal love and trust shared by squadron colleagues, friends and aerial colleagues whose lives and operational success depended on each other's professional skill and expertise.[18] That 'complete sense of purpose and absolutely one hundred per cent loyalty to the death', Geoff Cornish explained, 'binds you, takes away selfishness and brings co-operation with other people'. Not only did brotherhood underpin squadron life and successful aerial operations, but their 'great friendships' sustained them throughout captivity.[19]

Australian fraternity was not necessarily based on a shared national identity. While 351 Australian airmen passed through the gates of Stalag Luft III before the January 1945 evacuation, there were never that many Australians in the camp at the same time. Nor were they in the same compound. In September 1942, for example, only forty Australian officers and forty NCOs were among the 2,507 allied airmen spread between two compounds.[20] In July 1943, after the NCOs were sent to Stalag Luft VI, Heydekrug, the British contingent of 663 included only 53 Australian officers and three NCO orderlies.[21] The Australians' friends were just as likely to be British, Canadian, Polish, or American. As Cy Borsht recalled, as well as himself and Australians Bruce Lumsden and John Dack, his roommates included 'New Zealand, there was South Africa, there was United States Air Force. That's as disparate a group as you can get'.[22]

---

15 Bryce FA: 'Jock Bryce's POW Diary 1942–1945', 143.
16 AR: Jennifer Walsh, interview 29 April 2017.
17 AR: Arnel, interview 12 November 2015.
18 AAWFA: Austin 0382, 5 June 2003.
19 AAWFA: Cornish 1388, 2 July 2004.
20 NAUK WO 224/63A: Red Cross and Protecting Powers reports, 13 September 1942.
21 NAUK WO 224/63A: Red Cross and Protecting Powers reports, 26 July 1943.
22 AR: Borsht, interview 28 January 2016.

Their common Australian background however, was a factor in some strong friendships. Most of the Australian NCOs in Centre Compound bunked together.[23] Harry Train and his officer friends in East Compound considered Block 64 to be a 'fairly good Australian centre'.[24] Some designated their rooms 'Anzac Cove' or 'Australia House'.[25] Reginald 'Reg' Kierath (also known as 'Rusty' to his friends) particularly appreciated national and school connections within his new room. 'I have now moved into a room with two other Australians … I went to Shore with John Williams, knew him in the [Middle East] and also came across him in Durban on one occasion. … The other bloke was at Scots, Ian McIntosh … It is certainly a great improvement to live with a couple of chaps that I have something in common with.'[26] Jimmy Catanach relished his squadron connections. He shared his room with navigator, Bob Anderson, and Tony Gordon, a fellow pilot from 455 Squadron RAAF, who had been captured just before Catanach joined the squadron. We 'do our own cooking and are very thankful for comforts of the Red Cross as added luxury'.[27]

Social welfare was an intrinsic part of life in Stalag Luft III. Mirroring the organisation of a standard RAF station, Stalag Luft III's administrative structures benefited 'the community', Alan Righetti recalled.[28] Although established on capitalist principles, Foodacco, the camp trading mart, was an example of economic social welfare.[29] So too were the rules implemented by each room and block to ensure harmonious living arrangements and equitable sharing of rations.

A fundamental aspect of kriegie brotherhood was a clear sense of altruism. After an influx of new prisoners created a strain on medical resources, 'somebody [took] up a collection of white shirts for the wounded to sleep in while in hospital'.[30] With winter approaching, the former Buchenwald internees were given extra clothing.[31] Long-term inhabitants also shared cigarettes and rations with newcomers. All books coming into camp via the Red Cross, other service organisations, and family were appropriated by the library. Recipients had first call on them but could not keep any reading material: they were for general circulation unless appropriated by the escape organisation. Airmen scrupulously divided rations and Red Cross parcels. Some altruistic acts had an intimate dimension. In a time of almost desperate rationing in January 1945, 'the blokes had saved up their semolina and everything' to make Rex Austin's 21st

---

23 Younger, *No Flight From the Cage*, 66.
24 Arnel archive: Train, 'A Barbed-Wire World', 15 April 1943, 40–41.
25 Anzac Cove: Preen FA: Albert Hake to Noela Hake, 28 February 1944; Australia House: Wickham, *We Wore Blue*, 174–175.
26 Kierath FA: Reg Kierath to Ada Kierath, 19 September 1943.
27 SOR JCC: 2013.CAT050, James Catanach to Dad Syb. Da and Heather, 16 October 1942.
28 AAWFA: Righetti 0984, 16 September 2003.
29 'The Inside Story of "Foodacco"' in 'Scangriff', (Winston, ed.), *Spotlight on Stalag Luft III*, 29–36.
30 NLA FERG/4550: *P.O.W.*, No. 37, 15 February 1945, unattributed, undated letter, 12.
31 Burgess RC: Raymond Perry, 'War Diary', undated, 49.

birthday cake. They also fashioned the key from precious cardboard and silver paper salvaged from cigarette packets.[32]

Deductions from RAF pay went into a communal fund to purchase musical instruments, sports kit, and items from the camp canteen. Some money was diverted to the escape organisation to bribe guards. While imprisoned officers received an allowance in Reichsmarks from the Germans, NCOs did not. Accordingly, every officer's pay was levied to provide funds for the non-commissioned officers in Centre Compound and other camps, as well as those employed as orderlies in order to, as Tony Gordon put it, 'ameliorate the lot' of the NCOs.[33] Non-commissioned officers did not just receive charitable largesse, they gave as well. Under the Geneva Convention, they were not obliged to carry out physical labour. Some Centre Compound kriegies, however, volunteered for work parties to clear the ground before construction began on North Compound. All 'money earned was put in the Camp Welfare Fund.'[34] Charity extended beyond barbed wire. Funds were also allocated to the wives and relatives of foreign nationals living on the continent.

Kriegie fraternity enabled many of the Australian airmen to relieve the strains of incarceration and effectively negotiate captivity. Whether they liked it or not, RAF Station Sagan was home for the duration. As such, the Australian airmen made the most of it, and, as best they could, created 'our kriegie home', as Timbury 'Tim' Mayo described it in a watercolour sketch of 'the room I shared with ... fellow POWs'.[35]

The 'small courtesies of everyday life, so easily forgotten, were practised', Laurie Simpson reported in an official debrief shortly after liberation. These ensured that the airmen generally kept on 'good terms with each other through the long waiting days'.[36] 'We now batch [number censored] per room', John Osborne told his family. 'Three chaps are from home, two NZ and the balance GB. Combination is as peaceful as one could expect under such confined conditions.'[37] But camp relationships were not always congenial. In such close living conditions, there was 'plenty to argue about', Alex Kerr recalled, 'especially if people haven't got anything to do and time is on their hands'.[38] There were 'little niggles', irritations and arguments over nothing at all or 'mercenary little things'.[39]

---

32 AAWFA: Austin 0382, 5 June 2003.
33 NAUK AIR 40/269: Stalag Luft III reports and nominal roll, Stalag Luft III Communal Fund. Quote: AWM 54 779/3/129: 11 PDRC post-liberation debrief, Gordon.
34 AWM 54 779/3/129: 11 PDRC post-liberation debrief, Adrian Condon.
35 Quote: Mayo FA: Mayo, 'Our Kriegie Home Looking In', November 1943 and 'Our Kriegie Home Looking Out', 10 January 1944.
36 AWM 54 779/3/126 part 1: Simpson, POW statement, 31 July 1945.
37 NAM JOC: John Osborne to family, 11 July 1943.
38 AAWFA: Kerr 1489, 3 March 2004.
39 'Niggles' from AR: Arnel, interview 23 June 2016. 'Mercenary little things' from NLA FERG/4550: *P.O.W.*, No. 8, 15 September 1942, unattributed letter, 29 April 1942, 5.

Sometimes, the tensions became almost unbearable in crowded rooms with no privacy. Loud-mouthed and domineering characters grated. So too did those who thought themselves 'superior to the colonials' or the morose types who kept to themselves.[40] 'People who were moody and solemn were unendurable', recalled Jock Bryce.[41]

The biggest threat to communal harmony was personality conflict. Generally speaking, Jock Bryce and Bill Fordyce lived with a fairly even-tempered group. Their room had the usual sort of arguments which soon blew over. Bryce and Fordyce, however, did not get on. They kept their mutual 'vague dislike' at bay to a certain extent but Bryce never went out of his way to make things easier. After a period of considerable tension in the early summer of 1944, their ill-feeling 'magnified rapidly into something stronger'. Bryce 'lost all control, for the only time during all my months as a prisoner, and resorted to violence'. Not only was it a 'breach of taste practically unknown in any prison camp I was in', it created a rift between their little brotherhood of airmen. Bryce does not elaborate on the form his aggression took but we can assume it was physical given the 'strained and nervous' atmosphere following the blow up. Certainly, life in the small room was difficult with two of its complement not speaking to each other and all walking on eggshells wondering if Bryce would again erupt. The RAF's Michael Calver, 'a natural humourist', did his best to create an uplifting environment but not even his good cheer could remedy the situation. Equanimity was only restored when Fordyce moved to another room. 'Thereafter the little community was peaceful.'[42]

When the airmen were pushed closer to the edge in times of extreme stress, fraternal bonds unravelled. In those situations, society's rules were not always observed. Laurie Simpson observed that 'if the POW is fairly well fed he can look on his lot with a much clearer eye and can "take it" much more philosophically'. But hunger could make men 'irritable and develop a quite intolerant and narrow-minded attitude over relatively small matters'.[43] There were many hunger-related squabbles. In times of strict rationing and food deprivation, portions were scrupulously split and rules were developed to ensure equitable sharing. Some who transgressed those rules felt intense guilt. 'Whilst room cook I took a slice of bread, margarine and jam and afterwards felt it wasn't mine – it belonged to the room', *Wilfred Mosse* confessed.[44] Some prisoners became obsessed about their own allocation. They indicated their preoccupation with food and rations by detailing in their wartime log books their food parcel largesse and

---

40 AAWFA: Winn 1508, 4 March 2004.
41 Bryce FA: 'Jock Bryce's POW Diary 1942–1945', 155.
42 Bryce FA: 'Jock Bryce's POW Diary 1942–1945', 155.
43 AWM 54 779/3/126 part 1: Simpson, POW statement, 31 July 1945.
44 DVA MX124472-02: clinical report from psychiatrist, 28 October 1965.

nutritional content as well as the German rations. Jack Morschel referred to the Red Cross parcel as 'A kriegie's weekly salvation.'[45] Such was their sensitivity over rations that, when 'the odd case of stealing' occurred, cordiality and courtesy disappeared; 'arguments and then fisticuffs' ensued, recalled Alex Kerr.[46] Discord was long lasting when members of one usually easy-going room hid a piece of chocolate. It was meant as a joke, Alec Arnel recalled, but was recognised only in hindsight as 'a silly thing to do, because a piece of chocolate was absolutely gold'. The chocolate owner's immediate reaction was that there was a thief in the room. The pranksters confessed, the chocolate was returned, but the joke's victim did not forgive easily or quickly.[47] While theft from the Germans was condoned and encouraged under the auspices of the escape organisation, taking from fellow kriegies was not tolerated.[48] In some rooms, thieves were shunned.[49] Some were punished severely or even brutally. Kerr told the story of how in one camp 'a couple of chaps had a hatchet ready to cut a fellow's hand off because he was caught stealing some bread'. He conceded that 'that was very far-fetched, but usually it would amount to beating a chap up'.[50]

While the *act* of stealing from POWs was not tolerated, there was, in some cases, a compassionate understanding of *how* men in extremis could break fundamental social tenets. In 1941, deprivation in Oflag X-C, an army camp at Lübeck, assailed the kriegies' sense of human dignity. The loss of weight, sickness, and fear of starvation had 'a terrible effect on us all', recalled Justin O'Byrne. 'It was my first experience of the survival instinct becoming dominant to all others and to see fine officers of the Black Watch, Coldstream Guards and other fine regiments waiting to share the discarded peelings and black portions of potatoes was a new "low" in the graph of my experiences.'[51] For 'something to look forward to', O'Byrne's friend, Patrick 'Les' Dixon, had been saving a potato for his birthday. Every time he came across a bigger one he swapped it and ate the smaller one. Just before his birthday, when Dixon's anticipation was greatest, another prisoner stole the potato and devoured it. It was 'unforgiveable' for 'anyone to steal anything else from a fellow prisoner', recalled O'Byrne. 'The ferocity that Les used on showing his anger at having lost his potato! He got [the thief] down, and we had to physically drag him away from his throat, because of his anger in this man doing such a dastardly thing.' Without condoning either the theft or Dixon's response, O'Byrne compassionately tried to explain how two

---

45   AWM PR00506: Morschel, wartime log book [unpaginated].
46   AAWFA: Kerr 1489, 3 March 2004.
47   AR: Arnel, interview, 23 June 2016.
48   AAWFA: Austin 0382, 5 June 2003.
49   AR: Arnel, interview 27 November 2014.
50   AAWFA: Kerr 1489, 3 March 2004.
51   O'Byrne FA: O'Byrne, 'Nine o'clock above!'

reasonable men could breach the normal societal boundaries. 'It gives an idea of the relativity of values ... of life itself, how it's a primitive and basic thing to have food when you're hungry; your stomach needs food.'[52] O'Byrne's uncensorious comments suggest that he was fully aware of how men could be pushed to the edge of their humanity not just because of what he had witnessed, but because he, too, had been close to it.

Despite these threats, the affective and service bonds of the brotherhood of airmen were strong and the Australian airmen generally enjoyed cohesion in captivity. Recalling their fractious relationships decades later, roommates tended to readily excuse the 'squeaky wheels' and even their own conduct. As John Dack remembered, they were 'one of us' and had to be tolerated.[53] The differences experienced by the 'brothers-in-captivity' in their interminable, forced intimacy were, as Ron Mackenzie recalled, 'probably not much more marked than those that plague brothers-by-birth.'[54] When physical survival was at risk, however, civility and discipline disintegrated, thus indicating that, for some, not all responses to captivity arose from a need to mitigate, moderate, or even clear-headedly navigate captivity. Indeed, some reactions to the most challenging circumstances were visceral or calculatedly selfish, arising from the darkest side of human nature. Ultimately, kriegie fraternity underpinned survival in Stalag Luft III. Ingenuity ensured their relative comfort.

Alan Righetti developed close bonds with his 3 Squadron RAAF comrades and fellow kriegies. Many friendships lasted a lifetime. Courtesy of Alan Righetti.

---

52 NLA O'Byrne, 'Reminiscential conversations', Tape 50.
53 Dack, *So you Wanted Wings, Hey!*, 91
54 Mackenzie, *An Ordinary War 1940–1945*, 43.

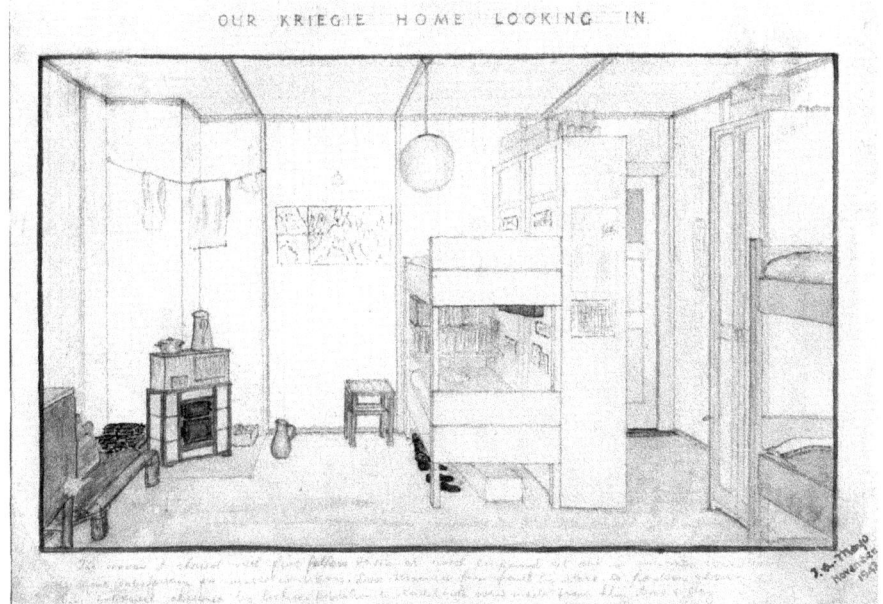

'Our kriegie room looking in,' November 1943, watercolour sketch by Tim Mayo. Tim, an observer with 12 Squadron RAF whose Wellington had been downed near St Nazaire, France, shared his room with five fellow POWs. Here, he depicts it *'in manner considered most satisfactory for winter conditions.'* Courtesy of Peter Mayo.

'Our kriegie room looking out,' 10 January 1944, water colour sketch by Tim Mayo. Mayo noted that the colours in this picture were *'much too clean looking and room much too tidy in appearance!'* Courtesy of Peter Mayo.

Although both Hampden pilots with 455 Squadron RAAF, Tony Gordon's and Jimmy Catanach's service did not overlap – Gordon was captured a month before Catanach joined the squadron. Nonetheless, the pair who both hailed from Melbourne, became roommates and firm friends. This photographic record of that friendship was so important that, when Gordon sent a copy to his sweetheart, Rosemary, he told her to 'hang onto' it. Tony never got over his friend's death. 'Jim was my good friend and was one of those murdered by the Germans after the GREAT ESCAPE.' Courtesy of Drew Gordon.

Chapter Five:

KRIEGIE INGENUITY

Within weeks of arriving in Stalag Luft III, Reg Kierath proudly declared to his mother that he had been put on his room's cooking roster and had 'even made a cake'. Ada no doubt had her own well-worn cook books. Nonetheless, her son shared his special recipe:

> Ingredients: six biscuits (Sao type) margarine, bread crumbs, powdered milk, raisins. Method: Grate finely the biscuits and bread into a fine flour and then add milk powder. Add the raisins and some water and stir the whole lot like hell … Icing can be made from cocoa, condensed milk, and margarine.[1]

Perhaps Ada was surprised by her son's new-found culinary expertise – Kierath's 'even made a cake' implies he thought she might be taken aback by his news – but it was pure common sense to embrace typically feminine tasks such as cooking, cleaning, and mending. Someone had to do the 'house work' and talking about it in letters normalised it. Kriegie domesticity signalled to homefolks that the Australian airmen, like Kierath, were 'beginning to settle down to the ways and habits of a regular prisoner of war.'[2] Even so, the airmen remained emotionally connected to their families in their 'real homes' and 'real lives' outside combat and captivity. 'Would that I were here', Tim Mayo wrote above a sketch of his home sent to his mother.[3] The Australian airmen maintained those nostalgic links through correspondence with family members but they also did it by emulating their mothers, sisters, and wives to create their own domestic environment. They, however, demonstrated an entirely masculine take on kriegie domesticity to ensure their essential masculinity was not overtly threatened.

Each room's space was carefully conserved. The kriegies precisely laid out their rooms' floorplans.[4] The privacy of bunks was not breached and seats were allocated at tables. This rigid spatial organisation was not just because of the room size. It reflected a desire to restore calm after the disruption of their ordered operational lives and, on a practical level, the disarray following German room searches. They decorated their rooms with photographs, maps, artworks, and books. Their decor reflected and, at the same time, reminded them of their pre-war homes and spick and span service accommodation.

---

1 Reg Kierath to his mother, 5 July 1943.
2 Reg Kierath to his mother, 28 May 1943.
3 NAA A705 166/5/818, Currie: Grace Mayo to Isabel Currie, 29 September 1942.
4 Burgess RC: Robert Mills, wartime log book, 14.

To ensure a fair distribution of labour and tasks, the airmen drew up rosters and allocated duties. They scrubbed and cleaned lockers, peeled potatoes, mended clothes, and did the laundry. Like Kierath, they managed rations, planned recipes, cooked for their fellows, and, in some compounds during times of fuel shortages, donated bed boards to supplement the briquette supply for their stoves.[5] While each room had a 'stube fuhrer' – room leader – quartermasters and cooks occupied the most important positions in domestic hierarchies.[6] They stood in the stead of mothers and wives as they carefully prepared food for their camp family. Others also took turns catering for every-day meals as well as special occasions such as birthday parties and Christmas celebrations.

Good cooks and quartermasters enhanced social cohesion within rooms and ensured a more comfortable existence. Those who skilfully carried out those tasks were praised. John Dack and his roommates 'were most fortunate' in having Bruce Lumsden as cook and Englishman 'Nobby' Clark as quartermaster. They did 'fantastic jobs with what was available.'[7] In a light-hearted article in *The Australasian*, Bill Fordyce publicised the kitchen skills of Hugh Lambie and James Vaughan, as well as the distillery talent of Laurie Simpson, the 'brew fuhrer.'[8] But 'woe betide the "cook of the week" if he doesn't do his best,' Allen Mulligan told his mother, Eulalie. 'He takes a big razzing.'[9]

Like Reg Kierath, airmen did nothing to hide their home-making expertise when writing to loved ones. They used it as conversational gambits with their womenfolk and offered it as demonstration that they could apply what they had learned at the family hearth to their own kriegie home. Domestic references in letters also assured recipients that they were safe, coping well, making the most of their circumstances, and managing their time. Tony Gordon asked his Aunt Mag to send knitting needles, a 'housewife' – a small case for needles and thread – and a ball of wool.[10] One man reported that he had 'manufactured a blanket out of old socks, scarves, jumpers, etc'. It was easy enough to fashion the 'crochet needle from a toothbrush handle,' he wrote. Using it 'was a bit hard for a while, but the fingers adjusted themselves to it.'[11] 'I have settled into doing my share of the chores,' wrote Alec Arnel. 'I do the washing and cleaning up in my turn.'[12]

Kierath was not the only one to boast of culinary prowess. 'After many weeks of saving, I made the Mess Christmas cake last week,' George Archer told his

---

5 Lumsden FA: Bradbeer and Lumsden, 'The Complete Tour', Lumsden, letter 10 June 1988.
6 'Stube fuhrer': Todd FA: Ken Todd, wartime log book, 11; 'position', Dack, *So you Wanted Wings, Hey!*, 83.
7 Dack, *So you Wanted Wings, Hey!*, 86.
8 'Sketches in a Prison Camp', *The Australasian*, 11 August 1945, 12.
9 'How our prisoners in Germany fill in the day', *Australian Women's Weekly*, 17 April 1943, 10.
10 Gordon FA: Gordon to Aunt Mag, 31 May 1942.
11 NLA FERG/4550: P.O.W., No. 19, 16 August 1943, unattributed letter, 30 May 1943, 10.
12 Arnel archive: Arnel to Margery Gray, [undated].

family. '14 lbs – From appearances it's excellent.'[13] Justin O'Byrne turned fruit into jam and confided his magic ingredient – 'orange drink crystals for sugar'.[14] In sharing recipes and menus of which they were obviously proud, the airmen sought parental approbation for their achievements. Some also looked to their future. 'The old cooking game is still going strong, and I've got some really hot recipes now. I'll give you both a treat when I come home', Alexander Smith told his parents.[15]

The Australian airmen's assiduous domesticity seems at odds with their martial identity, yet kriegie domesticity was in no way emasculating. It was an extension of air force discipline. All airmen were expected to maintain their billets on training stations, and, while officers on operational stations enjoyed the services of orderlies, NCOs had to tidy up after themselves; they sewed on their own buttons and took care of minor repairs. It was a matter of pride to stitch on wings, rank insignia, and overseas service chevrons. In camp, wearing and caring for their uniform emphasised that they were still active servicemen.

Despite this, some kriegies were unsettled by the gendered nature of their domesticity. They feared it did not entirely reflect their masculine or martial selves. Accordingly, they undermined their competency by making fun of it. Even as Alexander Smith planned a post-war feast for his family, he joked about being 'afraid you might suffer from indigestion after one of my meals'.[16] As well as writing out the recipe for his iced cake, Reg Kierath humorously included a significant instruction in the method: 'hope for the best'.[17] William Kenneth 'Ken' Todd ironically depicted his new domestic situation by including an RAAF recruitment poster ('Adventure in the Skies. Join the RAAF') in a drawing of a kriegie (perhaps himself) washing plates.[18] Seemingly poking fun at the Geneva Convention which provided that officers were not obliged to work, a series of drawings in Torres Ferres' wartime log book captioned, 'Oh no, we never had to work', includes examples of a POW performing what could be seen as traditionally women's housework: making the bed, sweeping the floor, and carrying water jugs and packages. The anonymous artist's apparent recognition of the value of women's work, however, is secondary to emphasising the sketched-kriegie's essential masculinity: the man making the bed and sweeping the floor is magnificently bare-chested.[19]

---

13 Equivalent to 6.35 kilograms. Archer FA: Archer to his mother, 17 December 1944.
14 O'Byrne FA: Justin O'Byrne to family, 29 October 1943.
15 NLA FERG/4550: P.O.W., No. 13, 15 February 1943, [Alexander Smith], 16 June 1942, 11.
16 NLA FERG/4550: P.O.W., No. 13, 15 February 1943, [Alexander Smith], 16 June 1942, 11.
17 Reg Kierath to his mother, 5 July 1943.
18 Todd FA: Ken Todd, wartime log book, 'Stooge' 16.
19 AWM PR90/035: Ferres, wartime log book, 67.

Despite the benefits of their competent domesticity, the Australian airmen recognised that, as a consequence of it, captivity straddled two gendered worlds: the civilian domestic front and the martial world of RAF Station Sagan. Yet, as indicated by Bill Fordyce's image of Leonard 'Len' Netherway on kitchen duty neatly attired in battledress with wings insignia and polished boots, the kriegies were ultimately comfortable with this duality.[20] It reflected a sensible, pragmatic and determined approach to managing their environment which was not at odds with their martial identity. Symbolically, in drawing on domestic skills (including tending to their uniforms), they indicated that they were upholding their active, operational stance. They also emotionally connected to home and their female role models. In making fun of their own efforts they revealed their high spirits and signalled that captivity was not getting them down. They would not, however, usurp the traditional female role of family cook when they returned home. Their homemaking skills were for the duration only. John Osborne was adamant that he would hang up his apron at the end of the war. 'It's quite a job housekeeping for this family and I have no further desire to manage house.'[21]

Homemaking may be perceived as a feminine task but the home handyman was a traditionally male role. Next to the cook and quartermaster, the most esteemed person on the kriegie domestic front was the 'tin basher'. More than just a handyman who could repair everyday utensils, dextrous kriegies who fashioned items out of tin cans or other metal objects exemplified ingenuity, creativity, and masculinity. They played a central role in Stalag Luft III's physical comfort. Roderick Ferry rigged up a 'bush bucket-shower'.[22] Others built chip heaters and stoves. The Australian airmen used whatever they had to hand or could scrounge to fashion kitchen and table ware, mugs and plates, biscuit grinders, and jugs. Doug Hutchinson and his friends in Belaria Compound 'make all our own cooking utensils and are becoming quite craftsmen at the job'.[23] Some became so skilled that tin bashing evolved from the purely utilitarian; aesthetic form became as important as function.

Tin bashing skills underpinned the camp's social life. George Archer sketched 'Simo's Masterpiece', a brewing distillery designed by Laurie Simpson.[24] The theatre chippies' creations 'passed beyond expectation, being really good'. Their designs were accurate 'to the last degree in realism even to the production of Jacobean furniture, old masters, lounges, telephones, wirelesses', recorded Ken

---

20 Netherway FA: Netherway, wartime log, Bill Fordyce, 'Bloody Stuff's Cold', 25.
21 NAM JOC: John Osborne to family, 11 July 1943.
22 NLA FERG/4550: P.O.W., No. 16, 15 May 1943, unattributed letter, 28 April 1943, 10.
23 Hutchinson FA: Doug Hutchinson to Lola Hutchinson, 18 August 1943.
24 Archer FA: Archer, wartime log book, 24.

Todd.²⁵ Centre Compound's Peter Stubbs' tin bashing skills were particularly valuable. At both Stalag Luft I, Barth and Stalag Luft III he built and maintained a radio. One of Stalag Luft III's doctors asked Stubbs and his handy friend, Englishman John Bristow, to build a lamp that could be used for operations. The medico's next request was 'for a more ambitious instrument – a pneumothorax machine' to collapse tuberculosis patients' lungs.²⁶

As well as contributing to the communal good, much kriegie ingenuity was dedicated to supporting the escape organisation. Some needle-workers were obliged to surrender their sewing kits to Albert Hake, George Russell, and their fellow compass-makers.²⁷ Skills developed to maintain uniforms were deployed in the tailoring department which fabricated German uniforms and civilian clothes for escapers. Tom Wood 'spent a bit of time making shorts, altering uniform trousers and the like. Quite time consuming, unpicking and re-using the cotton!'²⁸ Some tin bashers manufactured tunnel ventilation lines out of food cans. Others, including Tony Gordon, built lamps, portable heating stoves, and torches for tunnels. They also repaired radios, made uniform badges for the tailors, and carried out any necessary metalwork. Carpenters were particularly busy. Using Red Cross parcel packaging, those in East Compound constructed the vaulting horse used in the October 1943 Wooden Horse escape. North Compound's carpentry crew, headed by John 'Willy' Williams, and including Malcolm 'Mac' Jones and Reg Kierath, appropriated bed boards to shore up escape tunnels and make tunnel trolleys.

Practical and ingenious work could exist alongside ostensibly feminine domestic tasks. As Kierath particularly exemplified, creative cooks could also be industrious carpenters. Those with sewing skills were key operatives behind the escape organisation's scenes. Working for comrades within their rooms and for the broader camp community fostered cohesion and strengthened the kriegies' brotherly ties. Filling time so productively helped them bear captivity. So, too, did knowing that they had not been forgotten.

---

25   Todd FA: Ken Todd, wartime log book, 25.
26   Stubbs, 'Low-level Attack', in Walley (ed), *Silk and Barbed Wire*, 5–9, 13–14.
27   NAUK WO 208/3283: SLIII Camp History, Part I East (Officers') Compound, 26, 33; Alexander, 'Australian compass makers and more'.
28   3 Squadron RAAFA: 'Tom Wood Diary', 34.

Kriegies put on brave faces when communicating with family. They wanted to convince loved ones that they were making the best of life behind barbed wire. In April 1942, a bearded Tony Gordon sent this picture to his sweetheart, Rosemary, assuring her that 'it's really me behind the scrub'. Courtesy of Drew Gordon.

Captured in April 1943, it didn't take Reg Kierath of 450 Squadron RAAF long to 'settle down to the ways and habits of a regular prisoner of war'. Within a month of arriving at Stalag Luft III, he was on his room's cooking roster and sending his mother his special cake recipe. Courtesy of Peter Kierath.

John Williams, captured shortly after his appointment as Commanding Officer of 450 Squadron RAAF, had proved himself an aggressive Western Desert pilot. In camp, he ably headed the escape organisation's carpentry department. Courtesy of Louise Williams.

PART THREE: BRIDGING THE DIVIDE

Chapter Six:

NOT FORGOTTEN

May Fraser's anguish was palpable. Was Donald alive? Or had he died in action? She wrote to her son's friend, Ted Garside, and asked him to 'honestly tell me what you think of his chances of still being alive'. She tried 'to hope that he may be a POW and if he came down over the land there may be a chance that he is'. But, she confessed to Garside, 'I am very afraid of the sea'. May's dread was all-encompassing. It 'just goes on and on in my head, and makes me fear very much, that I will not see my son again.'[1]

From the first news that an airman was missing, families responded viscerally: shock, denial, distress, and a sense of helplessness. They were overwhelmed by uncertainty. Severe emotional reactions arose from trepidation that, rather than 'missing', their loved ones were in fact dead. Many suffered physically and psychologically; emotions were embodied. 'I haven't been well, the worry and anxiety always sends my blood pressure up', May confided.[2] Doug Hutchinson's wife, Lola, was 'breaking my heart'.[3] She dramatically lost weight.[4] Fathers also felt the emotional strains. Reverend Walter Betts' apprehension over the fate of his son, Wesley, was apparent to the Department of Air's official who minuted their conversations. 'Rev Betts called anxious…' 'He is anxious to send a cable to his son.' 'I assured him.'[5]

While Sophie Johnston had no doubt she would see her son, Eric, again, that certainty eluded many.[6] May Fraser anticipated 'the worst … in my heart I am very afraid'.[7] She, like countless others, experienced anticipatory grief, along with its stark emotions of shocked numbness and incredulity.[8] Extended family, friends, and colleagues responded to the 'anticipation of loss'.[9] They sent condolence-like letters which, even as they adhered to an accepted social formula, offered solace, sympathy, and empathy. As well as social niceties, these supportive articulations recognised and partly assuaged emotional pain. Family friend Dorrie Power extended to Doug Hutchinson's parents the comfort of an

---

1 Fraser FA: May Fraser to Ted Garside, 1 April 1943.
2 Fraser FA: May Fraser to Ted Garside, 10 April 1943.
3 Hutchinson FA: Lola Hutchinson to Doug Hutchinson, 1 October 1943.
4 Hutchinson FA: Lola Hutchinson to Doug Hutchinson, 31 October 1943.
5 NAA A705, 166/5/530 Wesley Betts, minute sheet.
6 AR: Evelyn Johnston, interview 18 October 2016.
7 Fraser FA: May Fraser to Ted Garside, 1 April 1943.
8 Raphael, *The Anatomy of Bereavement*, 50–51.
9 For 'anticipation of loss' refer Damousi, *The Labour of Loss*, 66.

all too common travail. 'There are not many of us who are not sharing the same worry.'[10] Lola was overwhelmed by the concern of fellow workers and customers as strengthening expressions of sympathy flooded in: 'You know Doug it has taken this trouble to make me realise how many true friends we have. … Gee sweetheart it's good to know people think so much of my husband.'[11]

Religious families turned to God and their faith communities. Frank and Jess Hutchinson's friends had a 'strong feeling of faith and trust in God' that Doug 'would return to us.'[12] Religion, however, was not a panacea for all. Evelyn Charles, who for five months had no knowledge of the fate of her sweetheart, Eric Johnston, would often quietly sit in the back of Melbourne's St Paul's cathedral. One day, 'there was a couple … She was breaking her heart. Absolutely. And I couldn't stand it. So I got up, I went to work. … and do you know, I never, ever went back.' Evelyn had felt alienated from both church and a potentially shared experience. 'I hadn't worked out whether they were mourning someone or whether they were missing someone. Whether they were like me.' Perhaps too, she was unwilling to identify herself as a grieving woman. While Evelyn experienced little emotional support from church or family, she and Sophie Johnston were mutually supportive.[13]

Clinging to hope was a natural, positive reaction to bad news. It made waiting endurable and, was for many, emotionally fortifying. Despite having no direct knowledge of the circumstances of Donald's last action, May Fraser was keen to accept the 'little gleam of hope' offered by Ted Garside when he gave his opinion of her son's chances of survival. 'I am trying to keep my chin up and believe like all the rest of my family that Don is a prisoner.'[14] Anticipation of good news for Evelyn Charles, however, alternated with uncertainty. 'I had no idea. … all there was were tears and hope and days when I think yes, and no, no, it's not going to happen. Up and down.'[15] Even so, Evelyn, like others who sent letters 'out into the blue', continued to write to their loved ones.[16] 'I suppose I am a bit crazy writing these letters when I haven't any definite news of you sweetheart, but I just know that you are all right and that by the time these reach their destination you will have arrived back safely.'[17]

Communications – whether official or private – between Australia and Germany were uncertain. As a clerk in the Department of Air's Casualty Section

---

10   Hutchinson FA: Dorrie Power to Jess Hutchinson, 9 August 1943.
11   Hutchinson FA: Lola Hutchinson to Doug Hutchinson, 1 October 1943.
12   Hutchinson FA: Joy and Bill of West Wyalong to Frank and Jess Hutchinson, 15 August 1943.
13   AR: Evelyn Johnston, interview 18 October 2016.
14   Fraser FA: May Fraser to Ted Garside, 10 April 1943.
15   AR: Evelyn Johnston, interview 18 October 2016.
16   AR: Arnel, interview 10 December 2015.
17   Johnston FA: Evelyn Charles to Eric Johnston, 2 October 1944.

explained to Walter Betts, German administration and communications were often disorganised because of allied bombing raids.[18] Sometimes advice took weeks, even months. That long waiting was 'most unbearable' for Charles Fry's fiancée, Beryl Smith.[19] 'The last three months' for Evelyn Charles 'have seemed like three long years to me'.[20] While Evelyn fretted until official word came through, some families were not content to wait. They took the initiative and made their own enquiries. Some, such as Walter Phelps, wrote to the Red Cross.[21] Ethel Righetti contacted the YMCA.[22] Herbert Adams travelled from Sydney to Melbourne especially to receive 'particulars' from the Casualty Section about his son, Denis.[23] Others, like Englishwoman Freda Pollard who lived in Lancashire and had heard nothing from her fiancé, Kenneth Wright, wrote to RAAF Headquarters in London.[24] Julia Osborne was so anxious during the month-long wait for confirmation of her son John's status that she consulted a psychic who assured her he was alive.[25]

Confirmation of safety was 'a great event'.[26] It was received 'with gladness and thanksgiving'.[27] May Fraser was overjoyed when advised that Donald was 'reported safe'.[28] Her initial grief-like reaction then changed to one of acceptance.[29] For many, the happy news signalled a return to their usual household, work, and social duties. Their letters, full of life's minutiae reflect their attempts to get back to normal and to allay their ongoing anxiety for their absent men. Women's letters also highlighted a cultural response. As Dorrie Power's letter indicates, many were in the same situation. Life had to go on. 'We'll just have to wait now till the war is over', Lola Kerwin declared to a reporter when she heard that her brother, Basil, had been captured.[30] 'It has been a long time now darling', Beryl Smith told Charles Fry, 'but even if it is as long again (which I don't think it will be) you will still find me waiting for you.'[31] No one, however, passively marked time. Love and responsibility were not put on hold. Families and partners worked ceaselessly to make captive lives more tolerable.

Long-distance nurturing was expressed by writing letters and preparing parcels. The kriegies were desperate for mail. While epistolary contact was

---

18   NAA A705, 166/5/530: Wesley Betts, minute sheet.
19   Fry FA: Beryl Smith to Charles Fry, [undated, c. 27 August 1941].
20   Johnston FA: Evelyn Charles to Eric Johnston, 6 October 1944.
21   MHRC CPA: Mrs A.E. Simonett, Director, Red Cross Bureau for Wounded, Missing & Prisoners of War to Mr W.J. Phelps, 24 July 1944.
22   NAA A705 166/35/8 Righetti: minute sheet.
23   NAA A705, 166/3/314 Adams: minute sheet.
24   NAA A9301 403176 [Wright], Freda Pollard, [undated] to RAAF Overseas Headquarters.
25   AR: Carlene Scifleet, interview 9 June 2016.
26   Mayo FA: Eric Mayo to parents, 3 June 1942.
27   Fry FA: Beryl Smith to Charles Fry, 14 August 1941.
28   A705, 166/14/311 Fraser: Senator Sampson to Langslow, Department of Air, 22 May 1942; telegram to Mr H. Fraser, 19 May [1942].
29   AR: Barbara Fotheringham, interview 26 June 2016.
30   'Reported Prisoner of War. Pilot Officer Kerwin', *Queensland Times* (Ipswich), 9 December 1940, 4.
31   Fry FA: Beryl Smith to Charles Fry, 31 May 1944.

mainly the province of female relations, male friends and family members also sent regular heartening missives. 'Great joy today,' wrote Justin O'Byrne. 'I have received letters from Dad, Brendan, Ray's five, Tom's two, Pauline, Kath and Pam and am absolutely delighted.'[32] The large quantity of mail handled by the Red Cross alone – which posted its millionth letter from Australia during 1943 – demonstrates that close and extended families needed to sustain their links to their absent loved ones. (Stalag Luft III's Harold Longworth was featured as the recipient of that milestone letter.)[33]

Parcels and letters provided solace to the sender through the act of writing, selecting and packaging; they were physical representations of love and concern, and fulfilled families' deep-seated need to help the absent airmen in any way they could. 'Darling, I am doing absolutely everything possible for you,' Beryl Smith told Charles Fry.[34] While parcel contents addressed the airmen's physical requirements, letters meant so much more than just the news they contained. They bridged the spatial, temporal, and emotional divide between home and prison camp; the daily trivialities – the evocation and recollection of them – connected the airmen to pre-captivity lives which they could still recognise. 'Do you remember the last crop of potatoes that were planted ... and how the boys used to pelt them at anyone going along,' Eva Green asked her son, Errol.[35] Letters were so precious that James McCleery mounted one from his sister, Laura, in his wartime log book: 'first news from home'. Laura had known he would be 'anxiously waiting on letters' and had written almost as soon as she heard he was missing, assuring him that all at home were well and that she and others would send comfort parcels.[36]

One of the greatest hazards to the well-being of prisoners of war was the fear of being forgotten.[37] Mail was vital proof that homefolks had not forgotten their loved ones. Family, romantic partners, and friends constantly reassured the airmen of their continued place in their lives and hearts. 'I do hope you receive our mail,' Eva Green told Errol. 'We never miss to write twice each week. ... You are never from my thoughts for many moments of the day. My first thoughts in the morning and the last at night.'[38] 'Please don't feel neglected or forgotten,' Beryl Smith pleaded with Charles Fry, 'as I am thinking of you every minute of the day and night.'[39]

---

32 O'Byrne FA: Justin O'Byrne to family, 24 November 1943.
33 'Million Letters', *Daily News* (Perth), 23 October 1943, 15.
34 Fry FA: Beryl Smith to Charles Fry, 31 January 1942. For psychological need to provide aid, refer Bomford, 'Fractured Lives', PhD thesis, 65.
35 Green FA: Eva Green to Errol Green, 21 June 1942.
36 AWM PR88/160: McCleery, wartime log book.
37 Newman, 'The Prisoner-of-War Mentality', 8–9.
38 Green FA: Eva Green to Errol Green, 28 June 1942.
39 Fry FA: Beryl Smith to Charles Fry, 30 October 1941.

Women also ensured their menfolk were publicly remembered. Lola Hutchinson constantly talked about her husband and passed on news of his well-being when she heard from him. Eulalie Mulligan was one of many mothers who allowed family letters and photographs to be published in newspapers or POW magazines. Frederick Archer relayed George's regards to relatives, neighbours, a member of his Masonic lodge, and 'all at the office and the crowd at Brighton'.[40] Brothers and sisters also made certain that their captive siblings did not recede from public memory. Lola Kerwin and Bill Poulton were just two who sent news of their brothers (Basil Kerwin and Warwick Poulton) and copies of their letters to the papers.[41] Richard Winn's mother, Betty, proudly wore the white gold brooch her son had given her before he embarked.[42] Mothers and wives wore Female Relatives' Badges.

Without the standing of a wife and, accordingly, not entitled to the Female Relatives' Badge, Beryl Smith highlighted her connection to a serviceman by wearing the Caterpillar Club Badge which Charles Fry sent to her. It was a deeply personal tangible link to her fiancé, 'because it is the only thing I have belonging to you which I can wear and I am very proud indeed to wear it.'[43] In some ways, too, the badge represented Fry: 'I am wearing the Caterpillar badge with its eyes pointing to mine, darling.'[44] In doing so, as historian Joy Damousi notes, Fry's fiancée created 'a presence out of ... absence.'[45] Beryl assiduously cultivated that imagined presence. She promoted Fry's service beyond their family and friendship circle. She fed items about him to newspapers; provided details to 'the Official War Historian for incorporation in their records of deeds by Australians'; and made enquiries to the Minister for Air regarding Fry's omission from the Honour Roll contained in the Australian War Memorial's 1943 publication, *RAAF Log*.[46]

Wives, fiancées, and sweethearts worried over their partners' health and well-being. 'Do you know at times I nearly go crazy, wondering what you are doing and if you are alright', Lola Hutchinson told Doug.[47] They feared their partners would forget them or turn away from them romantically. Loneliness and misery overwhelmed; they craved contact. 'It is over two months since I received your last letter-card, Chas', wrote Beryl, 'and words cannot express my anxiety to hear

---
40 Archer FA: Archer to his mother, 16 October 1943.
41 Reported Prisoner of War. Pilot Officer Kerwin', *Queensland Times* (Ipswich), 9 December 1940, 4; 'Prisoner still full of fight', The *Australian Women's Weekly*, 10 July 1943, 10.
42 Johnson, 'From Choirboy to Dogfighter'.
43 'To a typist came a gold caterpillar', *The Sun* (Sydney), 7 November 1943, 4. Quote: Fry FA: Beryl Smith to Charles Fry, 29 October 1943.
44 Fry FA: Beryl Smith to Charles Fry, 31 May 1944.
45 Refer Damousi, *The Labour of Loss*, 121.
46 Jeff James, RAAF Recruiting Drive Committee NSW to Beryl Smith, 9 September 1943; Fry FA: Beryl Smith to Editor, *The Sydney Morning Herald*, 20 December 1943; Fry FA: Beryl Smith to Charles Fry, 15 March 1944; Minister for Air to Beryl Smith, 15 April 1944.
47 Hutchinson FA: Lola Hutchinson to Doug Hutchinson, 29 April 1944.

from you again.'[48] 'I have missed your letters darling', Evelyn Charles told Eric Johnston. 'I can only hope that the next few days will bring some happy news for us all.'[49]

Women's own letters to absent menfolk served a particular purpose. Through them, they could assuage their emotional pain. Lola Hutchinson decided she 'mightn't feel quite so miserable if I sat down in front of the fire and talked' to her husband 'for a little while.'[50] Letters from their partners became precious artefacts in their own right even as they reignited memories and kept alive affective connections. Women cheered themselves up by dipping into them. 'Do you know sweetheart', Lola told Doug, 'I've reread all your letters so many times and particularly the one you wrote on 25 March', their fifth wedding anniversary.[51]

Nostalgia was a powerful emotion which imbued many couples' letters. It enabled a sense of togetherness, but also reflected a sexual tension which was constantly at odds with the women's role as emotional nurturers and kriegie supports. 'My dear I've been listening to a good program on the radio, they have been playing lots of new numbers and one of them, a favourite of mine, is "Every night about this time"', wrote Lola Hutchinson. 'It's funny but when I hear it played I always think of you, somehow the words bring back memories.'[52] Nostalgia is not the exclusive domain of the past: it also looks to the future. 'Am intensely looking forward to your return Charl – all my love is yours', Beryl Smith confided to her fiancé.[53] Future-looking nostalgia also focused on marital intimacy, expressed by women obliquely in descriptions of the contents of their glory boxes, or more overtly, such as Lola's joyous, 'How my heart skips a beat when I think of the day when once again I can feel your arms around me.'[54] Nostalgic tokens such as photographs spanned the emotional divide and imaginatively brought the women's loved ones into their presence. 'It is really marvellous to see your dear face again Charles and it makes me feel much closer to you, if that is possible', Beryl enthused. (She always carried five photos of Fry in her wallet.)[55] As for the photograph Doug Hutchinson sent to Lola just before he was taken prisoner, 'well I think it is so like you that my heart aches every time I look at it and I might add it's here in front of me now.'[56]

---

48 Fry FA: Beryl Smith to Charles Fry, 18 May 1942.
49 Johnston FA: Evelyn Charles to Eric Johnston, 2 October 1944.
50 [50]Hutchinson FA: Lola Hutchinson to Doug Hutchinson, 7 August 1945.
51 Hutchinson FA: Lola Hutchinson to Doug Hutchinson, 3 July 1944.
52 Hutchinson FA: Lola Hutchinson to Doug Hutchinson, 27 February 1944.
53 Fry FA: Beryl Smith to Charles Fry, 4 March 1943.
54 Hutchinson FA: Lola Hutchinson to Doug Hutchinson, 18 September 1944.
55 Fry FA: Beryl Smith, letters to Charles Fry, 23 April 1943; Charles Fry, 5 July 1945 (3) (five letters in wallet).
56 Hutchinson FA: Lola Hutchinson to Doug Hutchinson, 13 October 1943.

Lola's letters reveal that she and Doug had enjoyed an active and satisfying sex life. She often reminded him of it as well as her own attractiveness.[57] 'My dear you should see me now', she wrote. 'It's terribly hot and I'm lying on the floor with only a pair of scanties, a floral skirt and a white open neck blouse on.'[58] Loose fitting scanties, or French knickers, as Lola liked to inform Doug, were just one of the 'many undies and what nots' she had packed into her glory box for her post-return trousseau.[59] Hutchinson, however, was too circumspect or worried about who else was reading his censored mail; he failed to respond to his wife's sexual provocation. Lola reacted. After receiving a series of emotionally tepid missives, she made it clear she expected her husband to take an equal part in keeping alive their pre-war ardour.[60] Lola's evocative image of sexy knickers and open-necked blouse eventually incited a response: 'I must say your description of how you were coping with the hot weather was rather vivid. Almost distracting to me.'[61] While Lola elicited sexual responses from her husband, Charles Fry did not acknowledge his fiancée's demure reference to her feminine physicality when she posted him a photograph of herself in a swimming costume. Beryl never indicated how she felt about Fry's lack of reaction, nor of his failure to respond to her more direct overtures, such as, 'I am just living for the day of your return, Charles my dearest, and then "WHOOPEE".'[62] She did, however, feel the strain of perennially cheery and sexless letters, and imagined her fiancé felt it as well.[63]

*****

The Prisoner of War Relatives' Association (POWRA) provided a formal mechanism for kinfolk to seek and obtain solace. Founded in January 1942 by Sydney Smith, the father of a prisoner of war, it raised funds for Australian POWs in Europe and Japan, lobbied the government about their conditions, and became a powerful support organisation with branches around the country; it had 9,000 paying members by 1943, including families of the airmen in Stalag Luft III.[64] As well as regularly meeting, visiting, and exchanging news, the mainly female members shared anxieties about their menfolk and their joy on hearing from them. They received the organisation's monthly magazines which included extracts from official POW reports as well as letters and photographs sent in by families. Beryl Smith scoured them for details about Charles Fry's camps so she could gain a sense of his new life. It was a false impression, however. POWRA's

---

57 Hutchinson FA: Lola Hutchinson to Doug Hutchinson, 25 December 1943, 1 January 1944, 13 February 1944, Monday 3 July 1944; 26 November 1944.
58 Hutchinson FA: Lola Hutchinson to Doug Hutchinson, 1 January 1944.
59 Hutchinson FA: Lola Hutchinson to Doug Hutchinson, 16 July 1944.
60 Hutchinson FA: Lola Hutchinson to Doug Hutchinson, 6 February 1944.
61 Hutchinson FA: Lola Hutchinson to Doug Hutchinson, 1 May 1944.
62 Fry FA: Beryl Smith to Charles Fry, 6 September 1943. Quote: to Charles Fry, 5 March 1943.
63 Fry FA: Beryl Smith to Charles Fry, 12 December 1944.
64 'War Prisoners Relatives' Association, *The Advertiser* (Adelaide), 13 May 1943, 4.

relentlessly upbeat representations of fit, happy, ingenious men making the most of their captivity through sport, theatre, education, and other worthy time-filling pursuits would have misled many concerned relatives. The airmen, however, endorsed these comforting depictions. 'The Red Cross seems to paint our life here as a bed of roses', Harry Train, recorded in his diary. 'Perhaps it is just as well that way.'[65]

POWRA facilitated the formation of genuine friendships and supportive bonds. They sent the mother of one Stalag Luft III airman to visit Lola Hutchinson. 'She has promised to ring me or come in to see me again next week.'[66] Lola often asked Doug to pass on greetings from other mothers and wives to his fellow prisoners.[67] 'Should you know Gus [Fraser] tell him I've met his wife and that she is well and eagerly awaiting his home coming.'[68] Sometimes, however, contact with other wives caused consternation. 'Do you know sweetheart I've not had any mail from you for months. I can't understand it as Mrs Horsley and Mrs Greenaway have both had mail quite recently.'[69]

The responsibility for prisoner comfort reached beyond the immediate family to include friends and friends of the family, work colleagues, employers, old schools, church congregations, benevolent organisations, members of hospitality schemes, and others concerned with the prisoners' well-being. Together they relieved the strains of captivity through letters and comfort parcels. While 'the Red Cross keeps us supplied with most necessities now and things are not so bad as formerly', Thomas 'Tom' Leigh was grateful to 'have received another parcel from Yvonne.'[70] London's Rotary Clubs adopted 'by correspondence' Australian Rotarians to whom they would send books, cigarettes, and 'regular friendly cheery letters.'[71] A journalist at the Frankston *Standard* called on 'any local people who care to oblige Digby Young' by sending reading material and tinned foods to 'leave them in the safe keeping of the Red Cross.'[72] Tim Mayo's sister-in-law's mother donated £100 to the Red Cross in London to fund a parcel for Mayo in addition to comforts for wounded prisoners.[73] Even Wing Commander Harry 'Wings' Day, the Senior British Officer at the newly opened Stalag Luft III, wrote to the families of the first arrivals to solicit their assistance in obtaining books, sports gear, and musical instruments via the Red Cross.[74]

---

65   Arnel archive: Train, 'A Barbed-Wire World', 17 November 1942, 35.
66   Hutchinson FA: Lola Hutchinson to Doug Hutchinson, 14 November 1943.
67   Hutchinson FA: Lola Hutchinson to Doug Hutchinson, 14 May 1944.
68   Hutchinson FA: Lola Hutchinson to Doug Hutchinson, 9 July 1944.
69   Hutchinson FA: Lola Hutchinson to Doug Hutchinson, 14 September 1944.
70   Bligh FA: Tom Leigh to H.E.W Barker, 26 October 1942.
71   Quotes: AWM PR88/160: McCleery, Douglas Martin to James McCleery, 22 August 1944, mounted in wartime log.
72   'Prisoner of War. Frankston Footballer-Pilot', *Standard* (Frankston, VIC), 21 March 1941, 1.
73   NAA A705 166/5/818 Currie: Grace Mayo to Isabel Currie, 29 September 1942.
74   NAA A705 166/5/818 Currie: Wing Commander HMA Day to Grace Mayo, 24 March 1942 (copied to Isabel Currie).

The Dominion and Allied Services Hospitality Scheme offered holidays for servicemen in Britain. Cy Borsht recorded how he and his fellow crewmembers were 'adopted' by 'Mum Longmore' and her family.[75] Many of the schemes' hosts developed caring relationships with their temporary charges. Accordingly, some airmen asked their hosts to be their next of kin in the event of their deaths.[76] Others called on them to act on their behalf during captivity. They agreed, and the prisoners' families, in turn, acceded to their loved ones' requests to formally designate those caring people *in loco parentis* for the duration. Even without official UK next-of-kin status, British friends sent letters, comforts, and cigarettes. So too did Canadian host families. While family acted for their menfolk from love or familial responsibility, others were prompted by altruism, a sense of charity, or perhaps simply a desire to make captive lives more comfortable and bearable. The motivation of Margaret Archibald, a distant relative of Charles Fry, was clear. 'May I assure you', she wrote to Beryl Smith, 'that my sisters and I are doing all we can to help Charles. We leave no stone unturned if we think there is a possibility for help for I make no bones about this – our men who are prisoners need it.'[77]

Recognising the financial impost he had placed on his UK next of kin (as well as the drain on their rations), George Archer asked his parents to send parcels of chocolate and dried fruit to Harold and Dot Gibbs. 'I'm sure they would greatly appreciate it. So would I.'[78] Beryl Smith also contributed to costs borne by British benefactors.[79] In doing so, she, and other Australian families, felt 'we are all doing what we can' by vicariously providing for their menfolk.[80] Mothers made donations in their sons' names and sent extracts from their letters praising the work of the Red Cross to newspapers, some of which were published. Doug Hutchinson asked Lola to 'do me a favour and donate five pounds' to the Red Cross, 'and tell them it is in appreciation of the fine work they are doing for us lads over here'.[81] (She did so in early 1944.[82]) Beryl fund-raised for POWRA, and joined the Voluntary Aid Detachment. Others similarly assisted their loved ones by participating in the Red Cross' general war-related work. Lola Kerwin was secretary of Ipswich's Prisoner-of-War Adoption Scheme committee.[83] Some women's work was intergenerational. Both May Fraser and her daughter, Alison Fotheringham, were members of the local Red Cross branch, run by Alison's

---

75   Borsht Archive: Borsht, 'A Life Well Lived', 15.
76   Alexander, 'Miss Celia Macdonald of the Isles "who has been a particularly good friend"', 15–25.
77   Fry FA: Margaret Archibald to Beryl Smith, 23 June 1942.
78   Archer FA: Archer to family, 2 June 1943.
79   Fry FA: Beryl Smith to Charles Fry, 18 May 1942.
80   Fry FA: Beryl Smith to Charles Fry, 31 May 1942.
81   Hutchinson FA: Doug Hutchinson to Lola Hutchinson, 18 August 1943.
82   Hutchinson FA: Lola Hutchinson to Doug Hutchinson, 1 January 1944.
83   'News of the Day. Prisoner-of-War Fund', *Queensland Times*, 8 August 1942, 2.

mother-in-law, Nellie, whose son was a prisoner of the Japanese.[84] Alison's daughter, Barbara, contributed to her school's Junior Red Cross penny-a-week fund.[85] Despite these and other fund-raising efforts, the Australian Red Cross did not send parcels to POW camps. They provided money to the International Committee of the Red Cross and the Canadian and American Red Cross organisations.[86] Those who did not know about the cooperative arrangements were disconcerted by the lack of Australian comforts. It seemed to them that they had been forgotten. Ken Carson's son, John, recalled that his father 'was always upset' at receiving nothing from the Australian Red Cross.[87]

Some squadron bonds remained firm as former comrades remembered their captured colleagues. No. 12 Squadron RAF set up a fund to supply extra comforts.[88] So too did 460 Squadron RAAF.[89] Bill Fordyce, however, felt abandoned by 458 Squadron RAAF which 'never wrote to you in prison camp, they didn't keep up contact with you. If you are in a prison camp you're dead.'[90] As officer-in-charge of the RAAF's Overseas Casualty Section, William Melville perhaps made up for any squadron deficiencies. Conscientiously, with understanding and sympathy, he corresponded with Australian prisoners of war 'on all matters' relating to their captivity; some even became 'my very real friends.'[91] In doing so, Melville provided a voice for them within the RAAF, and was able to act directly on their behalf, including on conditions of service, promotions, comforts, and even allotments to the airmen's wives or mothers. '[Y]ou should not hesitate to submit any further matters on which you may require information or assistance, when everything possible will be done on your behalf', he told James McCleery and many others.[92] He reinforced that the airmen prisoners of war were still valuable members of the air force fraternity. Significantly, he demonstrated that the RAAF had neither forgotten, nor neglected its men.

As one of the first Australians to return from a German prisoner of war camp, Charles Lark, who had been medically repatriated in October 1943, recognised his privileged ability to provide up-to-date details about the well-being of his fellow prisoners. Within days of arriving in Australia, he requested from the Casualty Section contact details for the families of his closest friends within Stalag Luft III and visited as many as he could. The RAAF made clerical

---

84 AR: Barbara Fotheringham, interview 26 June 2016.
85 AR: Barbara Fotheringham, letter, [undated, received 4 July 2016].
86 Oppenheimer, *The Power of Humanity*, 108.
87 Carson, 'Brisbane's Ken Carson: Prisoner of the Axis. Part Ten', 21.
88 NAA A9301 404382 [Alexander Smith], Flight Lieutenant FT Neal to The Secretary, Prisoners of War Department, London, 3 February 1943.
89 Arnel archive: Train, 'A Barbed-Wire World', 22 July 1942, 20.
90 Fordyce in Billett, *Memories of War*, 210.
91 Kierath FA: Squadron Leader WM Melville to Mrs Ada Kierath, 20 June 1944.
92 AWM PR88/160: McCleery, wartime log book, letter, Melville to McCleery, 17 August 1944.

staff available to assist in writing to those who lived too far away for personal meetings. When they heard Lark was back in the country, some families wrote to the Casualty Section asking for news of their loved ones.[93] Others directly importuned him such as Douglas McLeod's fiancée, Jean Yelland, to whom Lark passed on a message from McLeod who had 'especially asked me to send his love to you ... and I know how much he looks forward to your letters.'[94] A note from one of his fellow prisoners published in the POWRA magazine with Lark's address may have prompted others to get in touch.[95] As time passed, Lark met, at their behest, the loved ones of men he had never known in camp, such as Eulalie Mulligan, Lola Hutchinson, and Beryl Smith. Lark often gave a rose-tinted gloss to POW life which was treated sceptically by some, including Beryl who was usually only too keen to believe overly-positive depictions of camp life. According to Beryl, Lark had told Eulalie that the men built sand hills in front of their huts, and pretended they were 'sunbaking at Bondi and Coogee. Would it were true!'[96] (It possibly was. The man-made sand dune may have been a means to hide in plain sight soil excavated from a tunnel.) Although Lola appreciated Lark giving her a sense of her husband's experiences, she was not comforted: 'Charles tells me not to worry as he feels sure you will be home with me soon, but it's all right for people to tell one that, it's so much harder to believe.'[97]

Kriegies with partners could not rely solely on the good natures of the handful of medical repatriates to pass on news and loving messages. They tried to foster their own long distance relationships from behind barbed wire.

---

93 NAA A705 166/26/670 Lark.
94 NAA A705 166/26/670 Lark: Lark to Jean Yelland, 17 January 1944.
95 NLA FERG/4550: P.O.W., No. 29, 15 June 1944, unattributed letter, 16 January 1944, 2.
96 Fry FA: Beryl Smith to Charles Fry, 21 January 1944.
97 Hutchinson FA: Lola Hutchinson to Doug Hutchinson 16 January 1944.

Chapter Seven:

ROMANTIC LIVES

Max Dunn had not seen his fiancée, Barbara Paton, for over three years when he composed his poem, 'Longing' in March 1944. He missed her intensely. 'How long must we await the days of everlasting bliss?' he asked. 'When will I hold you in my arms? / When will you seek my kiss?' He tried to keep Barbara's presence in his imagination but he was reminded too much of her absence. 'When I gaze upon your photo, / When I dream about your eyes, / I sigh for every wasted year / Which now behind me lies.' Dunn was not alone in begrudging 'the fleeting minutes / Every second we're apart.'[1] 'Being without the company of women was certainly a deprivation we all felt', recalled Alec Arnel.[2] There was more to it than just a physical, sexual, and emotional absence that had to be endured. Those with wives, fiancées, and sweethearts dreaded that love would not survive separation.

The airmen did not surrender responsibility for maintaining their romantic relationships. Attached kriegies wrote letters articulating how much they missed their partners. They perpetuated the exclusivity of their relationships by peppering missives with pet names, endearments, and frequent iterations of love. 'Darling I am alive and very well', Charles Fry declared to Beryl Smith, 'and am patiently awaiting the day when we shall be together again.'[3] While all correspondence to prisoners of war was censored, that knowledge bound lovers together in secret recollection of their most intimate moments. 'Never forget that what I said to you before I had to come over here still stands and I will come back to you as soon as ever I can', Eric Johnston told his sweetheart, Evelyn Charles, while still on operations.[4] In a coy attempt to disguise his feelings from both German and Australian censors, Albert Hake confided to his wife, Noela, that 'My thoughts are much the same as your own. The answers too.'[5]

Not only did letters remind loved ones of enduring love, their shared nostalgia created a pathway to reunion. 'This morning I gathered a large bunch of blue cornflowers from around the compound', wrote Doug Hutchinson to Lola. 'Somehow, when I see beautiful flowers, I always connect them with you, my dear. … Do you remember how happy you were when picking flowers from our

---

1 Dunn, *Poems of Norman Maxwell Dunn*, 'Longing', 17.
2 AR: Arnel, interview 2 March 2017.
3 Fry FA: Charles Fry to Beryl Smith, 23 August 1941.
4 Johnston FA: Johnston to Evelyn Charles, [no date, 1944].
5 Preen FA: Albert Hake to Noela Hake, 3 March 1943.

garden ... Those days will come again, but till then all I have are the memories.'[6] This letter, written shortly after D-Day, sparkles with the joy of love remembered, the 'lightning flash' of sheer, overwhelming elation, the passion the Hutchinsons shared, and Doug's assurance that in the wake of the allied invasion he and Lola would be together imminently.[7]

While letters ensured that romantic lives continued, Hutchinson, who had written to Lola almost weekly before captivity, often felt constrained. 'I would give anything to write a nice long letter to you ... There are many things about which I could write pages just as I used to do but they will just have to wait.'[8] Officers were only allowed three 26-lined letter forms and four 7-lined postcards per month. NCOs were given two letter and four postcard forms. Accordingly, affection was tempered by pragmatism as the airmen rationed and prioritised their correspondents. Charles Fry placed his fiancée and mother on an equal footing. 'I want my very limited supply of letters for you and mother and a few cards for business letters for London.'[9] Fry also expected Beryl and his mother to exchange his letters. Albert Hake firmly told Noela that 'I have so many letters to answer that I can only afford you one a month.'[10] The airmen adopted strategies to make the most of their allocation. Some scrounged spare letter forms. Others saved theirs for a two or three part missive. To coincide with their third wedding anniversary, Hake wrote three letters to Noela over two days.[11] Some co-opted their womenfolk to act as their amanuenses. 'Darling, would you please write to [a former neighbour] and thank her from me', Fry implored Beryl.[12] Jimmy Catanach found a less romantic but still useful solution. As he had to write to 'others in England', he asked his father, stepmother Sybil, and former nanny, Winifred Munt, to let him 'include Heather' in his letters to them.[13] We do not know how Heather Ebbott reacted to sanitised, communal letters. Lola Hutchinson, however, objected to anodyne communications: 'Darling do write me a nice love letter, the ones I've had lately make me feel as though you are my brother or something like it anyway.'[14]

Some, like Guy Grey-Smith and Ronald Baines extended their epistolary conversation to their diaries, as if they were speaking directly to their wives. 'How oft I have thought of you today darling and sent you all my love', Grey-Smith told

---

6   Hutchinson FA: Doug Hutchinson to Lola Hutchinson, 12 June 1944.
7   Quote McMahon, 'Finding Joy in the History of Emotions', in Matt and Stearns, (eds), *Doing Emotions History*, 109.
8   Hutchinson FA: Doug Hutchinson to Lola Hutchison, 20 June 1944 (first letter).
9   Fry FA: Charles Fry to Beryl Smith, 3 February 1942.
10 Preen FA: Albert Hake to Noela Hake, 20 February 1943.
11 Preen FA: Albert Hake, letters to Noela Hake, 28 February 1944 (first letter) and (second letter), 1 March 1944.
12 Fry FA: Charles Fry to Beryl Smith, 3 February 1942.
13 SOR JCC: 2013.CAT054, James Catanach to 'Dad, Syb and Da', 27 September 1942.
14 Hutchinson FA: Lola Hutchinson to Doug Hutchinson, 6 February 1944.

Helen-in-his-diary.[15] This continuous imaginary conversation was a particular boon to Grey-Smith who was able to gain immediate absolution for any infelicities, such as 'the awful letter' he wrote one day before mail call. 'Now I have received two lovely letters from you darling just to prove that I am just a silly kriegie – for they are lovely letters darling & I only feel such an ungrateful person.'[16]

Letters and imaginary diary conversations did not narrow the emotional distance between camp and home. Relationships still suffered the effects of separation. Censorship as well as the many months spanning a 'conversation' were constant annoyances. (Beryl Smith recorded when she received each letter. One she wrote to Charles Fry on 7 July 1943 was acknowledged in his of 29 November 1943, which she received on 4 March 1944.) Insecurity and active imaginations provided their own threats to relationships. Albert Hake 'dreamed last night you loved someone else'. He hinted at his fears of infidelity. Two days before his third wedding anniversary (1944 was a leap year) he told Noela, 'I shall sing my nightly theme song "I wonder who's kissing her now".'[17] Despite their commitment to sustaining their union through letters, the Hutchinsons' relationship was haunted by rumour, innuendo, and misunderstandings. Hutchinson's mother alleged that Lola had been unfaithful and it seems Lola accused her husband of the same.[18] 'As to the reference to myself and women, well, if I ever said such a thing, it was just pulling your leg. Believe me, because, never, since I left home, have I taken any woman out.'[19] Over a year passed before they resolved the matter but, regardless of the basis of their complaints, neither Doug nor Lola held grudges; their marriage withstood the emotional challenges of captivity.

Some letters reminded of how little those who had rushed into marriage really knew each other. Ronald and Irene Baines had had a whirlwind courtship, conducted mainly on leave because of their different postings; she was a WREN officer (Women's Royal Naval Service) stationed in Alexandria and he was a fighter pilot in a western desert squadron. They had met in April 1942, he proposed on 27 July, and they married on 13 October. 'God only knows how we'll get on after all this time … can she remain in love with me – of course I think so – typical male ego.'[20] Baines, who, in the early stages of imprisonment had received few letters from Irene, had to convince himself of the stability of their brief marriage. 'Wrote to Irene yesterday' and 'asked why she has never asked me if I wanted anything or my tastes, it's strange that she continues to maintain that

---

15 AWM PR05675: Grey-Smith, diary, 26 May 1943.
16 AWM PR05675: Grey-Smith, diary, 19 October 1942.
17 Preen FA: Albert Hake, letters to Noela Hake, 28 February 1944 and (second letter).
18 AR: Robert Douglas Hutchinson, interview 19 December 2016.
19 Hutchinson FA: Doug Hutchinson to Lola Hutchinson, 5 November 1943.
20 Baines FA: Baines, wartime log book, 18 November 1944, 20.

thoughtless attitude.'[21] Not appreciating the responsibilities of his servicewoman wife, he had earlier mused, 'I don't know why, maybe it is kriegie mentality, but I often feel her letters are just dashed off, in a few spare moments during a busy day.'[22] Baines' grandson, Stuart, suggests a deeper reason for Irene's slapdash communications. When her husband was first captured, she did not cope very well. She wrote infrequently and emotionally 'disappeared' for some time. She grieved bitterly when abandoned by a former partner so, Stuart speculates, had perhaps disconnected from Baines, thus protecting herself from the potential grief of another abandonment.[23] While Irene's apparently insensitive notes were dispiriting, they were, overall, welcome. After failing for some time at the 'mail stakes', Baines finally received 'nine marvellous letters from my little lass.'[24]

Letters could signal the end of relationships. There 'was an issue of mail, and, in my hands I held a letter which, even before I opened it', Calton Younger recalled, 'I knew was the dreaded "Mespot"': his fiancée had broken off their engagement.[25] The equivalent of a 'Dear John' letter, 'mespot' entered the servicemen's lexicon during the Great War when lengthy service in Mesopotamia had had its deleterious effect on relationships. Younger was not alone in receiving a 'mespot'. Other men were equally distraught at the loss of their emotional lifelines. Alec Arnel, while on operational service, received a letter from Margery Gray in which she told him she was considering a proposal of marriage from another man. He was devastated. 'It was an awful sense of the rope's broken and I'm falling'. A pre-war teetotaller, Arnel drank too much and took risks in the air until Margery wrote to say she had declined the offer.[26]

Change was a constant relationship hazard. 'I only hope that you haven't changed', Ronald Baines wrote.[27] 'I can see that you have not lost those characteristics I found so loveable – don't ever change, dear girl', Arnel begged Margery.[28] Mutability in their partners, however, was inevitable. 'You are certainly changing darling. I can follow it through the tone of your letters', Albert Hake noted.[29] The airmen dreaded the consequences: would their womenfolk still love and need them?[30] His fiancée reassured Charles Fry that all was well. 'I am just the same Beryl as you have always known.'[31]

---

21 Baines FA: Baines, wartime log book, 8 January 1945, 22.
22 Baines FA: Baines, wartime log book, 24 September 1944, 19.
23 AR: Stuart Baines, interview 9 July 2015.
24 Baines FA: Baines, wartime log book, 16–17.
25 Younger, *No Flight From the Cage*, 116–117.
26 AR: Arnel, interview 12 November 2015; Quote: interview 23 June 2016.
27 Baines FA: Baines, wartime log book, 24 September 1944, 19.
28 Arnel archive: Arnel to Margery Gray, [undated, c. Christmas 1944].
29 Preen FA: Albert Hake to Noela Hake, 8 September 1942.
30 Arnel archive: Arnel to Margery Gray, 21 May 1945.
31 Fry FA: Beryl Smith to Charles Fry, 15 May 1943.

The kriegies relied on their loved ones for emotional solace, constantly pleading for letters, photographs, and reminders that they were still loved and needed. They became increasingly more dependent on them by asking for physical comforts like books, newspapers, clothes, cigarettes and chocolates. Some welcomed this role reversal. 'She is going to be a wonderful wife', Ronald Baines wrote of Irene. 'The way she handles things, organising etc. Amazed me. I'll be perfectly content to let her look after everything.'[32] Others fretted about how their womenfolk were coping without them but accepted, albeit reluctantly, that they were unable to provide immediate support and guidance. Others, however, found it difficult to accept.

Despite encouraging his wife's independence and individuality, and telling her, 'I have confidence in your ability to handle affairs and question nothing', Albert Hake queried and undermined Noela's decisions.[33] He 'wish[ed] with all my heart I could be near to advise you.'[34] There is no doubt Hake loved Noela and that she provided genuine support during his captivity. To a certain extent, too, Noela accepted her husband's place as the dominant partner; she sought his approval in some matters and acquiesced to his requests. Even so, her growing maturity and ability to manage her life without him further destabilised Hake's sense of masculinity as he realised he could play no active part in their marriage as the primary decision maker, provider, and planner of their joint future.[35] Hake was also concerned about his ability to father children. While he and Noela had decided not to start before Hake embarked for overseas, it became his 'constant regret we hadn't organised a family before I left. Selfish I know and contrary to what I expressed but darn it all darling, I'm getting old.'[36] As time passed, Hake's letters suggest that he felt estranged from the easy intimacy he and Noela had shared, and that he would not be able to enjoy a healthy sexual relationship when he returned. Hake's sense of emasculation arose from his recognition that as time passed his chances of becoming a father were fading, although he was only 27 years old. Indicating his perception that his union had devolved into a platonic, rather than romantic marriage, he penned 'Cheerio Pal' as his final salutation in nine of the 25 extant letters written to Noela after leaving Australia.

*****

Letters did not entirely make up for the physical absence of women. Like many, Charles Fry had lost all his photographs. In his first letter home after capture,

---

32 Baines FA: Baines, wartime log book, 1 September 1944, 18.
33 Preen FA: Albert Hake to Noela Hake, 30 June 1942.
34 Preen FA: Albert Hake to Noela Hake, 17 November 1943.
35 Preen FA: Albert Hake to Noela Hake, 8 September 1942, 4 June 1943 and 29 June 1943.
36 Preen FA: Albert Hake to Noela Hake, 25 December 1943.

he asked his fiancée for more.³⁷ Mail from and to Germany seemed to take an eternity and it was almost six months before he received one. 'It was lovely, Beryl. It is the only snap or photo of any kind that I possess.' But it was not nearly enough. 'I would like some more.'³⁸ Later, an artist in Fry's room reproduced a photograph of Beryl 'in what is known as dry pointing ... darling the likeness is wonderful.'³⁹ Albert Hake revealed a similar creative streak. When he received a snap of Noela, he 'suddenly remembered I used to be a bit of an artist ... so set to work and made a coloured enlargement of you.'⁴⁰

Denied the physical presence of women, the kriegies imaginatively brought their loved ones into camp. Requests for photos were familiar refrains in letters home. Unattached men asked for snaps of their families and friends to maintain familial and social connections. For husbands, fiancés, and sweethearts, however, images helped maintain romantic bonds. At their most basic level, photographs enabled the recipient to remember what their loved ones looked like. From an affective perspective, they created a direct link to home. They evoked memories and desire. They imaginatively brought the physical presence of loved ones into their midst. They ameliorated the tensions of emotional separation. 'My Darling Lola', Doug Hutchinson wrote. 'Words fail me concerning the photo. I think it is the best one I have ever had of you. Darling you look absolutely beautiful and I can't keep my eyes off it.'⁴¹ Ronald Baines used one as a cure for 'Those Kriegie Blues' when he glued a picture of a relaxed, smiling, and swim-suited Irene into a thought bubble above a drawing of an obviously depressed Baines sitting slumped on his bunk.⁴² Yet, even as they rekindled memories and offered a tangible connection to their womenfolk, photographs exacerbated the physical strains. The image of Irene perhaps reminded Baines of their brief honeymoon before he was captured. Hutchinson's photograph of Lola made him 'realise what a lot of life I am missing and what a lovely wife I have.'⁴³

Their beloveds haunted the airmen's slumbers. 'I dreamed about you last night darling', Doug Hutchinson wrote. 'I don't remember the whole dream. All I remember was that we were ever so happy.'⁴⁴ 'I've dreamt of you and home for the last three nights so realistically', Albert Hake told Noela, 'that when I awake I can't recognise my surroundings.'⁴⁵ During their ordeal in Buchenwald concentration camp, Keith Mills thought of his girlfriend 'whenever things

---

37 Fry FA: Charles Fry to Beryl Smith, 10 August 1941.
38 Fry FA: Charles Fry to Beryl Smith, 3 February 1942.
39 Fry FA: Charles Fry to Beryl Smith, 29 April 1944.
40 Preen FA: Albert Hake to Noela Hake, 24 August 1942.
41 Hutchinson FA: Doug Hutchinson to Lola Hutchinson, 5 March 1944.
42 Baines FA: Baines, wartime log book, 'Those Kriegie Blues', 95.
43 Hutchinson FA: Doug Hutchinson to Lola Hutchinson, 5 March 1944.
44 Hutchinson FA: Doug Hutchinson to Lola Hutchinson, 18 July 1943.
45 Preen FA: Albert Hake to Noela Hake, 31 December 1942.

looked really black' and Eric Johnston 'lay awake for hours thinking' of Evelyn Charles.[46] Demonstrating how their imaginings sustained them, when they arrived at Stalag Luft III, both men copied into their wartime log books an unattributed poem entitled 'Day Dreams', in which 'We dream of wives and sweethearts dear / So far away and yet so near / We dream of them each day & night / And pray for the end of this struggle & fight.'[47] Dreams, however, were capricious. They did not come on demand, and could be distressing. 'In dreams I feel your lips on mine, / I see your rounded breast: / And then I wake to guards and wire! / Antithesis of rest', Max Dunn wrote of his fiancée, Barbara.[48]

Some men mentally ranged beyond the prison camp to reunite with their loved ones. Their romantic reveries or controlled fantasies were important coping mechanisms.[49] 'It's eleven o'clock where you are now', Johnston wrote to his sweetheart before his capture, 'and I think to myself if Evelyn's on day shift she will be up at Central and if "she" is on night's "she" will probably be just getting out of bed now.'[50] Given how thoughts of Evelyn sustained him at Buchenwald, it is likely Johnston continued to connect himself to her in this way. After capture, Alec Arnel transported himself away from the POW camp to Margery Gray and home in what he called 'dreamy time'. This 'gave me a sense of well-being that provided me with more hope, that someday [going home to her] would be a reality.'[51] As Arnel did not consider himself to be a whole person without Margery, 'dreamy time' enabled him to imaginatively reunite with her so 'I should be myself again'.[52] Even before capture, Arnel thought of Margery 'as being "HOME"'.[53] In captivity she became his lodestar steering him homewards as well as his emotional lifeline.[54] 'Soon I am coming back to see you smile again.'[55] Arnel's potentially fatal reaction to Margery's 'mespot' thus represented more than just breaking up with a sweetheart. He had lost his image of home. 'Almost the reason for being.'[56] Women and home were intertwined for others as well. 'Home (that's a wonderful word) (because it means you Darling)', Len Netherway told his wife, Mavis.[57] Ronald Baines linked dreams of 'my little lass' with 'home, comfort and security.'[58]

---

46 Keith Mills FA: Keith Mills to Phyllis Mills, 22 July 1945; Johnston FA: Johnston to Evelyn Charles, 27 May 1945.
47 Johnston FA: Johnston, wartime log book, 10; Burgess RC: Keith Mills, wartime log book, 3.
48 Dunn, *Poems of Norman Maxwell Dunn*, 'Longing', 17.
49 Ursano and Rundell, 'The Prisoner of War', in Jones et al., *War Psychiatry*, 435.
50 Johnston FA: Johnston to Evelyn Charles, 21 February 1944.
51 AR: Arnel, interview 23 June 2016.
52 Arnel archive: Arnel to Margery Gray, 22 June 1944.
53 Arnel archive: Arnel to Margery Gray, 14 April 1944. Original emphasis.
54 AR: Arnel, interview 23 June 2016.
55 Arnel archive: Arnel to Margery Gray, [undated].
56 AR: Arnel, interview 23 June 2016.
57 Netherway FA: Len Netherway to Mavis Netherway, 15 June 1945.
58 Baines FA: Baines, wartime log book, 'The Usual Day at Stalag Luft III', 60.

Wedding anniversaries elicited poignant romantic memories. They enabled husbands to relive their special days. 'Our third anniversary of our wedding darling', Guy Grey-Smith reminisced with Helen-in-his-diary. 'I lived through once again our ceremony & our send off.'[59] Albert Hake remembered his anniversaries and reread all Noela's old letters. For him though, they did not kindle happy memories. 'Made myself mournful, etc.'[60] 'Today is our fifth wedding anniversary', Doug Hutchinson recalled to Lola. 'I've been thinking of you all day long, and I'll think of you all tonight even when I'm asleep.'[61] Lola also wrote to her husband on that significant day. They were divided temporally as well as spatially but their synchronicity brought comfort (when they realised it) and reinforced their closeness. The belief that they were mentally harmonised across the hemispheres overrode the reality of time zone differences. Penning her letter to Charles Fry on her 27th birthday, Beryl Smith commented: 'It is nice to feel that we are thinking of each other at the same time.'[62] Guy Grey-Smith simultaneously 'felt' his wife, Helen, 'thinking of me' on their wedding anniversary.[63] Alec Arnel particularly found comfort in pre-planned synchronicity. 'Each night for just a minute we can stop for our moment', he told Margery before he embarked. 'In our moment we can think of each other and then – together – kneel before [God] and ask his blessing.'[64]

*****

Imagination was not enough. The kriegies missed the physical presence of women. 'We had a wonderful theatre', Bill Fordyce recalled.[65] Condoned by the *kommandant* on the understanding that the kriegies would not use any materials and tools issued to them for construction and productions for escape enterprises, the Germans allowed them space for both shows and behind-the-scenes work, facilitated rental of costumes and props the kriegies were unable to manufacture, and procured musical instruments for orchestras and bands. They also took their seats in the audience.[66]

The theatre played an immeasurable part in Stalag Luft III's cultural and creative life. It linked the airmen to the normality of their pre-war existence. New shows were highly anticipated. Kriegies competed for opening night tickets and theatre-lovers were not restricted to their own compound's productions. As well as enjoyably filling time for actors and production crew, shows were a

---

59 AWM PR05675: Grey-Smith, diary, 19 October 1942.
60 Preen FA: Albert Hake to Noela Hake, 3 March 1943.
61 Hutchinson FA: Doug Hutchinson to Lola Hutchinson, 25 March 1944.
62 Fry FA: Beryl Smith, letter Charles Fry, 5 March 1943.
63 AWM PR05675: Grey-Smith, diary, 19 October 1942.
64 Arnel archive: Arnel to Margery Gray, 2 April 1941.
65 AAWFA: Fordyce 0523, 19 June 2003.
66 Walton and Eberhardt, *From Commandant to Captive*, 85–87.

'tremendous fillip to morale' as they transported audience members from the dull monotony of camp.⁶⁷ For many, the theatre relieved the tension of their cares; escapism and laughter made life easier to bear. Productions also provided the kriegies with the opportunity to create the illusion that women were once again in their midst. They mingled with faux females at camp gala and sports days and entered illusory worlds inhabited by women courtesy of the camp theatre crowd. Englishman Dominic Page, as Miss Anne from *The Dover Road*, with a 'perfect figure', looked fetching in slacks and 'a very brief sun top', while cutting the ribbon to officially open the Sagan Races on 5 September 1942.⁶⁸ A 'lass from the Red Cross selling flags did a remarkable business' from the punters, George Archer recorded.⁶⁹ A 'barmaid' served drinks on at least one occasion and, during one Centre Compound performance, a German guest could barely believe that the 'ravishing lady' who joined him at interval was one of the prisoners.⁷⁰

Costumiers and makeup artists attempted to make those acting female roles look as realistic as possible. The actors spent hours perfecting their craft to ensure convincing portrayals. Responses to these illusions were complex. The 'ladies were the most remarkable achievement', Jock Bryce recalled.⁷¹ 'We certainly have some excellent girls in the shows, it would surprise you', Albert Hake told Noela.⁷² Reg Giddey ardently stressed to his family that the 'shows would amaze anyone – and especially the chaps who play the feminine parts, who have to be seen to be believed.'⁷³ Despite ribbing in the earliest performances until audiences became used to men acting as women, reality was suspended for the duration of the productions and the airmen were once again men interacting with women.⁷⁴ Their qualifiers ('remarkable') and riders ('it would surprise you' and 'seen to be believed') however, suggest a tension in their appreciation of the female impersonators. This is further revealed in some men's inconsistent use of quotation marks: 'One of the "girls" from "Dover Road"… was at the races … She looked very attractive.'⁷⁵ This was not uncommon, as prisoners grappled with the 'grammatical challenge' of describing the 'actresses'.⁷⁶ The use of feminine pronouns and nouns reinforced acceptance of the faux female persona in an all-

---

67 AR: Arnel, interview 27 November 2014.
68 Quotes: NLA FERG/4550: *P.O.W.*, No 12, 15 January 1943, unattributed letter, 9 September 1942, 8; Archer FA: Archer, 1942 Diary, Addendum at beginning of diary, beginning 1 February 1942.
69 Archer FA: Archer, 1942 Diary, Addendum at beginning of diary, beginning 1 February 1942.
70 Barmaid: Fordyce FA: Fordyce, wartime log book, unpaginated photographic section, Comber, 'Well – here's happiness! – On thirty bob a week!', Sagan 5 February 1944; 'Ravishing lady': Mackenzie, *An Ordinary War 1940–1945*, 64.
71 Bryce FA: 'Jock Bryce's POW Diary 1942–1945', 172.
72 Preen FA: Albert Hake to Noela Hake, 8 September 1942.
73 'Letter from Germany. Flying-Officer Reg. Giddey Writes Home', *Gloucester Advocate* (NSW), 21 January 1944, 2.
74 AR: Arnel, interview 21 February 2018.
75 NLA FERG/4550: *P.O.W.*, No 12, 15 January 1943, unattributed letter, 9 September 1942, 8.
76 Rachamimov, 'Small Escapes: Gender, Class, and Material Culture in Great War Internment Camps', in Auslander and Zahra, (eds), *The Material Culture of Conflict and Displacement*, 182.

male world.[77] Some airmen, however, revealed that they were fully aware that the male actors were nothing more than female impersonators skilfully playing a part. 'Good imitation women', Keith Carmody recorded.[78] 'The "girls" are practising their ballet steps very thoroughly', Reg Kierath informed his mother.[79]

Photographs of shows demonstrate the impersonators' skills. Illustrations in wartime log books, however, present a different perspective. They reveal that feminine masquerade did not wholly subdue masculine characteristics. In Bill Fordyce's watercolour of Canadian Gordon King, the hourglass-figured King is in full makeup, wearing sheer scanty underwear (including brassiere with a pert prosthetic and clearly visible nipples), and sits decorously with legs crossed away from the viewer to hide any giveaway bulge. Yet he is unwigged, sports a buzz cut, and his sandaled feet are the same size as those of Fordyce-the-makeup-artist. The tag line, 'My God, it was a terrific struggle, though', reveals that the transformation of King from physically hardened male to a feminine-physiqued faux female was not easy.[80] Calton Younger also presents an admixture of feminine and masculine in his parodic cartoon of a homely, strong-calved prima donna throwing a tantrum with his caption, 'Any more of this temperament from young Bill and we'll have to get a new leading lady'.[81]

Some scripts and characters were subversive. Kenneth Gaulton recalled one which touched on anxieties relating to decreased libido and virility. 'There were two bulls, the old bull and the young bull looking at all these cows. And the young bull says to the old bull, "come on, let's run down and fix them". And the old bull says "no, let's walk down and we'll fix them all". And this brought the house down.'[82] Fordyce's sketch of Fabius from the play *Messalina* (penned by Australian Wemyss Wylton Todd and British kriegie David Porter) declaring 'with you I'd fling myself down anywhere!' asserted male sexual supremacy. That is until the viewer (and audience of *Messalina* and any other play with a sex scene) realised the biggest joke of all: that the actor desired to lay down with another man.[83] That destabilising joke was also in the traditional 'love drama', as George Archer described Merton Hodge's comedic *The Wind and the Rain*, with its 'too many love scenes to suit a Kriegie audience'.[84] All tastes were catered for 'with straight plays predominating', recalled Jock Bryce.[85] Several productions, however, were not quite 'straight'. Plays such as Noel Coward's

---

77   Smaal, *Sex, Soldiers and the South Pacific, 1939–45*, 21.
78   Barker, *Keith Carmody*, 60.
79   Kierath FA: Reg Kierath to Ada Kierath, 16 August 1943
80   Fordyce FA: Fordyce, wartime log book, 59.
81   Younger, *Get a Load of this*, [42].
82   AAWFA: Gaulton 1276, 3 February 2004.
83   Fordyce FA: Fordyce, wartime log book, 5.
84   Archer FA: Archer to family, 17 December 1944.
85   'Bryce FA: 'Jock Bryce's POW Diary 1942–1945', 173.

Design for Living, Oscar Wilde's *The Importance of Being Earnest*, and Terence Rattigan's *French without Tears* contained distinctly homosexual themes or subtext. *Messalina*, featuring Emperor Claudius' scantily-clad wily courtesan and a 'sparkling' court life that was 'Bacchanalian in the extreme', was both camp and heterosexually risqué.[86] Some plays challenged the traditional male/female hierarchy. Emasculated male characters were at the mercy of more powerful females such as Shakespeare's murderous Lady Macbeth, Joseph Kesselring's poison-wielding Brewster sisters (*Arsenic and Old Lace*), and Oscar Wilde's imperious Lady Bracknell (*The Importance of Being Earnest*). Productions such as *Messalina* and A.A. Milne's *The Dover Road*, another comedy which commented on fidelity, potentially played to fears that womenfolk at home may cuckold or move on from their absent lovers.

*****

Historian Iris Rachamimov argues that performances by female impersonators created a 'safety valve'. Reality in the abnormal single-sex society was suspended as faux females provided a condoned outlet for sexual tension without challenging its basic order.[87] Yet, while Bill Fordyce recalled that no one was ever tempted by even the most convincing 'actresses', some portrayals of sirens, vamps, or ingénues stimulated sexual desire.[88] Some, as Calton Younger recalled, were 'seemingly easy in their consciences' when enacting their desires.[89] Other kriegies were mortified by their homoerotic responses. When a performer 'brushed past me in full stage dress' during rehearsal, Ron Mackenzie over-reacted, suggesting more than simply discomfort. Mackenzie 'turned … to curse, found myself starting to apologise, woke up and cursed probably more vigorously than was strictly warranted'.[90] While the theatre challenged the kriegies' heterosexuality on a number of levels, it offered, for the majority, uncomplicated 'wonderful entertainment'. Most, like Alec Arnel were not 'titillated by it all', or by the impersonators. Performances ended at curtain fall and 'I didn't go to bed dreaming about them'.[91]

The theatre, like the imaginations of husbands, fiancés, and sweethearts, brought women into the airmen's midst. In some ways their feminine fabrications were comforting. In others, they were potentially disruptive. While the Australian airmen enjoyed the theatrical offerings – and some like Albert Comber and Bill Fordyce contributed their talents – the illusion faded. Female

---

86   Quotes: Arnel archive: Arnel to Margery Gray, 15 September 1944.
87   Rachamimov, 'Disruptive Comforts of Drag', 364, 375.
88   AAWFA: Fordyce 0523, 19 June 2003.
89   Younger, *No Flight From the Cage*, 116.
90   Mackenzie, *An Ordinary War 1940–1945*, 64.
91   AR: Arnel, interview 23 June 2016.

characters did not offer the emotional connection and female sympathy many craved. Moreover, female impersonators could stimulate unwelcome physical responses. In addition, some scripts, theatrical iconography, and jokes subverted the airmen's virility and place in the traditional sexual hierarchy even as they provided a means to laugh at that subversion. While imaginary and theatrical faux females inhabited kriegie minds and lives, they did little to solve the vexed issue of how to satisfy physical needs.

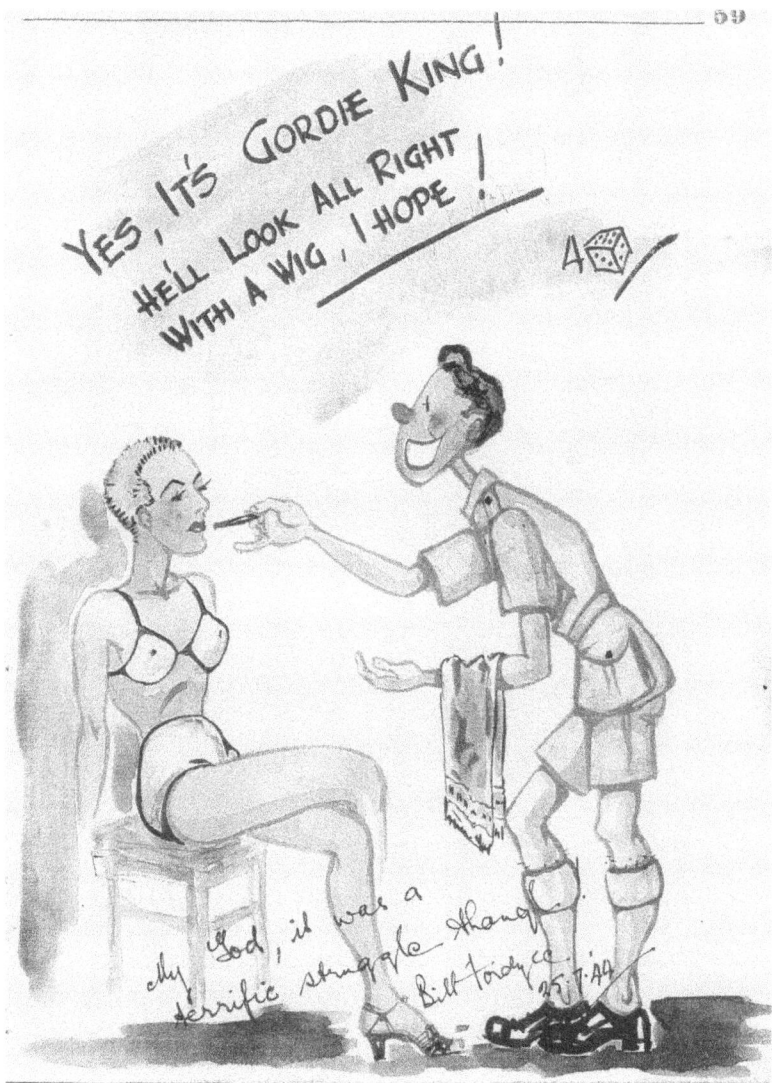

Bill Fordyce recorded the transformation of Canadian Gordon King for a theatre production. Judging by Bill's note, it wasn't an easy task! Courtesy of Drew Gordon, and with permission of Lily Fordyce.

Doug and Lola Hutchinson had married in March 1939. Thinking of their shared time together made captive life easier. 'Do you remember how happy you were when picking flowers from our garden ... Those days will come again, but till then all I have are the memories.' Courtesy of Robert Douglas Hutchinson.

Chapter Eight:

SEX

The walls of Bill Fordyce's fantasy illustration of Block 119's Christmas 1943 bar (complete with sozzled POW and kegged kriegie brew), are decorated with a poster of a smiling member of the Women's Auxiliary Air Force – a WAAF – declaring 'My dear! He's *twice* the man on Worthington', a famous English brewed beer. Another depicts two red-cheeked blondes (one looking as glazed-eyed as the inebriated kriegie) with the legend, 'Guinness makes loose women tight'.[1] Fordyce also painted a drunk-and-passed-out airman in the streets of Cairo dreaming of a bare-breasted woman.[2] Partnered or not, men missed sex and what it meant for their masculine, sexual selves. So they did something about it.

Sexually objectified depictions of women were everywhere. Glamour-girl posters adorned rooms. The memory of marital love was brushed aside as one artist sketched in Ronald Baines' wartime log book a sexy, scantily clad 'popsie' with a come-hither glance and slipped-down shoulder strap who suggestively lifts a sheet on a rumpled bed.[3] A long-legged blonde sitting in a Red Cross box entitled 'Red Cross Comforts' graces James McCleery's wartime log book.[4] The American Red Cross' 1944 Christmas parcel enclosed '1 lge envelope containing two pin up pictures'.[5] Photographs of girls were discussed in some quarters 'with brutal frankness', as indicated by the scrum surrounding one chap pulling out 'a photo of my sister', in warrant officers Robert Anderson's and David Westmacott's *Handle with Care*, a collection of humorous sketches commenting on the lives of airmen NCOs in stalags Luft III and VI.[6]

These images had nothing to do with love. Indicating misogynistic tendencies, some saw women purely as objects of desire. While objectifying women, sexualised images served other purposes. As suggested in a cartoon by Calton Younger of a kriegie looking through barbed wire at a defiantly ugly, bucked-tooth woman, some feared that, when liberated from their all-male world, they would fail to recognise beauty. 'Gee, I'd forgotten women were so beautiful', ran

---

1 Gordon FA: Bill Fordyce, '119's Bar, Xmas 1943, Luft 3, Sagan', 28 March 1944 from unknown wartime log book, 59.
2 Fordyce FA: Fordyce, wartime log book, 11.
3 Baines FA: Baines, wartime log book, unknown author, 'Here's your Popsie Ronnie! Good Luck! X–9–44', unpaginated photographic section.
4 AWM PR88/160: McCleery, wartime log book, M. Hall, 'Red Cross Comforts', 5 September 1944, 59.
5 Burgess RC: Robert Mills, wartime log book, 19.
6 Anderson and Westmacott, *Handle with Care*, 28.

Younger's caption.⁷ Such a reaction was not impossible. In a late-life interview, Bill Fordyce averred that they 'hadn't seen a woman for so many years. We hardly knew what they looked like.'⁸ Pin-ups and photographs, then, assured some that they could indeed appreciate feminine loveliness. They also contributed to group cohesion and reinforced that, despite the exclusively homosocial environment, the airmen were still attracted to women and had not 'turned' homosexual.

A drawing by 'Bish' of a naked Prune-as-Adam in the Garden of Eden bashfully protecting his genitals from the lasciviously appraising gaze of an equally naked Eve, insinuates that the once-glamorous and sexually alluring airmen had been emasculated by captivity.⁹ To counter this, some men asserted their virility by big-noting sexual competency. They equated conquests over women with military prowess. One married Australian, who was apparently 'a bit of a lad', however, was particularly disliked because of his frequent references to his carnal adventures.¹⁰ Indeed, the 'sort of person who was like that wasn't popular at all', Alec Arnel stated. Those who spoke of their exploits were disruptive. To avoid any discomfiture, sex 'was almost a taboo subject', in Arnel's room. 'We didn't talk about it.'¹¹ Dirty jokes were also off limits in his and other quarters. But not all kriegies placed restrictions on their conversation. Ronald Baines recorded that, after the shutters were closed, they generally sat around reading 'or talking – usually about sex or food.'¹² On one occasion, the 'main topic' among George Archer's friends was 'lack [of] sex & women plus past air exploits'. Less than a fortnight later, 'food & sex – boy what a combination.'¹³ As disturbing as they were for some, sex talk and conquest boasts provided an outlet for sexual tension. They also confirmed the kriegies' former sexual success and suggested anticipated future marital (or extra-marital) potency.

Stalag Luft III housed the *Luftwaffe*'s central mail censoring facility which employed about 200 female censors. Few airmen caught a glimpse of them but those in the Belaria satellite (about five or six kilometres from the main compound) regularly saw women travelling to and from work. As Doug Hutchinson recalled, when the women cycled or walked along the road about ten yards from the fence, the prisoners lined up to watch. They had 'a competition to see who could [mentally] undress the girl and make her fall off her bike'. It was 'a great game'. The women, however, were 'embarrassed with the

---

7   Younger, *Get a Load of this*, [44].
8   AAWFA: Fordyce 0523, 19 June 2003.
9   Fordyce FA: Bethell, 'A Glimpse of Stalag Luft III (North Compound)'; 'Bish', 'Prune's First Boob'.
10 Simpson, 'OPS' *Victory at all Costs*, 351. Quote: Simpson, son of Laurie Simpson, who shared this man's room', AR: Andrew R.B. Simpson, email 21 March 2016.
11 AR: Arnel, interview 23 June 2016.
12 Baines FA: Baines, wartime log book, 'The Usual Day at Stalag Luft III', 60.
13 Archer FA: Archer, 1942 Diary, 25 November and 7 December 1942.

blokes staring at them. And they got some idea of what they were thinking.'[14] Hutchinson excluded himself from the group harassment, so perhaps his strong ties to his wife left him immune to the female censors' sexual allure, but he was not invulnerable to inflamed desire.[15] When Lola reminded Hutchinson of their active and satisfying marital intimacy, he was aroused but neither in response to Lola's stimulating image nor in regard to the harassment anecdote did he indicate what he or others did to satisfy thwarted passion.[16] Nor did Ronald Baines when he asked a future reader of his wartime log book to imagine the 'horrible physical reactions to barbed wire – guards – orders – restrictions, the mental oppressions – no natural outlets for healthy normal human beings', in a world of 'dreary monotony'.[17]

Like Baines and Hutchinson, the majority of airmen were silent on substitutes for those natural outlets. Bill Fordyce skirted the issue when his interviewer asked, 'What about solo relief shall we call it?' 'Not that I knew of you know. Maybe.'[18] Ron Mackenzie, a rare exception, was less coy in his memoir when he recalled that, 'there were many jokes, some of them very funny, about masturbation, and innumerable tales of heterosexuality and homosexuality.'[19] The Australians' silence emanates from the social and religious stigma attached to what was seen at the time as self-abuse.[20] Censorship of private wartime writings, the fact that diaries were often written with another reader in mind (such as a wife or 'posterity'), and the public nature of memoir and oral history, deterred the majority from directly addressing the subject. Some, however, were less reserved.

Keith Carmody recorded in his diary that he dreamed of a woman he deemed 'some piece of work'. Shortly after, he had 'another distressing dream.'[21] George Archer's wartime diary suggests that some of the airmen enjoyed sexual horseplay. On one night, a bar of chocolate was the prize for a 'strip tease'. Archer later wrote that one of his roommates was 'the most sexy chap [I've] met for ages.'[22] Such sexualised behaviour, as historian Yorick Smaal notes, is part of 'ritualised male bonding in institutional settings', not necessarily related to homosexuality.[23] By not denying it and emphasising the humour of their situation, as they so often did, Ron Mackenzie implied that at least some

---

14 AAWFA: Hutchinson 0540, 17 June 2003.
15 Hutchinson FA: Lola Hutchinson to Doug Hutchinson, 1 January 1944.
16 Hutchinson FA: Doug Hutchinson to Lola Hutchinson, 1 May 1944.
17 Baines FA: Baines, wartime log book, 5 July 1944, 15.
18 AAWFA: Fordyce 0523, 19 June 2003.
19 Mackenzie, *An Ordinary War 1940–1945*, 63.
20 Social stigma: Michael Kirby, Foreword, Bongiorno, *The Sex Lives of Australians*, ix–x.
21 Barker, *Keith Carmody*, 66.
22 Archer FA: Archer, 1942 Diary, 25 November and 7 December 1942.
23 Smaal, *Sex, Soldiers and the South Pacific, 1939–45*, 95.

kriegies accepted and even enjoyed masturbation as they solved the awkward problem of sexual frustration. At the most basic level, the need for 'solo relief' reinforced that their libidos were intact and that they remained virile. Some airmen, however, were uncomfortable when roughhousing verged too close to homoerotic 'exhibitionism'.[24] There may have been a certain amount of light-hearted joking about some of the 'prettier' young men who played female roles in the theatre, and 'you will be home or homo this year', but the majority of Stalag Luft III's kriegies appeared to be firmly heterosexual, and revealed a keen appreciation of women.[25] Horseplay and masturbation were condoned as long as it was clearly understood that they were heterosexual outlets.

*****

There was a perception of elitism surrounding the air force; many believed only the fittest, brightest, healthiest, specimens were recruited for aircrew.[26] The RAF, however, was reluctant to equate physical strength with courage. Aesthetic types could be just as strong, fearless, valorous, and effective airmen as those with athletic physiques;[27] even decorated fighter pilots who died in battle could be homosexual.[28] But homosexuality, for some, posed a threat to the air force's perceived physical and psychological exclusivity, escape-mindedness, and masculinity. Reflecting a general belief in Australian and British society and in POW camps that homosexuality was a disease, illness, or physical deficiency, Doug Hutchinson was adamant that aircrew were 'mentally strong, because they'd had a fairly good education, and they were the cream of the country'. As he saw it, that mental fitness precluded them from being homosexual.[29] Paul Brickhill omitted all mention of homosexuality from his accounts of life and escape in Stalag Luft III. His biographer indicated that this was because it had no place in a 'heroic escape narrative'.[30] Perhaps too, Brickhill and his publisher were pandering to social mores – same-sex relationships were illegal at the time in Britain and Australia.

But there may have been more to Brickhill's omission. Just after Brickhill submitted *The Great Escape* manuscript to his publisher, he enquired about treatment at London's Tavistock Clinic, a specialist mental health facility, which recommended that he consult a psychiatrist.[31] As well as a range of psychological

---

24 Quote: Younger, *No Flight From the Cage*, 116.
25 'Prettier' young men: Archer FA: Archer, letters to family, 25 November and 21 December 1942; 'home or homo': Burgess RC: Robert Mills, wartime log book, 10.
26 Paris, 'The Rise of the Airmen: The Origins of Air Force Elitism, c. 1890–1918', 123–141.
27 Francis, *The Flyer*, 129.
28 Bourne, *Fighting Proud*, 104.
29 AAWFA: Hutchinson 0540, 17 June 2003. General belief: Wotherspoon, '*City of the Plain*', 26, 103; Bourne, *Fighting Proud*, 61.
30 Brickhill, *The Great Escape*; Brickhill and Norton, *Escape to Danger*. Quote: Dando-Collins, *The Hero Maker*, 203.
31 NAA C139 NMX283109-01: Brickhill, Paul Chester – service number 403313 [DVA medical case file; box 59618]: undated report, Miss Tamplin, Tavistock Clinic [c. May 1950].

and emotional problems, the consultant found that 'sexually he shows a mixture of sadistic and passive, including homosexual trends'.[32] Reviewing his original notes twenty years later, the psychiatrist qualified that assessment; he considered that 'mention of a homosexual element is perhaps technical, in that it was part of an early phase and only later appeared in dreams'.[33] While Brickhill's life-time medical records make no other reference to his sexuality, rekindled memories and concerning dreams at the time of writing *The Great Escape* may have stimulated him to a firm silence on same-sex relationships within Stalag Luft III.

Other airmen's responses to homosexuality were contradictory. Even as they denied the existence of homosexuals in the air force and Stalag Luft III, some conceded their presence. In substantiating their claims that homosexuality in camp did not exist, Ron Mackenzie and Bill Fordyce pointed out the conditions which excluded it, such as lack of food, privacy, or opportunity.[34] In the same series of interviews, Justin O'Byrne asserted that, 'strangely, never ever did I see an airman in a situation where you could suspect that he was a homosexual' yet also referred to 'two young people, and both of them were Fleet Air Arm pilots' – members of the Royal Navy's air service – who pulled a curtain around their bunk to hide from prying eyes (if not flapping ears). Attesting to a shared belief that homosexuality did not equate to virility, O'Byrne and his fellow kriegies 'used to talk about them and say they were poofters'.[35] Richard Winn acknowledged gossip about the sexuality of female leads in theatre productions but asserted that 'there was no evidence of any homosexuality for all the time I was a POW – 2 years, 4 months'.[36] Indeed, he 'never heard or noticed anything to do with homosexuality'.[37] He, however, may have been naïve or not privy to the cues used by those seeking homosexual interaction. Moreover, codes of silence may have been at play.

Richard Osborn was quite frank in recalling that, during his brief tenure in the Belaria compound before his medical repatriation, one of the huts 'was known as the "buggery block" – a bit crude, but that explained exactly the status of its occupants who quite freely chose their own quarters to satisfy their own preferred lifestyle'.[38] Despite Osborn's vivid recollection, fellow Belaria inmate, Doug Hutchinson, was vociferous in his repeated denial of same-sex behaviour in the air force and in captivity. 'No, no. I never knew of any. Never knew of

---

32   NAA C139 NMX283109-01: Brickhill, Paul Chester – service number 403313 [DVA medical case file; box 59618]: letter Dr Alan Mason, Harley Street, London to Miss Tamplin, Tavistock Clinic, 1 June 1950.
33   NAA C139 NMX283109-01: Brickhill, Paul Chester – service number 403313 [DVA medical case file; box 59618]: Dr Alan Mason, Harley Street, London to Deputy Commissioner of Pensions, Australia House, London, 10 September 1970.
34   Mackenzie, *An Ordinary War 1940–1945*, 63; AAWFA: Fordyce 0523, 19 June 2003.
35   NLA O'Byrne, 'Reminiscential conversations', Tape 51.
36   Winn, *A Fighter Pilot's Diary*, 58.
37   AAWFA: Winn 1508, 4 March 2004.
38   Osborn, *Circuits and Bumps*, 254.

any at all.'[39] He believed there were no homosexuals in the air force because 'they were very careful in their selection of people ... you had to be just one hundred per cent before they let you into an air crew, with the result that the blokes that were prisoners, they were young people who were very fit, or they had been very fit.'[40] Contradicting his recollections of the Fleet Air Arm boys (although perhaps naval fliers did not count as 'airmen') Justin O'Byrne also believed the air force screened out homosexuals.[41] So too did Richard Winn. 'Air force selected so there won't be homosexuals in it.'[42] There is no evidence to support their assertions. Moreover, their own contradictory recollections refute them. Australian military services, including the RAAF, had no formal policy on homosexuality before the Second World War.[43] Questions regarding sexual orientation were not asked by recruiters or medical officers. Many homosexuals, like thousands of other young men, were attracted to the air force because of its image of glamour, excitement and adventure, and because they wanted to fly. They enlisted and were accepted.

None of the contemporary and late-life personal narratives, medical testimony, or oral history recordings I consulted 'out' any of Stalag Luft III's Australians. None of the authors of these private or public accounts identify themselves as homosexuals. Only two post-war medical reports referred to sexuality. One, as indicated above, noted Paul Brickhill's past 'homosexual trends'.[44] In the other case, a psychologist recorded his patient's 'basic bisexual characteristics'.[45] Perhaps none were homosexual, or perhaps they simply did not disclose their preference in a climate where ignorance, fear, and criminality of same-sex behaviour was socially and culturally legitimised for most of the twentieth century.[46] Certainly, being labelled a 'poofter' would have been enough encouragement to lay low. For some, the idea of homosexuality precipitated homophobic fear and shame. Afraid he would be branded a homosexual, Kenneth Gaulton 'never felt so embarrassed in my life' when, after a concert party, he stood at the urinal with 'a good looking fellow ... dressed up as a girl'.[47] Some, according to Canadian Kingsley Brown, were anxious about the effects of an all-male environment on their 'normal libido'. Consequently, one medical officer spent much time assuaging concerns that 'they were queer, or becoming queer' by assuring them

---

39 AAWFA: Hutchinson 0540, 17 June 2003.
40 AAWFA: Hutchinson 0540, 17 June 2003.
41 NLA O'Byrne, 'Reminiscential conversations', Tape 51.
42 AAWFA: Winn 1508, 4 March 2004.
43 Riseman, Robinson, Willett, *Serving in Silence?*, 13.
44 NAA C139 NMX283109-01: Brickhill, Paul Chester – service number 403313 [DVA medical case file; box 59618]: Dr Alan Mason, Harley Street, London to Deputy Commissioner of Pensions, Australia House, London, 10 September 1970.
45 DVA QMX034497-02: psychologist report, 12 December 1950.
46 Wotherspoon, 'City of the Plain', 39, 41, 52, 79; Bongiorno, *The Sex Lives of Australians*, 114.
47 AAWFA: Gaulton 1276, 3 February 2004.

that, if they were, 'they would have known about it beforehand.'⁴⁸ Others, such as Calton Younger, were mortified when they experienced homoerotic responses. After a 'night on the turps' at Stalag Luft VI, Heydekrug, Younger kissed one of the 'barmaids', a fellow prisoner in drag. Although enjoying 'the almost forgotten taste of lipstick', he was 'afraid that some unsuspected proclivities had been awakened in me'. It was 'a long time before I forgot my shame'.⁴⁹

Homosexuality threatened group harmony. It was 'completely taboo'.⁵⁰ Contravention of their rigid moral code resulted in friction. Again contradicting his assertion of no homosexuality in camp, Justin O'Byrne recounted a confrontation between a 'young fellow, a fine young bloke, an Australian' who 'was appalled' at the Fleet Air Arm fellows (mentioned above) hunkered down in a single bunk behind a curtain. The 'fine young bloke' was so upset about it that he felt he should 'speak to them strongly and try and stop them from this practice, or just show how opposed to it he was'. The Fleet Air Arm boys, however, 'stood up to him'. The group reaction was memorable. According to O'Byrne, it 'was almost like a tribal conflict'.⁵¹

Despite threats to masculinity, air force elitism, a traditional moral code, and group cohesion – as well as overt homophobia – some former prisoners pragmatically or disinterestedly tolerated same-sex behaviour. Rather than condemn or condone their 'preferred lifestyle', Richard Osborn in Belaria focused on the 'welcome … distraction from the boredom of normal camp life' of some homosexuals' theatrical pursuits.⁵² In early January 1943, rumour had it that there were 'a pair of lovers' in Alex Kerr's Centre Compound block. 'Nothing could be proved, and having neither the interest nor the inclination to investigate myself, I accepted the more or less circumstantial evidence offered by the scandalmongers.'⁵³ In the interests of Centre Compound harmony, Ron Mackenzie confirmed that 'people with obvious homosexual tendencies' were generally 'treated with courtesy and a sort of baffled sympathy'.⁵⁴ Tolerant heterosexual airmen throughout Stalag Luft III, however, appear to have been in the minority.

*****

Doug Hutchinson's obvious love and constancy for Lola perhaps explains his lack of interest in other women, yet he attributed it to his advancing years and

---

48   Brown, *Bonds of Wire*, 130.
49   Younger, *No Flight From the Cage*, 116.
50   IWMSA Bernard: 26561, June 2004 [no date].
51   NLA O'Byrne, 'Reminiscential conversations', Tape 51.
52   Osborn, *Circuits and Bumps*, 254.
53   Kerr, *Shot Down*, 2015, 139.
54   Mackenzie, *An Ordinary War 1940–1945*, 63.

deteriorating strength (he had recently turned 28 when liberated). 'Physically, I probably wouldn't have been up to it anyhow.' As Hutchinson explained, he was 'in pretty poor condition. When the war was ended, we hadn't been fed properly for a long time, and physically, you're just out of condition.'[55] Most sports had tailed off in the final months as a consequence of food shortages. Running had given way to walking around the perimeter.[56] Bill Fordyce also credited the absence of desire to reduced rations. 'I always thought that it was hunger that you never worried about that. Truly.'[57] Starvation, however, was not a perennial state, as Fordyce implied. His reply ignored the reality of periodic rather than constant food shortages, such as during the early days of captivity or when the Germans implemented reprisals for attempted escapes or other rule infractions. While those imprisoned in Buchenwald concentration camp were on a starvation diet, the hungriest time for the majority was during the latter months of the war, particularly during and after the forced marches, when many men experienced the full effects of starvation, including nutritional diseases and diminished libido. At that stage hunger did seem 'perpetual', as Ronald Baines recorded on 4 March 1945, and it was certainly a strain. Baines, who frequently wrote in his diary about his 'honeypot', mentioned Irene only three times between 1 January and 27 April 1945. 'Amazing how since we left Sagan, the main topic of conversation is food. ... Mail and sex have faded into the background ... unless man has a full belly, little else interests him.'[58]

As they had done before, the airmen laughed at their plight, illustrating their hunger-induced lack of sexual interest in wartime log books. Arthur Schrock drew a sleeping kriegie's dreams. Year one was of food. Year two was of a vampish siren. Year three was simply the sleeping prisoner.[59] Bill Fordyce's and Alex Kerr's wartime log books include images of a returned kriegie ignoring the embrace of a shapely, well-dressed consort in favour of a sandwich in hand and a well-stocked food trolley nearby.[60]

Those at home knew nothing of the drastic decline of the airmen's physical conditions. The Australians may have complained about lack of food – or joked about it – but they did not emphasise the debilitating effects of it. That was left to the privacy of their diaries. Instead, they presented a masculine body image to their close and extended families by promoting a narrative of wellness. They told their loved ones that they had emerged from combat, crash, or bale-out with few or only minor wounds. If they could not claim total recovery, they made light

---

55 AAWFA: Fordyce 0523, 19 June 2003; Quote: AAWFA: Hutchinson 0540, 17 June 2003.
56 AR: Arnel, interview 23 June 2016.
57 AAWFA: Fordyce 0523, 19 June 2003.
58 Baines FA: Baines, 'A Wartime Log', entry dated 4 March 1945.
59 Simpson RC: Arthur Schrock, wartime log book, 14.
60 Fordyce FA: Fordyce, wartime log book, 21; Kerr archive: Alex Kerr, wartime log book, 61.

of their condition or minimised its seriousness. 'Let me say that after spending seven weeks in hospital (Dutch), except for the loss of my right eye', as well as shoulder muscle damage from a cannon and splinters knocked from his cheek bone by a bullet which he mentioned in passing, 'I am once again enjoying good health', Charles Lark told his folks.[61] 'We were shot down, and I was wounded in a number of places, but after three weeks in hospital I am now on the mend and will soon be quite fit', Doug Hutchinson assured Lola.[62] Hutchinson, however, had taken shrapnel in his elbow, legs, and body, had sustained severe wounds to his foot, and later developed an abscess. Despite Lola's frequent requests for details he failed to describe their full extent. Even those previously interned in Buchenwald concentration camp declared they were in 'the best of health' and 'well and fit'. Their post-liberation medical reports, however, contradict their assertions. Most were seriously underweight and some conditions had been exacerbated by dysentery.[63] Attached and unattached alike stressed physicality and sexuality by demonstrating that they were strong and healthy immediately after capture and later, as they had settled in. 'Am quite fit and well', Paul Brickhill told a friend.[64] On no less than eight occasions, George Archer affirmed to his family that he was either 'very fit' or 'well and fit'. Variations of 'fit and well' were oft-repeated refrains, even from the (not quite) walking wounded such as John Vivash who had arrived in Stalag Luft III with two broken ankles.[65]

The Germans allowed some photography, or took photographs themselves for propaganda purposes. Pictures of smiling, bare-chested men, hale-looking groups, and of sports' days reinforced masculinity, sexuality, and virility. By depicting their fitness in letters – including references to escape attempts – and providing visual evidence of it, Stalag Luft III's kriegies revealed to their families that they had not been cowed or broken by captivity. So too did kriegie defiance, active disruption, and escape.

---

61 Lark FA: Charles Lark to Dear Folks, 22 August 1942.
62 Hutchinson FA: Doug Hutchinson to Lola Hutchinson, 8 August 1943.
63 First quote, *Hubert Atkinson*, 'Personal' column, *Mercury* (Mackay, QLD). Second quote, *Arnold Hibbert*, telegram, 30 May 1945.
64 AWM PR03099: Brickhill to Del Fox, 27 November 1943.
65 NAA A705, 166/42/92 Vivash: John Vivash to mother, 13 December 1944.

Regardless of how they actually felt, many of the kriegies were committed to convincing family and friends that they were 'fit and well.' Photos such as this, taken in East Compound c. October 1942, did much to perpetuate the myth that life in captivity was not all bad. Tom Leigh (left), Bill Moore, (centre) and Paul Sanders. Courtesy of Winifred Chevalier.

PART FOUR: ESCAPE

Chapter Nine:

DUTY TO ESCAPE

Soon after settling in, the airmen were addressed by the Senior British Officer or Man of Confidence. The first words of Belaria's SBO, Bruce Lumsden recalled, 'were clearly intended to galvanise us out of any apathy and meek resignation to our fate'. There is a sense of defeat in apathy, an emotion that encompasses loss of motivation and depressed listlessness. Reappropriating the frequently repeated German words, the Group Captain attempted to rouse the new arrivals' military selves by announcing 'as though giving an order' that, 'for you ... the war is <u>not</u> over'. While Lumsden and his fellow new boys 'were to stop short of acts of overt disobedience which could be punished', they were warned 'against any degree of compliance or co-operation with the Germans beyond what was necessary'. Most emphatically, the SBO instilled in them that 'it was our duty ... to make the enemy's task of imprisoning us as difficult and demanding on their resources as we could'. Lumsden and his friends soon 'learned some of the ways by which this could be done'.[1]

The kriegies' disruptive efforts demonstrated to the Germans that 'you have us here, but we're not going to let you walk all over us'. As such, as Alec Arnel asserted, they 'used whatever means' they had to undermine German authority.[2] Kriegie defiances included 'the fierce joy of goon-baiting', where they either individually or in concert provoked the German prison staff.[3] The editors of North Compound's gossipy *Scangriff* undermined Teutonic superiority: 'we always used to put a lot of garbage in it so they never knew quite what was true', recollected Bill Fordyce who illustrated the news sheet.[4] ('Scangriff' was a kriegie term which meant 'scandal sheet'.[5]) They deliberately broke rules. Rudolph Leu was one of many who risked playing cards out of hours. One kriegie was punished for conducting a secret meeting. A repeat offender had a penchant for malicious damage to his barracks.[6] Another was 'non-cooperative and aggressive'.[7] The airmen bribed guards and stole tools and supplies both to make life easier and to feed into the escape organisation. Many misbehaved during *Appell* – roll call – frustrating attempts to count their numbers. Smoking

---
1 Lumsden FA: Bradbeer and Lumsden, 'The Complete Tour', Lumsden, letter 8 April 1988. Original emphasis.
2 AR: Arnel, interview 2 March 2017.
3 Lark, *A Lark on the Wing*, 75.
4 AAWFA: Fordyce 0523, 19 June 2003.
5 *The Falkirk Herald* (Scotland), 8 January 1947, 4.
6 NAA A13950 POW identification cards.
7 DVA MX035229-02: letter to Deputy Commissioner, DVA, June 1984.

on parade, Ron Mackenzie recorded, was particularly annoying for the Germans as it was *unsoldatlich* – unsoldierly behaviour.[8]

Some constructed radios. Others stole parts, and maintained those vital links to the outside world. Transcripts from BBC news broadcasts were distributed to boost morale. A more formal scheme of anti-German propaganda was also implemented. In the wake of D-Day, Senior British Officer Group Captain Douglas Wilson devised a major defence strategy in North Compound dubbed the 'Klim Klub', after a brand of milk powder provided in food parcels.[9] When German capitulation seemed likely, Wilson ensured his men were trained in 'individual and collective protection' in the face of anticipated civilian violence. He prepared the prisoners to overpower their captors, take control of the camp, and make a mass escape to allied lines.[10] An ex-paratrooper instructed Ronald Baines and his fellows on 'how to disarm – break necks' and carry out 'other forms of unarmed combat'.[11] Similar schemes were set up in East and Belaria compounds.[12]

The kriegies' disruptive acts had consequences. Roll call took longer; the airmen were made to stand on parade in bad weather or until late at night. They were put in the 'cooler' – the camp's punishment cells – or confined to barracks. Red Cross parcels or mail were withheld. Some POWs were beaten. Threats, wounds, and collective reprisals did little to dent the ardour of their resistance, however. Rather than *unsoldatlich* behaviour, disruption lifted morale, strengthened group cohesion, and reflected air force pride and martial masculinity. The kriegies revelled in it.[13] 'Never during the whole of the War did I stop sticking my neck out', Sean Hanrahan declared 40 years later.[14] It was all part of showing that 'there was a fight in the British as much as ever there was', Justin O'Byrne asserted.[15] So too was escape.

As well as providing guidance on how to behave when captured and during interrogation, the 1936 first edition of *Air Publication 1548* urged an escape awareness; it did not impose a duty to escape. The RAF did not update the booklet at the outbreak of war but, given advice that 'opportunities for escape will present themselves', and the exhortation to 'keep your eyes and ears open for any

---

8   Mackenzie, *An Ordinary War 1940–1945*, 56.
9   Brickhill, *The Great Escape*, 244–245.
10 NAUK AIR 40/269: Stalag Luft III reports and nominal roll.
11 Baines FA: Baines, 'Shot Down', 12.
12 NAUK WO 208/3283: SLIII Camp History, Part I East (Officers') Compound, 41, Part III North (Officers') Compound, 32, Part V Belaria (Officers') Compound, 16.
13 Alexander, 'The Australian prisoner of war experience in Stalag Luft III, 1942–45', in Nicole Townsend, Kus Pandy, and Jarrod Pendlebury (eds), *Australian Perspectives on Global Air and Space Power: Past, Present, Future*, 23–33. See also Alexander, '"For you the war is (not) over": Active disruption in the barbed wire battleground', *From Balloons to Drones*, <https://balloonstodrones.com/2017/12/18/for-you-the-war-is-not-over-active-disruption-in-the-barbed-wire-battleground/>.
14 DVA NCX065122-02: personal statement, 17 January 1980.
15 NLA JMFC: Justin O'Byrne, 31 October 1986.

information which you think may be of value should you succeed in escaping', some of the earliest captive airmen inferred an onus to escape.[16] In this they were encouraged by MI9. Established on 23 December 1939 as a department of the British War Office, one of MI9's aims was to develop 'escape-mindedness', a perpetual vigilance to every opportunity to avoid capture or flee from enemy hands.[17] MI9 trained escapers and evaders, provided equipment, and established evasion lines in occupied Europe. Later, the RAF Intelligence School ran courses for station intelligence officers, who in turn trained operational airmen.

The duty to escape was formalised in *Air Publication 1548*'s June 1941 edition. The escape rationale was also defined: attempts 'have a very appreciable nuisance value'.[18] The duty was rescinded in the April 1944 revised and retitled edition but, as in the original booklet, an implied duty was urged by encouraging an alertness to escape.[19] The revision was a response to heightened security within Germany because of the 'threat' posed by allied prisoners of war. With the so-called 'Bullet Decree' of 4 March 1944, escaped prisoners (with the exception of British and Americans) were to be handed over to the German security services rather than returned to their camps. It also allowed for the execution of non-British and non-American escapers. In mid-September 1944, the Germans spelled out the ramifications of escape in a circular addressed 'To all Prisoners of War!' which declared that 'escape from prison camps is no longer a sport!' Absconders captured in newly designated 'death zones' would be 'immediately shot on sight'.[20]

Escape-mindedness was a running thread through wartime log books. Humorous images reflected wishful thinking. James McCleery and Cy Borsht had similar drawings of a guard patrolling above a diligent tunneller.[21] Emphasising the pipedream aspect of a successful escape in his variation of the theme, Eric Johnston drew two diggers about to break out just inside the barbed wire, directly underneath three guards. Reinforcing the hopelessness of escape for a man debilitated after two months in Buchenwald concentration camp, Johnston's log book also includes a turban-topped airman scaling a magic rope.[22] Making fun of their pre-capture intelligence briefings, McCleery drew a group of aircrew listening to a boffin declaring 'Escape! It's a piece of cake!!' Underneath, an airman looked hopefully over the warning line while a ferocious guard dog and handler waited to attack if he stepped across.[23]

---

16 *Air Publication 1548*, March 1936, front cover, 4.
17 Foot and Langley, MI 9, 34–35. Quote: 53.
18 *Air Publication 1548*, 2nd Edition, June 1941.
19 *Air Publication 1548: The Responsibilities of a Prisoner of War*, 3rd Edition, April 1944.
20 Quotes from poster.
21 AWM PR88/160: McCleery, 3; Borsht Archive: Borsht, wartime log book, 37. Borsht's image is captioned 'Escape!'. Original emphasis.
22 Johnston FA: Johnston, wartime log book, 9 and 29.
23 AWM PR88/160: McCleery, wartime log book, 23.

McCleery, Borsht, and Johnston were all captured after the 'Bullet Decree'; Borsht and Johnston arrived after the 'immediately shot on sight' poster was displayed. Even so, as these comic illustrations prove, they could dream and, in imagination, thumb their noses at their captors. While their drawings took the sting out of unfulfilled dreams they also rendered images and words safe from German censorship. Because of secrecy constraints, escape work was not often recorded, nor were details of secret escape and evasion lectures held in camp.[24] Some of the Australian airmen, however, referred to failed efforts in after-the-fact diary entries and letters home. Censors did not obliterate those accounts because they were interpreted as highlighting German success in foiling attempts; some demonstrated German post-escape disciplinary measures. 'M.G's brother got moved because he tried to escape, and last week I nearly got moved for the same reason', one man told his mother.[25]

Italian captivity presented few opportunities to escape.[26] Even so, some men tried. Albert Comber and others worked on tunnels at PG 78, Sulmona while other Australians disposed of soil and played games to distract the guards. Comber and fellow members of the 'escape team + tunnel-digging crew' worked underground for over two months. 'Dangerous earth falls increased with heavy rain which finally caused a cave-in … and thus discovery … Failure after months of hazardous, tedious effort!'[27] For many, the first real chance to escape came when Italy signed the armistice with the Allies. After moving to PG 19, Bologna, Comber was one who tried to take advantage of the post-Armistice disarray. He and eleven other Australians broke out not knowing they were surrounded by Germans. They were then machine-gunned and 'forced back into captivity. Failure again!'[28] Many allied prisoners in Italian custody, including airmen, escaped to Switzerland and France. Comber, Bill Fordyce, Ken Carson, Rudolph Leu and others tried to escape during the long transit from Italy to German camps in crowded cattle trucks. After spending three days whittling through the planks with a small pen-knife, Comber and a friend 'wriggled out & rode the buffers for 3 or 4 hours waiting to jump if the train slowed down'. They seized their opportunity but 'ran bang into a German patrol – prisoners after 2 hours of uncertain freedom. Failure again!'[29]

---

24   Green FA: Errol Green, MI9 'General Questionnaire' 23574, 18 May 1945.
25   NLA FERG/4550: P.O.W., No. 29, 15 June 1944, unattributed letter, 30 January 1944, 2.
26   Gilbert, POW, 75.
27   AWM: AH Comber, artist, letter 16 December 1990.
28   AWM: AH Comber, artist, letter 16 December 1990.
29   AWM: AH Comber, artist, letter 16 December 1990

MI9's historians deemed Stalag Luft III an escape-minded camp.[30] Rather than giving in to what Jimmy Catanach termed 'the futility of the existence',[31] many of the Australian airmen – including Catanach – joined the 'X' organisation, as the kriegies dubbed it.[32] It was 'a masterpiece of coordination', Justin O'Byrne recalled. Miners, carpenters, engineers, draftsmen and artists all had roles.[33] At Oflag X-C, Lübeck, O'Byrne had almost immediately joined the 'keenest and most energetic types ... working on tunnels'.[34] He soon found a place in Stalag Luft III's escape organisation, becoming a dedicated member of 'X'. 'German speakers, of which I was one, were detailed to make friends with the German patrols inside the camp, follow them about and eventually try to bribe them to bring in items needed from outside.' There was even a place for 'kriegies who had no special skill but were keen to help'.[35]

'X' oversaw escape work and mobilised camp resources towards officially sanctioned schemes. It was based on that established in Stalag Luft I, Barth by dedicated escaper, Harry 'Wings' Day. According to his biographer and fellow prisoner at Stalag Luft III, Sydney Dowse, Day's commitment to escape derived from his professional honour and pride as a soldier and air force officer.[36] Escape would enable him to 'return to the fight'.[37] Day stamped his personal philosophy over the 'X' organisation and led by example.[38] Designating 'escaping' as Barth's 'operational function', Day stressed that escape was an essential element of air force duty.[39] When Day and other members of Barth's escape committee were transferred to the newly opened Stalag Luft III, where Day became the camp's inaugural Senior British Officer, they set up the organisation anew. As well as being an active tunneller at Barth, Paul Royle was in charge of tunnel operations in the officers' compound.[40] He was one of many who joined the new iteration of the escape organisation when they moved to Sagan. After the more senior Martin Massey arrived, and thus assumed the role of SBO, Day continued to run the escape organisation with Massey's approval.[41] When Day and a large group of officers transferred to Oflag XXI-B, Schubin (now Szubin, Poland) in October 1942, Day appointed Roger Bushell – again with Massey's support – as head of Stalag Luft III's escape committee.[42]

---

30 Foot and Langley, *MI 9*, 108.
31 SOR JCC: 2013.CAT050, James Catanach to William Alan Catanach, 28 March 1943.
32 '"X" organisation': Brickhill and Norton, *Escape to Danger*, 6.
33 O'Byrne FA: O'Byrne, '*Mercury* Radio Roundsman'.
34 O'Byrne FA: O'Byrne, '*Mercury* Radio Roundsman'.
35 O'Byrne FA: O'Byrne, '*Mercury* Radio Roundsman'.
36 Smith, *Wings Day*, 62. 'Sydney Smith' was the *nom de plume* of former Stalag Luft III prisoner, Sydney Dowse.
37 Smith, *Wings Day*, 195–196.
38 Meale, 'Leadership of Australian POWs in the Second World War', PhD thesis, 166–167.
39 Smith, Wings Day, 81–82, 97, 133, 169.
40 NAUK WO 208/3334/1574: MI9/SPG/LIB Liberation reports, Royle.
41 White, *Extremes of Fortune*, 114.
42 White, *Extremes of Fortune*, 108, 115.

Bushell, as 'Big X', dominated the organisation during Day's absence and even after his return. While Day's leadership and own escape efforts derived from service idealism, Bushell's motives as reported by his confrères were selfish, reflecting a personal desire to escape at all costs. Scholar Katie Meale, who examined Bushell's leadership style, concludes that he was 'obsessed with escape'. Moreover, he was not a true 'team player', demonstrating a track record throughout his years of captivity of putting self-interest first.[43] Bushell's biographer, Guy Walters, posits that Bushell was also motivated by a sense of 'being fated to do something great'.[44] As such, Bushell autocratically redesigned and expanded Day's organisation to realise his ambitions and exercised total control over it. Stalag Luft III's official 'X' report asserts that the escape committee regulated 'practically 100 per cent' of the escapes within Stalag Luft III but Bushell gave the orders and made the final decisions.[45] He forbade all but authorised attempts. Four Australians who ignored the rules discovered his ire. They were given 'a good talking to ... and now as punishment we have to dig rubbish tips'. They were forbidden another attempt and 'promised it won't happen again'.[46] Accordingly, when North Compound opened on 27 March 1943, the 'X' organisation became the central focus of RAF Station Sagan's escape efforts.[47] While Bushell countenanced no unsanctioned plans for tunnel escapes, he approved some schemes because they would divert attention from his grand plan.[48] The other compounds had their own versions of the 'X' organisation. All Senior British Officers supported them and MI9 covertly assisted their efforts.

Every aspect of camp life except for the care of the sick was subordinate to the 'X' organisation, according to Aiden Crawley, official historian of the RAF's wartime escapes, and former Stalag Luft III kriegie.[49] Each new arrival was informed that if they wanted to help they were to give their name to their hut's escape representative. While preferences for any sort of work might be considered, volunteers were warned that they would be expected to perform any task for which they were suitable and physically fit. No one, however, would be instructed to undertake work which could endanger his life.[50] Australians such as Ken Todd reinforce MI9's assessment of Stalag Luft III's escape-mindedness. Todd later told his family how he and his companions attempted to escape from the Belaria compound three times. He knew it was stupid but considered it his

---

43 Meale, 'Leadership of Australian POWs in the Second World War', PhD thesis, 116–119.
44 Walters, *The Real Great Escape*, 29.
45 NAUK AIR 40/285: 'X' report, 25.
46 NLA FERG/4550: *P.O.W.*, No. 29, 15 June 1944, unattributed letter, 30 January 1944, 2.
47 NLA JMFC: Justin O'Byrne, 31 October 1986.
48 Meale, 'Leadership of Australian POWs in the Second World War', PhD thesis, 134–136 and 141.
49 [Crawley], *Escape from Germany*, 32. Originally published in 1956.
50 NAUK WO 208/3283: SLIII Camp History, Part III North (Officers') Compound, 9.

duty to try.⁵¹ Clarence 'Alf' Miners recalled that 'many harebrained schemes' in Centre Compound 'were put forward in all sincerity'. Most, however, were impractical, and, 'the proponents were persuaded not to try'.⁵² As Reg Giddey recalled, 'there were some weird and wonderful ideas' aplenty in other compounds too. He contemplated hitching a ride on North Compound's 'honey cart' (the sanitary waste wagon).⁵³ Geoff Cornish was one of North Compound's first escapers when he joined the 10 April 1943 gate walk-out scheme. Two months later, Ian 'Digger' McIntosh participated in the so-called 'delousing escape', one of a party of eighteen men escorted to the delousing shed by two fluent German speakers.⁵⁴ Hugh Lambie and a companion, 'fitted out for a break to Danzig', were captured cutting the wire.⁵⁵ Serial escaper Allan McSweyn swapped identities with an army private, worked as an orderly, made a nuisance of himself, and was transferred as a trouble-maker to Stalag VIII-B, Lamsdorf where, after some attempts, he finally made a 'home run'.⁵⁶ He was the only one of Stalag Luft III's Australian airmen escapers to make it back to England.

Many dug tunnels or participated in 'diversionary tactics' to distract the guards. The goons, however, were alert to this. According to Hec Henry, *Oberfeldwebel* Hermann Glemnitz told his subordinates that '"The sillier they appear to be acting – that's when they are up to gross mischief"'⁵⁷ including (although Glemnitz was not aware of it), Henry's own covert work. The ingenious Australian was one who helped make dummy rifles. He modelled his section in soap, then used silver paper and other oddments to complete it.⁵⁸ In addition to his duties in the carpentry department, Digger McIntosh, also made fake pistols.⁵⁹ Other escape-related activities in which Australians participated included writing coded letters to MI9, parcel diversion, look-out, soil dispersal, equipment manufacture or acquisition, forgery, and photography. Some even considered keeping fit to prepare for long-distance walking in the event of a successful break-out as escape work.

While there was a clear formal duty to escape between June 1941 and April 1944, an implied duty at other times, and active encouragement by Wings Day, Roger Bushell, and the 'X' organisation – what we would probably now refer to as 'peer pressure' – it seems, as Jock Bryce records, that few airmen captives

---

51 AR: Peter Todd, interview 13 October 2015.
52 Miners, The Wartime Memories Project.
53 Whittaker, 'The Men Marked X', *The Australian Magazine*, 26–27 March 1994, 40.
54 Walters, *The Real Great Escape*, 98.
55 AWM 54 81/4/135: MI9 report, Lambie.
56 NAA A9300 McSweyn, A F, Statement obtained from Flight Lieutenant A.F. McSweyn.
57 Henry FA: Henry cited in Joan Franklin, unpublished biography of Henry, 2005.
58 Henry FA: unattributed news clipping, October 1945.
59 Brickhill, *The Great Escape*, 80.

'were interested in "the duty of an officer to escape".'[60] Paul Royle, who when captured on 17 May 1940 became one of Australia's earliest prisoners of war, was one who denied duty or tying up German resources as justification for his dedicated escape work and repeated escape attempts.[61] Rather, he indicated an underlying rationale of self-interest.[62] 'We only thought of ourselves getting out.'[63] Reflecting a complexity of the impulse to escape where duty was only one among many reasons, and not necessarily the most important, Justin O'Byrne presented several other motives: to get out of a tedious environment and 'all the other sorts of debilitating influences that existed there'; the challenge; and being a hindrance to the Germans who had to 'smarten up their method of surveillance' to cope with them.[64] Bruce Lumsden was captured after the duty to escape was rescinded but he doubted whether duty, King, or country were ever real rationales for escape attempts. Rather, he recognised the human desire for freedom, that 'innate urge [which] impels the captive to look for an opportunity, and to calculate the chances'. He wrote that, even if 'the opportunity never comes, or the chance is never taken, it aids morale to play the game.'[65]

Frederick Seamer had a long devotion to escape before he helped form Centre Compound's escape committee, and then went on to head it in Stalag Luft VI, Heydekrug after the NCOs left Stalag Luft III in mid-1943. While not explaining his own drive to escape, Seamer recognised that 'desperate bids for freedom' were to 'escape from the monotony and boredom of camp life'.[66] For some, the taste of liberty, no matter how brief, was too much to resist. 'Three others and I went out for a few hours and got caught; too bad, eh, pet? But, gee, it was good to be free again.'[67] Before internment in Stalag Luft III, multiple-escaper Alex Kerr was drawn by the adventure combined with potential freedom. He felt 'triumph and excitement' when he and his companions had to live on their wits while on the run. 'It was an exhilarating feeling knowing you were winning a dangerous cat and mouse game' with the threat of disaster if you lost. 'The adrenaline was coursing through your veins almost continuously.'[68]

Emotions, rather than duty, underpinned some escape bids. Jock Bryce claimed that for some the 'misery of confinement and homesickness for one's friends are incentives as strong as any.'[69] Keeping busy, as well as their continuing

---

60   Bryce FA: 'Jock Bryce's POW Diary 1942–1945', 40.
61   SLWA: Royle, 4 March 2014.
62   IWMSA Royle: 26605, 2 December 2012.
63   SLWA: Royle, 4 March 2014.
64   NLA JMFC: Justin O'Byrne, 31 October 1986 (quotes); NLA O'Byrne, 'Reminiscential conversations', Tape 50.
65   Lumsden FA: Bradbeer and Lumsden, 'The Complete Tour', letter 7 December 1987.
66   AWM 54 779/3/126 part 1: Seamer, POW statement, [undated, c. June 1945.
67   NLA FERG/4550: P.O.W., No. 29, 15 June 1944, unattributed letter, 30 January 1944, 2.
68   Kerr, *Shot Down*, 195, 102, 149. Quotes: 195.
69   Bryce FA: 'Jock Bryce's POW Diary 1942–1945', 40.

service obligations as members of the air force helped mitigate their barely admitted deep humiliation. Sometimes there were no real motivations. The wartime editions of *Air Publication 1548* fostered opportunistic approaches to escape and men took their chances. Doug Hutchinson's Belaria friends hid in barrels waiting to be loaded onto a brewery truck: 'the blokes decided, here's an opportunity.'[70] On another occasion, Centre Compound's Kenneth Gaulton noticed an open gate with guards nowhere in sight. 'I walked straight out.'[71]

The great variety of disruptive acts including escape reinforced air force pride, service, and unity. They were vital elements in maintaining the battle against the Germans. Their efforts, in retrospect, were validated by von Lindeiner, Stalag Luft III's longest-serving *kommandant*, who acknowledged that the British – including Australians – 'were the most defensive [prisoners] against the Germans.'[72] The main focus of their defiances was the 'X' organisation. This gave rise to Stalag Luft III's myth of near-universal escape.

---

70 AAWFA: Hutchinson 0540, 17 June 2003.
71 AAWFA: Gaulton 1276, 3 February 2004.
72 Walton and Eberhardt, *From Commandant to Captive*, 63.

Paul Royle was in charge of tunnel operations in the officers' compound at Barth. The former 53 Squadron RAF pilot was also an active tunneller. Later, Royle joined Stalag Luft III's 'X' organisation. Stalag Luft I, Barth, c. 1941. Courtesy of Paul Royle.

Escape!', 1 March 1945, by Cy Borsht, in his wartime log book. Regardless of any actual or implied duty, many of the Australian airmen were wryly aware of the unlikelihood of a successful escape. Courtesy of Cy Borsht.

Chapter Ten:

THE ESCAPE MYTH

Shortly after arriving back in the United Kingdom, the newly liberated Terence Officer declared nearly 100 per cent commitment to escape among the Australians: 'The names of POWs who have tried to escape and even those who temporarily escaped include almost everyone, at some time.' He was one of them. A Hurricane pilot with 274 Squadron RAF, Officer crash landed in North Africa on 21 June 1941. Uninjured except for slight burns and cuts on his knees, he started walking but encountered an Italian police detachment. He shot three men, confiscated a bicycle, then made off for allied lines. Two days later, 'Lack of food and water resulted in stumbling into German lines, who took me to Germany as POW.'[1] Officer's assertion accords with the Australian airmen's narrative of wellness, and continuing stance as active airmen, but *did* almost every Australian attempt to escape? And what of the rest of Stalag Luft III's prisoners?

While some in Centre Compound, like Frederick Seamer, were keen to escape and formed an 'X' organisation known as 'Tally Ho' which mirrored that in other compounds and later flourished in Stalag Luft VI, Heydekrug, only a few non-commissioned officers were 'deeply interested' in escape.[2] Indeed, contrary to any official directives regarding duty of escape or implied duty, the majority of NCOs did not feel they were 'duty bound' to make the effort.[3] After realistically assessing the hazards of escape, Ron Mackenzie concluded that the odds were against him so decided he would not try.[4] Officer's declaration, written long after the Centre Compound NCOs had left Stalag Luft III, implies only a handful of exceptions to 'X' organisation membership. So too does George Harsh, an American serving in the Royal Canadian Air Force who was, for a time, North Compound's security officer and member of the 'X' organisation's executive committee. He recalled that only a few had to be coaxed into escape support work.[5] Drawing on his experiences of escape from a variety of camps, Wings Day assessed that 5 per cent of the prisoners were 'dedicated escapers' who willingly accepted any risk: 'fanatics who thought, dreamed and talked of

---

1 AWM 54 779/3/129: 11 PDRC post-liberation debrief, Officer.
2 AWM 54 779/3/126 part 1: POW statement, Top Secret report narrated by W/O F. Seamer, Chief of Escape Committee, [undated c. June 1945]; quote: NAUK WO 208/3283: SLIII Camp History, Part II Centre (NCO's) Compound, 17.
3 NAUK WO 208/3283: SLIII Camp History, Part II Centre (NCO's) Compound, 17–18.
4 Mackenzie, *An Ordinary War 1940–1945*, 43, 49.
5 Harsh, *Lonesome Road*, 196.

nothing else'. He considered that 20 per cent of the camp's population were 'hard-working escapers' who kept up a consistent effort, even as they contributed to life generally. While the majority, in his opinion, would only escape if the opportunity was presented to them, they were, however, happy to join the 'X' organisation and help those who were eager to escape. Only a small minority did not attempt to escape in any circumstance, or participate in the escape organisation. Day called those exceptions the 'non-escaping fraternity'.[6]

Abstainers did not enjoy the full support of their fellows. Aiden Crawley appeared sensitive to non-escapers – 'No one could blame those who decided escape was not worthwhile' – but it was a qualified sympathy. 'Provided they stuck to their guns and held their point of view with tolerance, they were often the most valuable members of the community'.[7] Day's position is inconsistent. According to his biographer, he assessed the non-escaping fraternity as 'realistic and well-balanced types whose moral resistance to captivity was above the average'. His use of 'fraternity' suggests that they had not been exiled from the air force and compound family and could provide useful assistance to the 'X' organisation. George Harsh, however, records that Day was not well-disposed towards those who did not share his enthusiasm for escape work. As Harsh tells it, Day charged him with the responsibility of ensuring that the airmen gave the 'Huns a bad time'. 'If any bastard – or group of bastards – gets in your way or hampers your work, I want to know about it. I'll have 'em court-martialled to the last man once the war is over! This is a military operation, and I expect it to be carried out as such.'[8] Others in recollection vilified those who did not participate in the 'X' organisation. Dedicated escaper Indian-born Bertram 'Jimmy' James, who made ten attempts, including the Great Escape, had no time for them, dubbing the not-interested 'irreconcilables'. Rather than being embraced in Day's fraternity, those men were, in effect, excluded from much of camp life and left to their own company; they were even encouraged to room together.[9] Later, they, along with homosexuals, were elided from the most renowned account of Stalag Luft III's escape operations, Paul Brickhill's *The Great Escape* because they had no place in the heroic narrative.[10]

Despite George Harsh's post-war hyperbole and assertions by Terence Officer and Wings Day, Aiden Crawley states that only about two-thirds of North Compound registered for the 'X' organisation.[11] That one-third who did not

---

6   Smith, *Wings Day*, 81–82.
7   [Crawley], *Escape from Germany*, 30.
8   Harsh, *Lonesome Road*, 195–196.
9   James, *Moonless Night*, 83–84.
10 Brickhill, *The Great Escape*; Dando-Collins, *The Hero Maker*, 203.
11 [Crawley], *Escape from Germany*, 252.

comprised a significant minority. Australian evidence also contradicts Officer's statement of 'almost everyone, at some time'. After liberation, airmen prisoners of war were questioned about their experiences at 106 Personnel Reception Centre, (106 PRC) Cosford (members of the RAF) and 11 Personnel Despatch and Receiving Centre, (11 PDRC) Brighton (RAAF). Their post-liberation debriefs asked if they had ever been captured and, if so, to state details, of any escape effort. Not all of the Australian debriefs are extant but, in the 295 I consulted (written by 85 per cent of Stalag Luft III's post-war survivors), only 28 per cent of the former kriegies reported escape-related work. Significant omissions include Albert Comber, Justin O'Byrne, Les Dixon, and Hugh Lambie, who all declared escape attempts in other testimony, as well as Bill Fordyce who was trapped in the tunnel when the Great Escape was discovered. Perhaps they, and others who were silent about their 'X' work, had interpreted escape in its narrowest form: escape to freedom. Or perhaps they considered escape-related work such as soil removal or stooging – logging German movements – too inconsequential to mention when compared to actual escape attempts. Yet, even looking at all of the available evidence for Stalag Luft III's 345 post-war survivors only about a quarter recorded escape attempts or escape-related work.[12]

Approximately 10 per cent of the Australian airmen specifically stated in post-liberation debriefs that they had made no escapes. Suggesting a valid basis for non-participation, the majority of reasons for non-involvement relate to changed circumstances after the Great Escape, pragmatism, and the physical and psychological states of some of the airmen. Many of that 10 per cent, along with some of the non-disclosers, would have been genuine non-escapers. A fifth of the Australian airmen had been captured after the Great Escape, including about 5 per cent who were taken after the mid-September 'immediately shot on sight' decree. After the duty of escape was rescinded in April 1944, prisoners in Stalag Luft III and elsewhere were advised of the fact via coded message. Many of the longer-term prisoners heeded the new instructions but most would not have needed them anyway. 'Generally speaking', Alan Righetti recalled, 'the great desire to escape had subsided amongst those of us involved. I, personally, would not have walked out if they had left the gates open.'[13] North Compound's 'X' organisation, however, was resurrected and, in about July 1944, a fourth tunnel – known as 'George' – was started under the theatre. There was no policy on mass escapes; they just wanted to get it started and see what happened.[14] The kriegies had not finished it before the snow came so it became a contingency tunnel,

---

12 Including post-liberation debriefs, camp histories, MI9 escape and evasion forms, POW statements held by the Australian War Memorial, oral history accounts, prisoner memoir or biography, medical testimony, and family recollection.
13 AR: Alan Righetti, email 4 January 2012.
14 Brickhill, *The Great Escape*, 244.

used for storing weapons, extra radios, and escape items such as compasses and food. According to Paul Brickhill, it would also serve as 'a bolt-hole in case the rough-stuff started' i.e. the Germans turned on them as the Soviet army advanced.[15] Very few knew about it; some, Righetti noted, had misgivings about starting it in the wake of the Great Escape.[16]

Some of the newly-captured considered they had already fulfilled their operational duty; captivity was their equivalent of 'tour expired'. For Alec Arnel who had been downed shortly after D-Day, there was 'no point at that stage in being heroic. I'd had enough of the war anyway, I'd had over four years of front line service … [and] I was tired, awfully tired of the war. So there was some self-interest in that I wasn't going to do anything dramatic unless the opportunity came'. Arnel was not alone. 'I found that it was pretty well the attitude … in the camp at that time: there's not much point us doing anything at the moment.'[17] As 1944 advanced, Arnel's reluctance to escape firmed into a survival instinct. 'I'm going to survive and keep trying to survive', he recalled. Indeed, 'not too many stuck their head out at that stage because we weren't going to help win the war'. (Their war-weary attitude, however, did not stop their *unsoldatlich* behaviour.)[18]

Some men were not physically capable of escape, including those who were temporarily or permanently debilitated during operations, bale-outs, aircraft crashes, or the unhealthy conditions they were exposed to on the run or during captivity. Pilot *Gerard Lane* was one of them. His Stirling bomber was shot down by enemy fighters over German territory. Forced to parachute out, his back smashed into a fence on landing. It was, he later claimed, a 'traumatic experience'.[19] He suffered pain then and intermittent backache during imprisonment. A nervous condition which had manifested earlier that year ('I had a nervous reaction to operational flying') 'due to stress of service' became more pronounced because of 'POW condition'.[20] Downed on 29 January 1944, Geoffrey Coombes spent four months in hospital for his knee which took eighteen months to heal.[21] *Cedric Brandon* was hospitalised for two months with second and third degree burns which required a skin graft. He arrived at Stalag Luft III in January 1945, two weeks before the camp was evacuated.[22]

---

15 Brickhill, *The Great Escape*, 245.
16 AR: Alan Righetti, email 4 January 2012.
17 AR: Arnel, interview 12 November 2015.
18 AR: Arnel, interview, 2 March 2017.
19 NAA DVA medical file: DVA Lifestyle Report, 12 September 1988.
20 NAA DVA medical file: DVA Medical History Sheet claim for war service related conditions: Nervous Condition and Lumbar Disc Lesion, 1 December 1970. Details deleted to protect identity.
21 AWM S00551 KMSA: Coombes, Geoffrey Bernard, 23 March 1989; AWM 54 779/3/129: 11 PDRC post-liberation debrief, Coombes.
22 AWM 54 779/3/129: 11 PDRC post-liberation debrief, Crump, *Brandon*.

Nor were those who were medically repatriated likely to have been involved in escape work. Charles Lark's wounds were much too serious; it was five months before he was fitted with a prosthetic eye. Another Australian who had developed pulmonary tuberculosis from exposure to the elements, malnutrition, and contact with virulent cases within weeks of capture, spent most of his internment in German hospitals.[23] None of the Australian airmen who had been incarcerated in Buchenwald were fit enough for an escape attempt from either Stalag Luft III or during the forced marches. One had rheumatism in both knees and a hip when he arrived at Sagan, and, by the time he was liberated, had lost almost 32 kilograms.[24] Earlier bad experiences on the run, perhaps, deterred others. Of ten men who made in-transit dashes and camp break-outs before arriving at Stalag Luft III, none tried again. Les Dixon was one who had a particularly hard time. He was hospitalised for three months after his nine days abroad.[25] Paul Brickhill was psychologically unable to participate in escape work. He reluctantly gave up tunnelling because of crippling claustrophobia.[26]

Psychological or physical limitations did not deter some men, however. Neither dread of confined spaces nor tunnel collapse discouraged Albert Comber or *Sean Hanrahan* who 'was buried on two occasions by falls in escape tunnels in pure sand and was extremely lucky to be rescued'.[27] Guy Grey-Smith hoped to use one of the tunnels he worked on in Oflag VI-B, an army camp at Warburg, despite being laid up after his crash with a broken jaw and leg that had healed two centimetres shorter.[28] Justin O'Byrne dug tunnels at Oflag X-C, Lübeck even when 'only receiving about 900 calories of food per day'.[29] He later developed Dupuytren's contracture at Warburg – a condition where the fingers are permanently contracted into a flexed position – but continued to dig.[30] Serious wounds during his last operation did not impede Alex Kerr's multiple attempts,[31] including at Stalag III-E, an army camp at Kirchhain, where he made two attempts including in the failed mass escape of October 1941.[32]

Many non-escapers made valuable contributions to the 'X' organisation and their kriegie community. Reeling from his 'unreasonable fear of tunnels mixed with the shame I felt because I always tried to avoid the actual tunnel digging when involved in attempts to escape', *Robin Sumner* opted 'for an open air job

---

23　DVA MX003452-01, 'Medical Board' at 7 RAAF Hospital, 17 January 1944.
24　DVA MX163729-01, MRU medical board, 25 October 1945.
25　AWM 54 81/4/135: MI9 report, Patrick Dixon.
26　ADB, Wilcox, 'Brickhill, Paul Chester (1916–1991)'; Dando-Collins, *The Hero Maker*, 104–105, 124–125.
27　AWM: AH Comber, artist, letter 16 December 1990; AR: Cath McNamara, interview 18 July 2016. Quote: DVA NCX065122-02: personal statement, 17 January 1980.
28　Gaynor, *Guy Grey-Smith*, 13; AWM PR05675: Guy Grey-Smith, diary, 29 May and 5 June 1942.
29　O'Byrne FA: O'Byrne, '*Mercury* Radio Roundsman'.
30　NLA O'Byrne, 'Reminiscential conversations', Tape 50.
31　Kerr, *Shot Down*, 143–144.
32　AWM 54 779/3/129: 11 PDRC post-liberation debrief, Crump; Kerr, *Shot Down*, 102–112.

such as "stooging" ... [and] manufacturing air pumping gear and other tasks for which I was better suited.'[33] While Harold Bjelke-Petersen had made several attempts to escape from previous camps, he put his physiotherapy and massage training at the disposal of Stalag Luft III's escapers and those prisoners suffering from pain; he was later commended for his 'valuable work'.[34] Ron Mackenzie carried out acts of sabotage.[35] Because of his physical limitations ensuing from a shot-up left foot (with a large piece missing), opportunistic attempts such as the would-be barrel exit would have been difficult for Doug Hutchinson. He, however, 'gave back' to Belaria's community. 'If you were asked to do something, you'd do it in any way that you could. As a matter of fact, you'd go looking for something to help somebody.'[36]

The 'X' organisation was lauded, after the war, as an officially endorsed, valuable aspect of the camp community.[37] As we have seen, not every airman, however was – or could be – involved. Terence Officer's statement of 'almost everyone, at some time' is one of the earliest iterations of what has become a myth of near-universal participation in Stalag Luft III's escape organisation.[38] While this myth had no place for physical debility and mental disturbance, it enabled former kriegies to collectively look back on their actions with pride and to make sense of perhaps the greatest tragedy of their captivity: the deaths of fifty airmen – including five Australians.

---

33 DVA NMX272113-01: letter to Deputy Commissioner, DVA, 21 November 1996.
34 Harrison RC: Recording by Warrant Officer Ross Thomas Breheny; NAUK AIR 40/269: Stalag Luft III reports and nominal roll, Section 45: Recommendations.
35 Mackenzie, *An Ordinary War 1940–1945*, 43, 49.
36 AAWFA: Hutchinson 0540, 17 June 2003.
37 NAUK WO 208/3283: SLIII Camp History, Part III North (Officers') Compound, 11.
38 AWM 54 779/3/129: 11 PDRC post-liberation debrief, Officer.

Chapter Eleven:

THE GREAT ESCAPE

Stalag Luft III is renowned for two escapes. Some Australians, like Justin O'Byrne, participated in both.[1] The first, in October 1943, was the Wooden Horse escape where three men from East Compound made it to Britain. When O'Byrne was not playing the harmonica to distract the guards, he disposed of spoil excavated from the tunnel.[2] Victor Wood forged the escapers' travel papers and John 'Jock' McKechnie's hands were scarred from the 'crude tools' he used when helping to fabricate the vaulting horse.[3] Richard Winn and others took turns jumping over it while tunnellers worked underneath.[4] Winn also joined the digging roster and took his turn removing the soil,[5] some of which ended up in bunkers on the golf course they had laid out themselves. If the escape route had not been discovered, George Archer (one of those who enjoyed a good game of golf) was in the next batch of prisoners hoping to use it. 'You do get disheartened,' he stated after the escape was blown. Reflecting his own sense of community however, he conceded that 'it was a great thing' that three airmen got out.[6]

The second, more notorious scheme, was the mass attempt organised by Roger Bushell which has come to be known as the Great Escape. It would take months to plan and execute but it would be worth it, the airmen believed. Manpower and matériel would be tied up for days, perhaps weeks, as the Germans searched for the escapers. It would create havoc.[7]

With East Compound's population continuing to increase, a new compound had to be built. Kriegies volunteered to help clear away tree stumps and Justin O'Byrne was one of those 'busy studying the layout and pacing off distances with the idea of eventually constructing tunnels for escape.'[8] The kriegies dug three tunnels known as 'Tom', 'Dick', and 'Harry'. 'Tom' was discovered by the Germans and 'Dick' was decommissioned and used to store excavated dirt and escape supplies. They then pinned their hopes on 'Harry'.[9] The grand scheme,

---

1 O'Byrne FA: O'Byrne, '*Mercury* Radio Roundsman'.
2 NLA O'Byrne, 'Reminiscential conversations', Tape 51.
3 Gordon FA: Dunstan, 'Diggers "relive" Years in German Prison Camp', *Herald* (Melbourne), 3 October 1951, unpaginated clipping.
4 Winn, *A Fighter Pilot's Diary of World War 2*, 52; Whittaker, 'The Men Marked X', *The Australian Magazine*, 26–27 March 1994, 40.
5 AAWFA: Winn 1508, 4 March 2004.
6 Archer FA, George Archer interview, 'Grandstand', ABC Radio, [undated] April 1993.
7 NLA JMFC: Justin O'Byrne, 31 October 1986.
8 O'Byrne FA: O'Byrne, '*Mercury* Radio Roundsman'.
9 NAA A1608 AT20/1/1 'War Records—Prisoners of War. Shooting of Air Force Personnel (POW) in Germany'. Summary of Proceedings of Court of Inquiry Held To Investigate The Shooting of Air Force Personnel at Stalag Luft III.

O'Byrne assessed, was 'a classic of perseverance, of ingenuity, of bravery and everything combined'.[10]

The plan was for 160 kriegies to sneak out via 'Harry', with forty reserves.[11] Choosing who would go was a complicated process. Some who played key roles in the 'X' organisation were guaranteed a chance at freedom. Others, with particular skills, were handpicked, but the majority were selected by ballot.[12] Torres Ferres, who had carried out stooge duties for Albert Hake in the compass-making department, helped the Senior British Officer draw lots for the '"lucky" escapees'.[13] Bill Fordyce, who 'hadn't done much towards the tunnel' and 'just put my name in with the mob' was pleased with the result. 'The fact I drew number 86 was very good. It was near the front'.[14] One-time stooge Alan Righetti, however, 'was so disappointed' when friends drew a 'lucky' ticket to escape and he missed out.[15] Not everyone involved in the escape preparations, though, was prepared to take the risk of an uncertain journey on foot or train through enemy territory. Len Netherway, who had helped remove soil from the tunnel, declined to go in the draw. As well as feeling too much responsibility towards his wife, Mavis, he was mindful of the limited chances of success.[16] Jock Bryce who had worked on 'Dick' before it was abandoned, was one whose name went into the draw but he, like many others, did not receive 'a ticket'.[17] Paul Royle, who had been employed on tunnel construction in East Compound before transferring to North Compound, and then carried out stooge and dirt disposal duties, was told that 'I was to be a member of the escaping party'. He and British pilot Edgar Humphreys decided to be partners. 'Between us we made plans for our journey outside'.[18] So too did six other Australians: Bill Fordyce, Albert Hake, Jimmy Catanach who spoke fluent German and was proficient in Norwegian, carpentry team members John Williams and Reg Kierath, and Tom Leigh.

As we have seen, there were many reasons for participating in an escape bid. While some thought it their duty to escape, believing a large-scale breakout would divert German resources into recapturing them, Paul Royle admitted late in life that the idea simply was 'not in my mind. No thought of it'. He, and others, he said, did it because they wanted to get out.[19] Love was perhaps a factor.

---

10 NLA O'Byrne, 'Reminiscential conversations', Tape 51.
11 NAA A1608 AT20/1/1 'War Records—Prisoners of War. Shooting of Air Force Personnel (POW) in Germany'. Summary of Proceedings of Court of Inquiry Held To Investigate The Shooting of Air Force Personnel at Stalag Luft III.
12 NAA A1608 AT20/1/1 'War Records—Prisoners of War. Shooting of Air Force Personnel (POW) in Germany'. Summary of Proceedings of Court of Inquiry Held To Investigate The Shooting of Air Force Personnel at Stalag Luft III.
13 AWM PR90/035: Ferres, 'A POW in Germany'.
14 AAWFA: Fordyce 0523, 19 June 2003.
15 AR: Alan Righetti, email 31 October 2008.
16 AR: Mike Netherway, interview 28 September 2016.
17 Bryce FA: 'Jock Bryce's POW Diary 1942–1945', 167–168.
18 NAUK WO 208/3334/1574: MI9/SPG/LIB Liberation reports, Royle.
19 SLWA: Royle, 4 March 2014.

There is a suggestion that Tom Leigh had a fiancée and Jimmy Catanach had a girlfriend;[20] he missed the companionship of women.[21] Quiet but fun-loving Albert Hake[22] missed his wife and wanted to return to her.[23] He had exhibited a rebel streak as a child and those who knew him (in hindsight) were not surprised that he had been so involved in the escape effort.[24] Noela had not seen that side of him, but who knows how much he had changed in the years they had been apart, she later admitted.[25] Love seemed to have made the risk acceptable. So too did his faith. Hake always 'believed that God would bring him through safely.'[26]

In his first letter as a POW, Albert Hake told Noela that he felt 'a cad ending up like this darling.'[27] Others were ashamed, such as Jimmy Catanach. 'My arrival in enemy territory was far from glorious,' he confessed to his brother, Bill. 'I force landed as a result of fuel shortage caused by a sequence of misfortunes, mostly due to my own foolishness.' Despite the circumstances, it had been a good landing 'and no one was hurt but that is small consolation.' Thinking about it, Jimmy admitted, 'gets me down a bit.' Perhaps the 'futility' of kriegie life[28] had been too much for him, too. Just one letter from Tom Leigh exists. He mentions no romantic ties but he listed those from whom he had heard recently. He had received only one note from his sister, and 'had no news' of his brother, except via friends. He sounded cheery enough as he passed on 'My love & kisses to Auntie' but lack of contact with his family must have depressed him. Tom was only 7 years old when his mother died and 13 when his father passed away in Shanghai. Two years later, living in England, he took the entrance examination for the Training Ship *Mercury* and was declared medically fit for sea service. In 1935, he was accepted as an apprentice aero engine fitter at the Royal Air Force's No. 1 School of Technical Training and later, into aircrew training, where he was mustered into gunnery. Separated from his parents and siblings for much of his young life, perhaps he simply wanted to renew the few affective ties he had.[29] And of course there was that grand sense of adventure that would have been hard for any airman to resist. Reg Kierath revealed no hint in his letters to his mother that he was involved in 'X' but he was so high spirited, loved life so much it is possible his venturing spirit lay at the heart of his decision to participate.

---

20 Vance, *A Gallant Company*, 201; SOR JCC: 2013.CAT054, James Catanach to 'Dad, Syb and Da', 27 September 1942; Alexander, 'Jimmy Catanach and Heather Ebbott', <https://australiansinsliii.blogspot.com/2016/10/jimmy-and-heather.html>.
21 SOR JCC: 2013.CAT050, James Catanach to William Alan Catanach, 28 March 1943.
22 Preen FA: Noela Hake, letter to Jonathan Vance, 30 September 1986.
23 Preen FA: Albert Hake, letters to Noela Hake
24 Preen FA: Jean Heckendorf, letter to Jonathan Vance, undated.
25 Preen FA: Noela Hake, letter to Jonathan Vance, 30 September 1986.
26 Preen FA: Noela Hake, letter to Jonathan Vance, 12 December 1986.
27 Preen FA: Albert Hake, letter to Noela Hake, 15 April 1942.
28 SOR JCC: 2013.CAT050, James Catanach to William Alan Catanach, 28 March 1943.
29 Bligh FA: family history details; Tom Leigh to H.E.W Barker, 26 October 1942; 'Thomas Barker Leigh', <https://kristenalexanderauthor.blogspot.com/2014/10/thomas-barker-leigh.html>.

We do not know why John Williams joined in, but he and Kierath were close friends and had worked diligently together in the 'X' organisation's carpentry department. Perhaps it was a joint decision to take their chances.

While Reg Kierath had managed to keep his plans secret from his mother (and Stalag Luft III's censors) in recent correspondence, Albert Hake dropped a hint that he might be planning something in his third wedding anniversary letter.[30] It was very oblique and easily missed. Lively, boisterous Jimmy Catanach, however, could barely control his excitement at the forthcoming attempt, telling a friend to 'Get my suit pressed'.[31] Nervous energy permeated the camp as their plans culminated. Stalag Luft III's 'biggest break ever' was scheduled for the night of 24–25 March 1944.[32] Paul Brickhill, who had been assigned to other important 'X' Organisation tasks, including security chief in the forgery department[33] and transcribing BBC news reports containing coded information,[34] was one who hoped to join the escape. Although dreading the underground trek to the tunnel entrance because of his claustrophobia, he was willing to take his chances. The escape organiser, Roger Bushell, however was not. Concerned that a panicking participant might delay proceedings, Bushell banned Brickhill and other claustrophobics from participating.[35]

Justin O'Byrne, who had transferred into North Compound in early 1944, was one of those who had been allocated a place in the escape. 'Eventually it was time to go' so he joined his friends in a line up which he thought 'was like a giant crocodile'.[36] Each prospective escaper was issued with maps, high energy escape food, and the tiny compasses Hake and fellow Australian George Russell had spent months making from melted gramophone records and magnetised sewing needles or strips of razor blades.[37] Some were garbed in disguised uniforms but Catanach, along with Royle and the majority of others, wore civilian clothes.[38] The moonless night was freezing. Snow covered the ground.[39] Roommates farewelled their friends; Canadian George Sweanor shook hands with, and wished Godspeed, to Tom Leigh with his 'cheerful, boyish face'.[40] Along with two others from his hut,[41] Leigh headed to Hut 104 where the entrance to

---

30 Preen FA: Albert Hake, letter to Noela Hake, 1 March 1944.
31 'Prison Camp Escapes Hinted in Letters', *The Daily Telegraph* (Sydney), 22 May 1944, 2.
32 Arnel archive: Train, 'A Barbed-Wire World', 24 March 1944, 50.
33 Dando-Collins, *The Hero Maker*, 113
34 Dando-Collins, *The Hero Maker*, 118
35 Dando-Collins, *The Hero Maker*, 124.
36 NLA O'Byrne, 'Reminiscential conversations', Tape 51.
37 NAUK WO 208/3334/1574: MI9/SPG/LIB Liberation reports, Royle; Alexander, 'Australian compass makers ... and more', <https://australiansinsliii.blogspot.com/2016/08/australian-compass-makers.html>.
38 SLWA: Royle, 4 March 2014; NAA A1608 AT20/1/1 'War Records—Prisoners of War. Shooting of Air Force Personnel (POW) in Germany'. Summary of Proceedings of Court of Inquiry Held To Investigate The Shooting of Air Force Personnel at Stalag Luft III.
39 Unless otherwise cited, general narrative of the escape is drawn from Walter, *The Real Great Escape*, Chapter Nine.
40 Sweanor, *It's All Pensionable Time*, 173.
41 Sweanor, *It's All Pensionable Time*, 167.

'Harry' was located. The regular occupants dispersed to other huts and, crowded together, each escaper awaited his turn to enter the tunnel. They carried only the bare necessities. 'Everything we had was in our pockets', or briefcases. All 'were nervous in some way or another', Royle recalled. 'We didn't want to be caught.'[42]

The first men made their way through 'Harry' at about 10.30 p.m. They were pulled from the hut to the discharge point on the wooden trollies John Williams and Reg Kierath had helped make.[43] But progress was immediately impeded. The boards across the exit shaft had swollen and could not be budged. When they were finally dislodged, the front men discovered that the tunnel was roughly 4.5 metres short of the tree line and the nearest guard tower was just under 30 metres away. More time was wasted figuring out how to safely cross the bare ground between the exit and the pine trees. Once the escapers started passing through, more delays were caused by blankets or cases getting stuck in the sides of the tunnel. Jimmy Catanach carried a case. Perhaps it had contributed to the hold-up.

Catanach, the 23rd to emerge from the tunnel, waited for escape partner New Zealander Arnold Christensen then set off towards Sagan's railway station. Williams, number 32, and Kierath, 35, did not follow them: their group headed off to a small station some distance from Sagan. The escape was well behind schedule when, at 2.30 a.m. on 25 March,[44] Paul Royle, the 55th kriegie, made it through.[45] 'It was very cold when we got out of the tunnel … and all we could see was pine trees up above and snow banked up against the trunks.'[46] It was exhilarating.[47] 'We'd got that far, an achievement.'[48] Then, 'I looked up at the stars, and … back at the watchtower and the barbed wire.'[49] After almost four years in captivity, the 30-year-old was free. He ran for the trees and waited with the others in his party for Edgar Humphreys. Then the ten airmen slogged off through the snow.[50] Hake, the 70th through, was followed close behind by Leigh, the 73rd. They, and others travelling on foot, were what the airmen termed 'hard-arsers'.

Royle had not thought much beyond the actual breakout. 'I don't know what our plan was, except we would head for Switzerland.'[51] After about an hour

---

42 SLWA: Royle, 4 March 2014.
43 SLWA: Royle, 4 March 2014.
44 NAUK WO 208/3283: Part III North Compound, 73 (Royle's statement).
45 NAUK WO 208/3334/1574: MI9/SPG/LIB Liberation reports, Royle.
46 SLWA: Royle, 4 March 2014.
47 Page, 'Centenarian Great Escaper', 37.
48 SLWA: Royle, 4 March 2014.
49 Page, 'Centenarian Great Escaper', 37.
50 NAUK WO 208/3334/1574: MI9/SPG/LIB Liberation reports, Royle.
51 Page, 'Centenarian Great Escaper', 38.

trudging through the snow, his group split up. He and Humphreys travelled south.[52] Others waited on and near the railway platform. Catanach and Christensen caught the 3.15 a.m. to Berlin; their ultimate goal was Denmark where Christensen had relatives. Williams and Kierath boarded their train at 5.00 a.m. Their party of twelve alighted five hours later at Boberröhrsdorf (now Siedlce, Poland) and, in smaller groups, went their separate ways, aiming for Czechoslovakia. We do not know where Hake and his escape partner, Porokoru Patapu 'Johnny' Pohe of New Zealand, were making for or what destination Leigh had in mind. We do not even know if Leigh travelled alone or with a companion.

Dawn approached and barely half those waiting had climbed into the tunnel. 'It was so light' by the time it was Bill Fordyce's turn that, he remembered, 'they decided that no one else could go through. So immediately I got into it they closed the tunnel down. No one went in after me.'[53] As Fordyce and those ahead of him made their way towards the surface, the scheme was discovered; shortly after Leigh had drawn his first breath of freedom and sprinted off into the trees, three escapers were arrested outside the tunnel and one nearby; seventy-six were on the run.[54]

The sirens blasted. 'People were screaming down the shaft to me get back: the Goons are here.' The German at the tunnel entrance started firing into the shaft. 'So the only thing I could do was turn round and go back', Bill Fordyce recalled.[55] As he made his way back to the hut, those awaiting their turn, including Justin O'Byrne and Albert Comber, 'sneaked back to our bunks'. For Comber, trying to make light of another disappointment decades later, this was yet another foiled escape attempt. 'Failure again!'[56] Alan Righetti remembered hearing shots fired. It 'was pandemonium' in Hut 104 as those awaiting their turn covered up or destroyed all traces of the enterprise.[57] Guards rampaged through the camp looking for signs of a tunnel. They were 'going absolutely berserk and firing guns everywhere', Fordyce recalled.[58] The Gestapo arrived the next morning and took control.[59] *Kommandant* Von Lindeiner was almost immediately relieved of command, and Erich Cordes stepped up to take his place.[60]

---

52 NAUK WO 208/3334/1574: MI9/SPG/LIB Liberation reports, Royle.
53 AAWFA: Fordyce 0523, 19 June 2003.
54 NAA A1608 AT20/1/1 'War Records—Prisoners of War. Shooting of Air Force Personnel (POW) in Germany'. Summary of Proceedings of Court of Inquiry Held To Investigate The Shooting of Air Force Personnel at Stalag Luft III.
55 AAWFA: Fordyce 0523, 19 June 2003.
56 AWM: AH Comber, artist, letter 16 December 1990.
57 AAWFA: Righetti 0984, 16 September 2003.
58 AAWFA: Fordyce 0523, 19 June 2003.
59 NAA A1608 AT20/1/1 'War Records—Prisoners of War. Shooting of Air Force Personnel (POW) in Germany'. Summary of Proceedings of Court of Inquiry Held To Investigate The Shooting of Air Force Personnel at Stalag Luft III.
60 NAUK WO 208/3283: SLIII Camp History, Part III North (Officers') Compound, 77.

Within hours a great search had been launched. Thousands from Gestapo units, the *Kriminalpolizei*, *Abwehr* and even the Hitler Youth scoured the countryside.[61] The *Grossfahndung* – the highest level of search – was, Justin O'Byrne considered, 'the biggest manhunt of the war.'[62] It was just the sort of major disruption they had wanted.[63] Meanwhile, the escapers had scattered in all directions, to Flensburg near the Danish border, northerly Danzig, Munich to the south-west, Saarbrücken on the French border, and the occupied French city of Metz a further seventy kilometres to the west.

At about eight o'clock in the morning, well after the escape had been blown back at Stalag Luft III, Paul Royle and Edgar Humphreys 'laid up all day', hiding from sight. The 'bitter cold [was] … exaggerated by our inaction.'[64] Twelve hours later, under cover of deep darkness, they resumed their trek. Somewhere around 2.30 a.m., they entered a small village and were stopped by three members of the German auxiliary police. They had been free for just 24 hours. Jimmy Catanach and Arnold Christensen had put about 530 kilometres between them and the camp before they were captured, along with Norwegians Halldor Espelid and Nils Fugelsang, at Flensburg. Catanach had been on the run for 45 hours. First on train and then on foot, John Williams and Reg Kierath had covered perhaps 80 kilometres when, about 50 hours after climbing from the tunnel, they and two companions were recaptured ploughing through the thick snow of the Jizera mountains, bordering Czechoslovakia. (Most of their party had continued by train.)[65] It is thought that Hake and Pohe, who both suffered excruciating frostbite,[66] had travelled less than 65 kilometres and had been free for about 72 hours before they were captured near Görlitz (a German town now located on the Polish border). No one knows for sure, but it seems Leigh had trudged but 24 kilometres from the camp, and had been free for less than 48 hours when he was caught somewhere in the Sagan area.[67]

*****

Adolf Hitler met with Hermann Göring, head of the *Luftwaffe*, Heinrich Himmler, leader of the *Schutztaffel*, and Wilhelm Keitel, chief of the *Oberkommando der Wehrmacht* on 26 March. He ordered that those who had been recaptured were to be shot. Keitel especially supported the plan. Although the airmen had been confined in a *Luftwaffe* facility under Göring's jurisdiction, Keitel wanted to 'set an example, otherwise we shall no longer be able to master the question

---

61 AWM54 1010/6/132 Part 1: Wielen; Walters, *The Real Great Escape*, 85–86, 155–156.
62 O'Byrne FA: O'Byrne, '*Mercury* Radio Roundsman'.
63 NLA JMFC: Justin O'Byrne, 31 October 1986.
64 Royle archive: Royle, 'Stalag Luft III', 1985, 5.
65 NAUK WO 208/3283: Part III North Compound, 61–62 (Green's statement); Williams, *A True Story of the Great Escape*, 31–32.
66 NAA A1608 AT20/1/1 Cablegram 2702, 14 June 1944.
67 Distances and hours free taken from Walters, *The Real Great Escape*, appendix 'The Escapers', 308–12.

of escapes'.[68] Such a barbaric act was not unprecedented. British commandos captured after the September 1942 Operation *Muskatoon* raid on Norway's Glomfjord power plant, for example, had been murdered by SS guards under the auspices of Hitler's Commando Order, issued on 18 October 1942. Felled by a single pistol shot fired into the back of each man's neck, the seven men were the first allied operatives killed under the Commando Order.[69]

The Great Escape captives were not commandos. Even so, they would face a similar fate. A list of the dead should be sent to Stalag Luft III, Keitel decided, and posted on the noticeboard for all to see. It would, he believed, deter potential absconders. Rather than burying the bodies as stipulated by the Geneva Convention, he declared, they would be cremated and the urns returned to camp; the ashes would be an 'intimidating example' of what prisoners could expect.[70]

---

68 AWM 54 1010/6/132: The Stalag Luft 3 War Crimes Trial Commencing at Hamburg 1st July1947 Part 1, Voluntary Statement by Adolf Westhoff.
69 Macintyre, Colditz: *Prisoners of the Castle*, 143–146.
70 AWM 54 1010/6/132: The Stalag Luft 3 War Crimes Trial Commencing at Hamburg 1st July1947 Part 1, Voluntary Statement by Adolf Westhoff.

Tom Leigh's 'cheerful, boyish face' remained a sad memory for one friend after farewelling the former 76 Squadron RAF air gunner as he entered the escape tunnel. Courtesy of Winifred Chevalier.

Chapter Twelve:

MURDER SQUADS

Paul Royle and Edgar Humphreys were held locally at first. In the morning, they were taken to Sagan and incarcerated in the town's gaol. As they were in mufti, without military identification, they were treated as civilians without benefit of the protections of the Geneva Convention.[1] They were moved to Görlitz prison at about midnight, along with twenty other recaptured escapers.[2] Up to six airmen were confined in each small, insanitary cell; they were fed little more than bread and water.[3] Albert Hake was with New Zealanders Johnny Pohe and Michael Shand.[4] Royle was separated from Humphreys who was put in a cell with Tom Leigh.[5] It was 'dirty and horrid ... absolutely appalling,' Royle recalled.[6]

Each airman was interrogated. While Shand was not beaten nor menaced in any way, he appears to have been the exception.[7] Henry Marshall, another of Leigh's cell mates, claimed that 'all through interview their attitude was very threatening.'[8] Most were subjected to a 'general atmosphere' deliberately cultivated to 'cause fear'; some were told they would be shot, others would never see their wives again.[9] Royle and the others watched as some of their fellow prisoners, including Humphreys and Tom Leigh, and Albert Hake and his cellmate Johnny Pohe, were led away. At the time, they assumed their comrades were on their way back to Stalag Luft III; they thought Hake was being taken to hospital for frostbite treatment.[10] Canadian Keith Ogilvie related decades later that he had whispered to Hake in the corridor before the five men disappeared, asking what was happening. Hake had no idea. Perhaps they were going to be interrogated again.[11]

---

1   NAA A1608 AT20/1/1: Shooting of Air Force Personnel (POW) in Germany. Summary of Proceedings of Court of Inquiry Held To Investigate The Shooting of Air Force Personnel at Stalag Luft III. [Summary of Proceedings.]
2   Royle archive: Royle, 'Stalag Luft III', 1985, 5 and Royle, wartime log, 34; NAUK WO 208/3283: Part III North Compound, 73 (Royle's statement).
3   NAA A1608 AT20/1/1: Shooting of Air Force Personnel (POW) in Germany. Cablegram 2702 from Berne [Protecting Power] to Foreign Office, 14 June 1944.
4   NAUK WO 208/3283: SLIII Camp History, Part III North (Officers') Compound, 74 (Shand's statement).
5   NAUK WO 208/3283: SLIII Camp History, Part III North (Officers') Compound, 66 (Marshall's statement).
6   IWMSA Royle: 26605, 2 December 2012.
7   NAUK WO 208/3283: SLIII Camp History, Part III North (Officers') Compound, 74 (Shand's statement).
8   NAUK WO 208/3283: SLIII Camp History, Part III North (Officers') Compound, 66 (Marshall's statement).
9   NAA A1608 AT20/1/1: Shooting of Air Force Personnel (POW) in Germany. Cablegram 2702 from Berne [Protecting Power] to Foreign Office, 14 June 1944; NAUK WO 208/3283: SLIII Camp History, Part III North (Officers') Compound, 75 (Thompson's statement).
10 NAA A1608 AT20/1/1: Shooting of Air Force Personnel (POW) in Germany. Cablegram 2702 from Berne, 14 June 1944.
11 Vance, *A Gallant Company*, 264. Ogilvie did not include details of this conversation in NAUK WO 208/3283: SLIII Camp History, Part III North (Officers') Compound, 74 (Ogilvie's statement).

The exact number encompassed by the 'Führer order'[12] or 'Sagan order'[13] as it is also known is uncertain but ultimately, fifty airmen, including the escape's instigator, Roger Bushell, and Australians Albert Hake, Jimmy Catanach, Tom Leigh, Reg Kierath, and John Williams, were taken away from various holding cells. At Görlitz, someone later noticed that the handcuffed group included officers of European-Allied nationality.[14] One was Czechoslovakian, another was Greek, and the majority were Polish. Perhaps they had been chosen because, as provided by the 'Bullet Decree' of 4 March, they were of non-British birth. The implication seems to have been that they had been picked because of their non-Aryan backgrounds. Hake's dark features could have seen him included on this basis, so too could Johnny Pohe, who was of Māori descent. It does not, however, explain why fair-featured Tom Leigh was among those taken. Leigh did have Polish Jewish ancestors but they were so far back – they had migrated to Hamburg, then England, in Napoleonic times before converting to Christianity – that no one would have even suspected, including Leigh himself.[15] Looking back, there appeared to be 'no rhyme or reason' for their selection.[16] Paul Royle could not see 'why one should live and not the other'.[17] According to Hans Merten of the Berlin *Kriminalpolizei* (criminal police), there was perhaps some method underlying the choice of who lived and who were handcuffed, taken to secluded spots and, as was later reported in one Australian newspaper, 'vilely murdered'.[18]

Merten later told war crimes investigators that he had witnessed Arthur Nebe, the *Kriminalpolizei*'s chief, scrutinising cards containing the personal details of the recaptured airmen. Nebe tossed some to Merten, telling him to check whether the men had wives and children. Meanwhile, Nebe sorted his own cards into two piles. After he had finished, he took Merten's. Merten recalled him looking at one of them, saying, 'He is for it'. He considered the next 'so young', and put the card in a different pile. Nebe looked at another one: 'Children? No!', Merten recalled Nebe exclaiming as he placed it on top of the first stack.[19] Can this story be true? Jimmy Catanach and George Wiley, for example, both in their early twenties, were shot. So too was Albert Hake, who was married. RAF bomber pilot Tom Kirby-Green and Polish airman Paweł Tobolski had sons.

---

12   AWM 54 1010/6/132: The Stalag Luft 3 War Crimes Trial Commencing at Hamburg 1st July1947 Part 1, Voluntary Statement by Adolf Westhoff.
13   AWM 54 1010/6/132: The Stalag Luft 3 War Crimes Trial Commencing at Hamburg 1st July1947 Part 1, Voluntary Statement by Wilhelm Scharpwinkel.
14   NAA A1608 AT20/1/1: Shooting of Air Force Personnel (POW) in Germany. Summary of Proceedings.
15   AR: Winifred Chevalier, interview 5 April 2014; 2 September 2015.
16   NAA A1608 AT20/1/1: Shooting of Air Force Personnel (POW) in Germany. Summary of Proceedings.
17   Edlington, 'The Great Escape Recalled', 15.
18   '"Vilely Murdered". Shot after Recapture. R.A.F. Officers' Escape', *The West Australian* (Perth), 28 February 1946, 7.
19   AWM54, 1010/6/132 Part 1: Merten.

Perhaps, in the context of explaining to war crimes investigators his part in the selection of those to be killed, Merten was trying to impart some sense to Nebe's seemingly arbitrary choices.

Rumours later abounded about the existence of a nominal roll with some sort of sign, like a cross, against the names of those to be killed. Peter Mohr, also of the Berlin *Kriminalpolizei*, attested 'with fair certainty' that there had been no such list. However, 'Some of the cards lay separated in an envelope. These were marked with a red cross'. They were, he added, 'the cards of officers already shot'. Mohr admitted that there were some Gestapo reports and lists which he thought summarised those details contained in the index cards. 'I cannot judge', however, 'whether the choice of the officers to be handed over to the Gestapo was made on the basis of the summaried [sic] list'.[20] Later, many POW identification cards compiled by the Germans were taken into British War Office custody, including location and movement cards. Those of the fifty Great Escapers are firmly stamped with a black cross in the top right hand corner to indicate their deaths.[21]

*****

Paul Royle was sent back to Stalag Luft III on 3 April and consigned to the cooler for three weeks.[22] Thirteen other recaptured airmen also spent time in the punishment cells.[23] But what of the other Australian escapers? While much detail relating to the deaths of the Stalag Luft III's kriegies was later uncovered by RAF police personnel and members of the War Crimes Interrogation Unit, there are many gaps because not all German witnesses could be interrogated or, if they were, had not seen the actual shootings or did not admit involvement. Even so, we have a general idea of what happened to Hake, Leigh, Kierath and Williams. Although some witness statements were tainted – facing a potential death penalty it was not in the perpetrators' best interests to tell the truth – we know much about the deaths of Jimmy Catanach, Arnold Christensen, Halldor Espelid, and Nils Fugelsang.[24]

The deaths of Albert Hake and Tom Leigh were 'masterminded' by Wilhelm Scharpwinkel, the Breslau Gestapo chief, and they were killed by members of the Breslau and Görlitz Gestapos.[25] (Breslau, then a German town, now Wrocław

---

20 AWM54, 1010/6/132 Part 1: Mohr.
21 Alexander, 'The "Kriegie" Personalkarte', Iron Cross, Vol. 15, December 2022, 88–97.
22 Royle archive: Royle, wartime log, 34.
23 NAA A1608 AT20/1/1: Shooting of Air Force Personnel (POW) in Germany. Summary of Proceedings.
24 AWM 54 1010/6/132: SLIII War Crimes Trial Part 2. Between November 1946 and June 1947, Kiel Gestapo officers, Johannes Post, Hans Kaehler, Oskar Schmidt, Walter Jacobs, along with their drivers Artur Denkmann and Wilhelm Struve, who had all been implicated in the deaths of Catanach, Christensen Espelid and Fugelsang, provided written statements to Alexander Scotland, officer commanding Britain's War Crimes Interrogation Unit. A seventh man, Franz Schmidt, was not interviewed; he had committed suicide on 27 October 1946.
25 Quote, Walters, *The Real Great Escape*, 216.

in Poland, is about 138 kilometres from Stalag Luft III as the crow flies.) Scharpwinkel and one of his underlings, Richard Hänsel, testified to war crimes investigators that they had witnessed six killings. According to Scharpwinkel, this was 'the first execution' of prisoners from Görlitz and Breslau.[26] Neither Scharpwinkel nor Hänsel named those who were shot but Guy Walters has surmised that they were Hake, Leigh, Johnny Pohe, Indian-born Michael Casey (of Irish descent), Canadian George Wiley, and British-born Ian Cross.[27]

After the six airmen were led away from the Görlitz cells, they were again interrogated and, according to Scharpwinkel, told that 'they had been sentenced to death'. A small detachment of Gestapo men, led by Walter Lux, manhandled the prisoners into cars and drove them along the road to Sagan. When they arrived at a predetermined location, the airmen were told to get out. The armed Gestapo men shepherded them into 'position' in a wooded area close to the roadside. The men stood side by side. Then, as Scharpwinkel put it, 'it was revealed to them that the sentence was about to be carried out'. The Gestapo chief was 'surprised' that the airmen 'showed considerable calm'.[28] This was later published in newspaper accounts which gave the impression that all fifty men had been shot at the same time. While emphasising the appalling nature of a mass execution by 'murder squad', it perhaps offered loved ones the comfort of a brave 'unflinching' death with friends by their sides.[29] Lux gave the order to fire. 'By the second salvo', Scharpwinkel stated, 'the prisoners were dead'.[30]

Hänsel, who was not present during the shootings, saw the bodies sprawled among the trees; he indicated they had been shot in the back, in the region of the heart. Hake, Leigh and their confrères were killed at about 3.30 p.m. Their corpses lay in the open for about five hours until they were collected by an undertaker and driven to Görlitz crematorium which officially took delivery at 11.30 p.m. Labels on six metal urns recorded that they were cremated on 31 March 1944.[31] (In a tragic coincidence which was only discovered in later decades through family research, Leigh's Polish Jewish ancestors had hailed from Görlitz.[32])

After capture, Kierath, Williams, Polish airman Jerzy Mondschein, and Londoner Leslie Bull, were taken to Reichenberg (now Liberec in the Czech Republic) where they were interrogated. At some point they met up with fellow escaper Ivo Tonder who later told war crimes investigators that he felt

---

26 AWM 54 1010/6/132: SLIII War Crimes Trial Part 1: Scharpwinkel, 19 September 1946.
27 Walters, The Real Great Escape, 216–217.
28 AWM 54 1010/6/132: SLIII War Crimes Trial Part 1: Scharpwinkel, 31 August 1946.
29 'Gestapo Chief Says Airmen Died Bravely', Advertiser (Adelaide), 8 July 1947, 1.
30 AWM 54 1010/6/132: SLIII War Crimes Trial Part 1: Scharpwinkel, 31 August 1946.
31 Hänsel cited in Walters, *The Real Great Escape*, 217–218.
32 Winifred Chevalier, interview 5 April 2014; 2 September 2015.

that Williams may have been aware that he was going to die. A serious and disciplined airman, Williams had proved himself an aggressive pilot and an able coordinator of North Compound's carpentry department. 'He was not normally a nervous man', Tonder considered. 'But he was clearly pale and scared.'[33] On 29 March, five days after the breakout, Kierath, Williams, Mondschein, and Bull were taken away.

We know nothing specific about the four airmen's deaths other than that they were shot. Their bodies were not put in coffins; the Gestapo officials present at the killings piled them into the back of a truck which was then driven to the crematorium at Brüx (now Most).[34] Crematorium records reveal that the shootings were premeditated. The document stating that the airmen's bodies were to be handed over for 'immediate cremation' was signed the day before they were killed. Other details were falsified. They 'were shot during an escape attempt', crematorium staff were advised. 'There is no third party to blame.'[35] Under Germany's Cremation Act, cremations had to be authorised, with approvals confirming the method of death. This too, stated that the airmen had been 'shot during an escape attempt'.[36] Before the corpses entered the furnace, a post-mortem was conducted by the local public health doctor. His certificate iterated the same cause of death. Even so, the examiner stated that, 'based on the post-mortem, there is no suspicion that the deceased did not die of natural causes'. (This service, and the lie, cost 5 Reichsmarks.)[37] Then, the four airmen's bodies were cremated; the Gestapo men watched as the clothed corpses were fed into the flames.[38] Their ashes were placed into four urns, labelled 6925–6928 (John's was 6295 and Reg's was 6928).[39] The Gestapo witnesses removed them on the same day.[40]

Jimmy Catanach, Arnold Christensen, Halldor Espelid, and Nils Fugelsang were captured in pairs in Flensburg on the night of 25–26 March: Catanach and Christensen together, and Espelid was with Fugelsang.[41] The four were photographed and interviewed at the *Kriminalpolizei* headquarters.[42] Early on the morning of 29 March, Fritz Schmidt, head of the Kiel Gestapo, ordered Johannes Post and his fellow officer, Oskar Schmidt, to find a secluded spot on the road between Kiel and Neumuenster where four men could be shot. After

---

33 Cited by Williams in *A True Story of the Great Escape*, 80.
34 War crimes testimony of Anton Sawethal, Brüx crematorium chief, cited by Williams in *A True Story of the Great Escape*, 224.
35 Kierath FA, Secret State Police, to the Crematorium in Brüx, [cremation order], 28 March 1944.
36 Kierath FA, The Mayor of the Town of Brüx, Record number 168/44 [re Kierath], 29 March 1944.
37 Kierath FA, Public Health Office Certificate, Kierath Reginald Victor, 29 March 1944.
38 War crimes testimony of Anton Sawethal, Brüx crematorium chief, cited by Williams in A *True Story of the Great Escape*, 224.
39 Kierath FA, Secret State Police, to the Crematorium in Brüx, [cremation order], 28 March 1944.
40 War crimes testimony of Anton Sawethal, Brüx crematorium chief, cited by Williams in *A True Story of the Great Escape*, 224.
41 See also Alexander and Ariotti, 'Mourning the Dead of the Great Escape: POWs, Grief, and the Memorial Vault of Stalag Luft III'.
42 AWM 54 1010/6/132: SLIII War Crimes Trial Part 2: Paul Linke.

they returned from scoping a suitable location, the Gestapo chief directed Post and Oskar Schmidt along with Hans Kaehler, Walter Jacobs, Franz Schmidt, and two drivers, Artur Denkmann and Wilhelm Struve, to fetch the prisoners from Flensburg.[43] The Gestapo officers were to interrogate them. Then, 'at the place previously decided upon', shoot the airmen. After laying out the plan to kill the prisoners and dispose of their bodies, Fritz Schmidt pledged his squad to the 'strictest secrecy'. They swore an oath and clasped hands to seal it.[44]

After interrogation, the Gestapo officers bundled the handcuffed airmen into two cars. Catanach travelled with Post and Kaehler. Christensen, Espelid, and Fugelsang followed but, at some point, the cars were separated. Catanach perhaps had no idea of what was in store. Post, apparently, chatted to him amiably in English throughout the trip. At about 5.00 p.m., Post, Kaehler, and Catanach arrived at the preselected spot, about 8–15 kilometres outside Kiel. The second vehicle was only moments behind. Catanach was ordered out and the driver moved off to block the entrance to any passers-by. Kaehler removed Catanach's handcuffs then retrieved a weapon from the car while Post and the Australian walked about.[45] Then, according to Post, 'Kaehler and I led Catanach to the meadow'.[46] At this point, Post's testimony is blurry, as is Kaehler's: neither admitted to shooting Catanach. Regardless of who pulled the trigger, the 22-year old 'fell forward and gave no further sign of life'; he had been hit from behind, between his shoulder blades.[47] The other car pulled up and Christensen, Espelid, and Fugelsang, still handcuffed, alighted and walked towards the dead man on the ground. They were 'startled' at the sight of Catanach's motionless body. Kaehler then heard Post call out to go ahead and fire. Within moments, they too were shot from behind. One, however, was still alive so Post ordered Kaehler to 'finish the prisoner off with a coup-de-grace shot'. Kaehler hesitated so Post grabbed his weapon and shot the dying man in the head.[48] Handcuffs removed, the four corpses were carried to the side of the road. They were uncovered, but hidden from view by a thick hedge.[49] It was a merciless, cruel and undignified death.

Post ordered Oskar Schmidt, Walter Jacobs, Franz Schmidt, and their driver Wilhelm Struve to guard the bodies. He and Kaehler then returned to Kiel to arrange for an undertaker who would ferry them to Kiel Crematorium.[50] A van, along with Kaehler, arrived about an hour later and the four corpses were

---

43 AWM 54 1010/6/132: SLIII War Crimes Trial Part 2: Post.
44 AWM 54 1010/6/132: SLIII War Crimes Trial Part 2: Kaehler; Struve.
45 AWM 54 1010/6/132: SLIII War Crimes Trial Part 2: Kaehler.
46 AWM 54 1010/6/132: SLIII War Crimes Trial Part 2: Post.
47 AWM 54 1010/6/132: SLIII War Crimes Trial Part 2: Kaehler.
48 AWM 54 1010/6/132: SLIII War Crimes Trial Part 2: Kaehler.
49 AWM 54 1010/6/132: SLIII War Crimes Trial Part 2: Kaehler.
50 AWM 54 1010/6/132: SLIII War Crimes Trial Part 2: Post.

shoved into two wooden boxes.[51] (We do not know if these were just boxes or if they were actually coffins as the German testimony had been translated into English.[52]) The crematorium was closed and the men had to wait at the gates while Oskar Schmidt negotiated a special opening. Schmidt handed over the bodies and the Gestapo men left.[53] Once incinerated, the ashes were placed in four metal urns labelled with the airmen's names.[54] A few days later, Jacobs took them back to Flensburg.[55] Then, along with papers and valuables found on the airmen, they were sent to Berlin.[56] Germany's capital was only a staging post. Next stop was Breslau. Once in his custody, Max Wielen, the head of Breslau's *Kriminalpolizei* headquarters, cleared a bookshelf and placed the urns behind a silk curtain.[57] This represented a strange admixture of honouring the dead and hiding from public view the evidence of what would later be deemed a war crime.[58] Finally, as Keitel had decreed, the urns were sent to Stalag Luft III, as were those of Albert Hake, Tom Leigh, Reg Kierath, John Williams, and forty-five other Great Escapers.[59]

---

51 AWM 54 1010/6/132: SLIII War Crimes Trial Part 2: Oskar Schmidt.
52 AWM 54 1010/6/132: SLIII War Crimes Trial Part 2: Jacobs.
53 AWM 54 1010/6/132: SLIII War Crimes Trial Part 2: Kaehler.
54 CWGC ADD 3/1/9 Prisoners of War, Treatment. Sagan: Major J. da Silva, Intelligence Group, Report on Graves of R.A.F. Officers at P.W. Camp, Sagan, 15 February 1946.
55 AWM 54 1010/6/132: SLIII War Crimes Trial Part 2: Kaehler and Jacobs.
56 AWM 54 1010/6/132: SLIII War Crimes Trial Part 2: Post.
57 AWM54, 1010/6/132 Part 1: Wielen.
58 Wielen was tried at Hamburg and found guilty of conspiracy to murder relating to all fifty airmen and sentenced to life imprisonment. Walters, appendix 'The Murderers', 316–20.
59 AWM 54 1010/6/132: SLIII War Crimes Trial Part 1: Wielen.

Jimmy Catanach, dressed in civilian clothes fashioned by the tailoring department and carrying a small case, was 'vilely murdered' shortly after this photograph was taken. Author's collection.

Jimmy Catanach's German POW identification card, like others of those killed in the Great Escape reprisals, is stamped with a black cross. The date – 25.3.1944 – is not the day of his death, as some assume, but the date he escaped from Stalag Luft III. TNA WO/416/60/290.

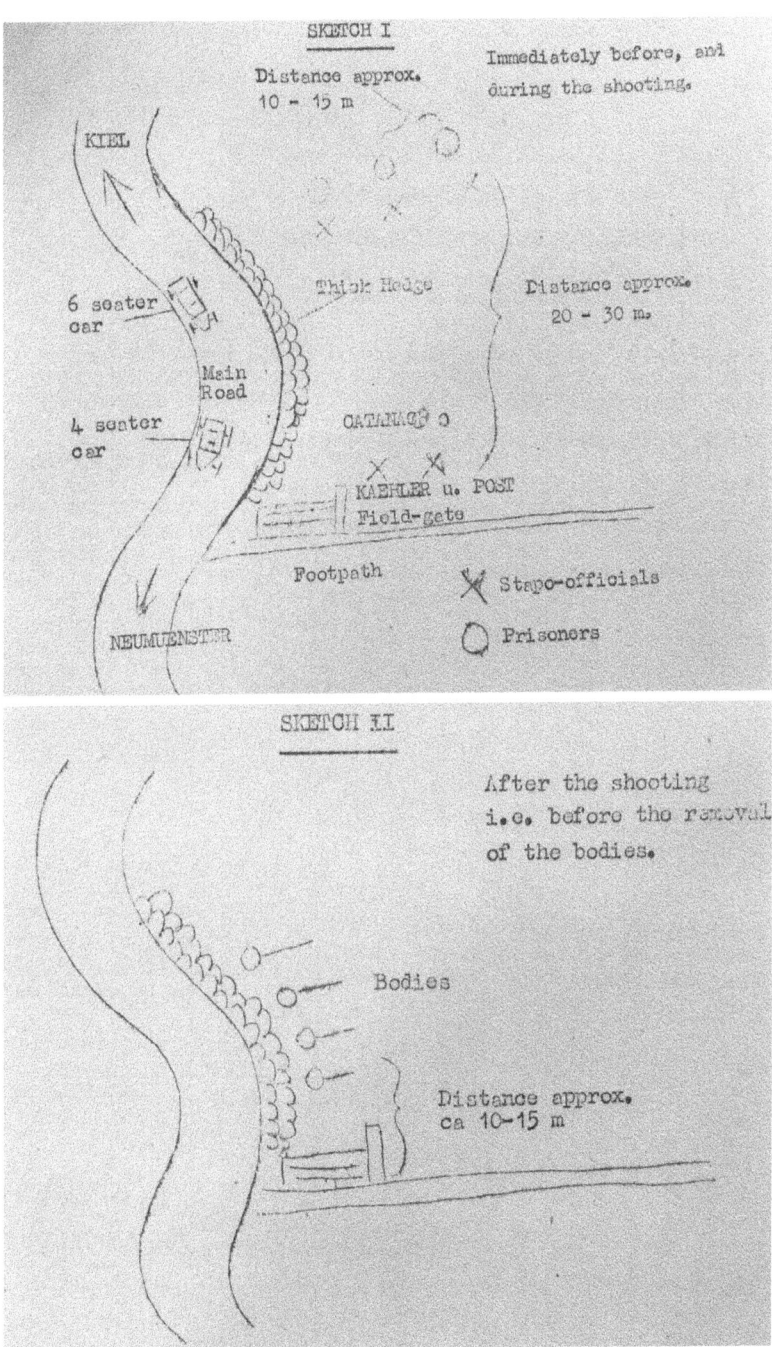

Sketches of Jimmy Catanach and his companions showing the positions before, during, and after their murder. They were drawn by witness and perpetrator Johannes Post as part of his war crimes testimony. AWM54/1010/6/132 Part 2.

The last photograph of a tired, unshaven John Williams in travel-stained clothes, taken at Reichenberg Police Station, shortly after recapture. Courtesy of Louise Williams.

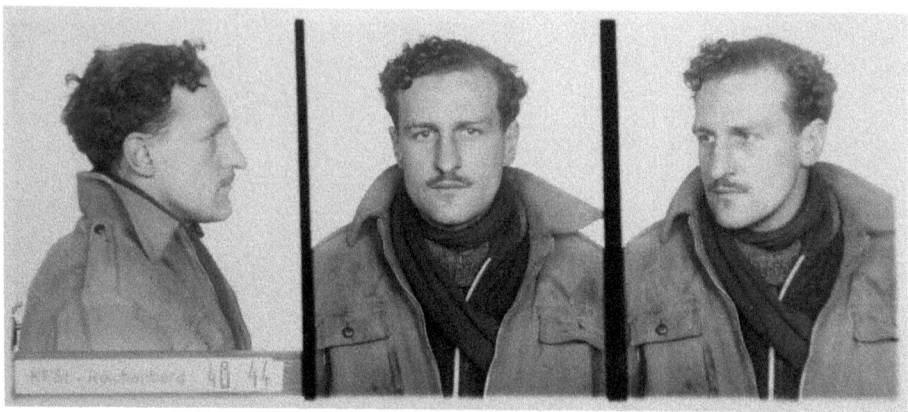

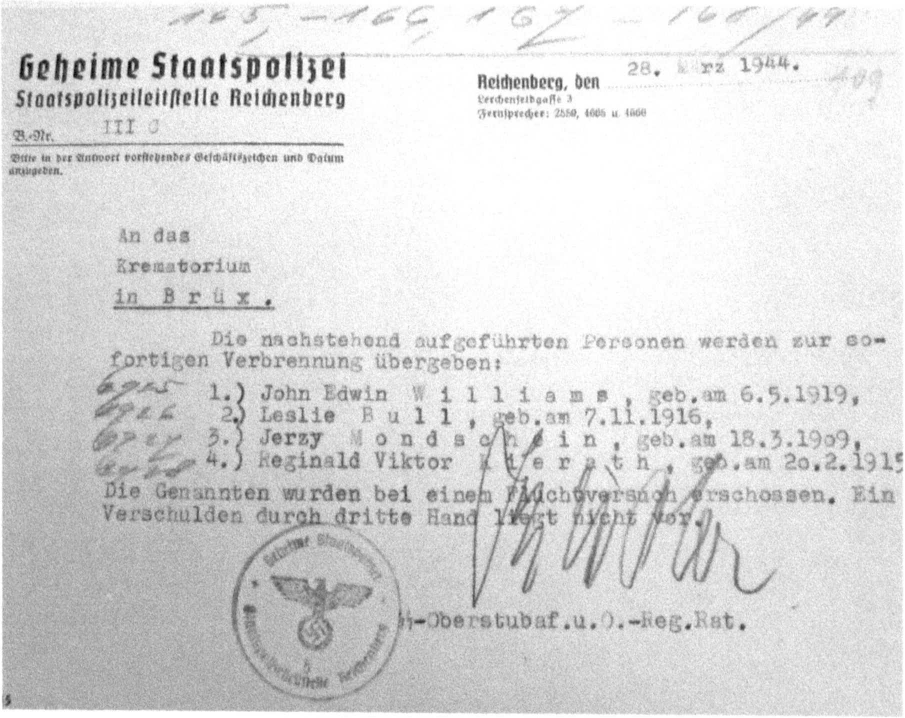

Geheime Staatspolizei
Staatspolizeileitstelle Reichenberg

B.-Nr. III C

Bitte in der Antwort vorstehendes Geschäftszeichen und Datum angeben.

Reichenberg, den 28. März 1944.
Lerchenfeldgasse 3
Fernsprecher: 2550, 4665 u. 4666

An das
Krematorium
in Brüx.

Die nachstehend aufgeführten Personen werden zur sofortigen Verbrennung übergeben:

1.) John Edwin W i l l i a m s , geb.am 6.5.1919,
2.) Leslie B u l l , geb.am 7.11.1916,
3.) Jerzy M o n d s c h e i n , geb.am 18.3.1909,
4.) Reginald Viktor K i e r a t h , geb.am 20.2.1915

Die Genannten wurden bei einem Fluchtversuch erschossen. Ein Verschulden durch dritte Hand liegt nicht vor.

SS-Oberstubaf.u.O.-Reg.Rat.

John Williams, Leslie Bull, Jerzy Mondschein, and Reg Kierath were 'handed over for immediate cremation.' German records falsely attest that they 'were shot during an escape attempt.' Courtesy of Peter Kierath.

Chapter Thirteen:

DEEP PERSONAL LOSS

Martin Massey ordered a general parade on 6 April 1944. North Compound's Senior British Officer had 'crushing news'.[1] Earlier that day, Von Lindeiner's replacement, *Kommandant* Erich Cordes had told Massey that forty-one escapers had been shot trying to evade arrest or escape after recapture.[2] None had been wounded. None had survived.[3] Massey had asked Cordes what had happened to the bodies; he wanted to give them the dignity of burial in the camp cemetery where others of their fellows lay. Cordes promised a list of names as soon as possible but was silent on the whereabouts of the corpses.[4] Massey now stood in front of the assembled airmen and uttered the devastating details.[5] The kriegies were 'visibly shaken and despondent'.[6] As well as shock, they felt 'deep personal loss'.[7] Emotions were high. 'Some of the hot-heads', Reg Giddey remembered, 'wanted to charge the barbed wire and guard boxes, but reason prevailed'.[8] The Germans could not have shot the escapers; it must be a hoax to discourage future breakouts, they thought.[9] Underlying disbelief was the fact that, as prisoners of war, they were protected by the Geneva Convention. Article 2 provided that captives were at all times to be treated humanely. Reprisals were expressly forbidden. Article 3 stated that they were entitled to 'respect for their persons and honour' – their essential human dignity could not be violated.[10] While many, as we have seen, had experienced hostile treatment on capture or harsh interrogations,[11] Germany generally treated British prisoners in accordance with the Convention.[12]

Massey declared that a memorial parade would be held that evening, to be attended by all of North Compound; similar parades were later held in other compounds. The grief-struck kriegies sang hymns and uttered psalms which called upon God to aid and comfort. The chaplain prayed that the 'souls of the

---

1 Arnel archive: Train, 'A Barbed-Wire World', 6 April 1944, 51.
2 NAUK WO 208/3283: SLIII Camp History, Part III North (Officers') Compound, 77.
3 NAA A1608 AT20/1/1: Shooting of Air Force Personnel (POW) in Germany. Summary of Proceedings.
4 NAA A1608 AT20/1/1: Shooting of Air Force Personnel (POW) in Germany. Summary of Proceedings.
5 See also Alexander and Ariotti, 'Mourning the Dead of the Great Escape: POWs, Grief, and the Memorial Vault of Stalag Luft III'.
6 Arnel archive: Train, 'A Barbed-Wire World', 6 April 1944, 51.
7 Arnel archive: Harvey, 'Over, Down and Out', 23.
8 'Gloucester Boy's Part in the Great Escape. Was one of the lucky ones', *Gloucester Advocate* (NSW), 29 May 1951, 1.
9 NAA A1608 AT20/1/1: Shooting of Air Force Personnel (POW) in Germany. Summary of Proceedings.
10 'Geneva Convention Relative to the Treatment of Prisoners of War (27 July 1929)', Jonathan Vance (ed.), *Encyclopedia of Prisoners of War and Internment* (Millerton: Grey House Publishing, 2006), 508.
11 Alexander, 'Emotions of Captivity', 104–106.
12 Oppenheimer, '"Our Number One Priority"', in Beaumont et al *Beyond Surrender*, 82.

faithful, through the mercy of God, rest in peace.' After Grace the 'Last Post' and 'Reveille' were sounded. 'Every prisoner wore a black diamond ... on his sleeve for the remainder of our term in prison', recalled Justin O'Byrne.[13] Even in the absence of their friends' bodies, the parade was a solemn affair, as much a military funeral as any they had attended before, whether in captivity or on operational or training stations.[14] Despite the absence of the bodies, Stalag Luft III's dead had been granted all the dignities of a regular death in service.

Two days after the memorial parade, Massey heard he was to be medically repatriated (this had been in train for some months).[15] Before he left, he formed a committee to gather and record evidence about the escape and the fate of those who had not been returned to camp. He would report the findings when he returned to Great Britain. (A court of inquiry was later held to consider the testimony.)

Paul Royle and others who had returned from Görlitz told what they knew, and what they thought had happened to those who had been taken away. They disputed that their fellows had been trying to escape from custody. They all knew it was futile to resist arrest. Royle claimed that if any 'had been shown an open door and told they could walk out all would have refused. Everybody was hungry, exhausted and the weather outside was hopeless'. Frost-bitten Albert Hake could barely stand, let alone escape.[16] It was illogical, they considered, for so many shootings to not result in even one wounding. Moreover, 'all Officers knew it was futile forcibly to resist arrest'. It was obvious, the committee concluded: the airmen had been 'murdered'.[17]

A list of the dead arrived which was pinned to the noticeboard. Rather than forty-one, it had forty-seven names.[18] Seeing the names was a shock. The kriegies' grief, still stark, was renewed. Many compiled rolls of the dead in diaries and wartime log books.[19] Eventually, fifty deaths were confirmed. There was some consolation, however, when the news came through secret channels that three of the escapers had made it back to England.

*****

Many of those shot by the Germans had been married; some, like Albert Hake, had paid allotments to their wives or mothers.[20] Recognising that the deceased

---

13   O'Byrne FA: O'Byrne, '*Mercury* Radio Roundsman'.
14   Bryce Cousens (ed), *The Log*, 5–6.
15   White, *Extremes of Fortune*, 137.
16   NAA A1608 AT20/1/1: Shooting of Air Force Personnel (POW) in Germany. Cablegram 2702 from Berne [Protecting Power] to Foreign Office, 14 June 1944.
17   NAA A1608 AT20/1/1: Shooting of Air Force Personnel (POW) in Germany. Summary of Proceedings.
18   NAUK WO 208/3283: Part III North Compound, 78.
19   Logbooks and diaries: Alexander, 'Emotions of Captivity', 251. See for example Baines FA: Baines, wartime log book, 37.
20   Preen FA: Albert Hake to Noela Hake, 10 September 1941.

airmen's next of kin might need financial assistance, North Compound personnel each subscribed an average of £5 to a special fund. A committee of adjustment was formed to gather the personal effects that had been left behind. Usually, putting possessions in good order and ensuring they were despatched to loved ones was a sign of respect but, as noted by historian Mary Louise Roberts, it diminished the connection with the dead; the once personal became impersonal.[21] Stalag Luft III's airmen had bitterly grieved, but they had started to move on. This was reinforced when the items were auctioned off. Rather than returning artefacts which next of kin would have considered tangible links to their loved ones, the dead airmen's possessions were used to increase the fundraising coffers: even in death the airmen provided for their families' welfare. It was a grand occasion. 'Some of the camp leading lights were invited to act as "guest auctioneers"', Laurie Simpson reported. Although the kriegies still mourned their friends – they would never entirely set aside their grief – 'the whole thing was carried out ... in a very light hearted spirit'. The 'bidding was generally very high, some prices being fantastic'. As a result, 'a substantial sum' was raised;[22] Noela Hake, for example, received two payments totalling £283. 4. 11d. The impressive sum was the equivalent of $22,933.27 in 2022.[23]

Not all personal possessions were sold. Comfort parcels addressed to the dead kriegies were considered communal property and divided up. RAF airman Vivian Kelly, 'one of the few who have suffered a particular dearth of clothes', benefited from Ada Kierath's last package. Despite the charitable efforts of his friends in camp who shared what they could spare, Kelly 'was beginning to feel very much in need'. He was touchingly grateful to Ada: 'I may tell you that the contents were never more welcome because it has been over two years since any clothing parcel had come my way'.[24] Before entering the escape tunnel, Alan Righetti's roommate, George Wiley, who had 'bad vibes about the whole thing' had charged him with returning his wristwatch and photos to his family in Canada if anything should happen.[25] Righetti was not the obvious choice as there were other Canadians in their hut who lived much closer to the Wiley home than the Australian but, recognising his roommate's need to place his possessions in safe hands, Righetti agreed to deliver them if necessary.[26]

---

21 Roberts, *Sheer Misery: Soldiers in Battle in WWII*, 134.
22 AWM 54 779/3/126 part 1: Simpson, POW statement, 31 July 1945; NAUK AIR 40/269: Stalag Luft III reports and nominal roll, Stalag Luft III Communal Fund.
23 Preen FA: W.E. Mann, Area Finance Officer, Department of Air, letters 18 October 1945 and undated to Noela Hake. Reserve Bank Pre-Decimal Inflation Calculator.
24 Kierath FA: Vivian B. Kelly to Ada Kierath, 3 September 1944.
25 AR: Alan Righetti, email 31 October 2008.
26 AR: Alan Righetti, email 27 April 2012.

Righetti wondered about the fate of his young friend but would have had no idea that Wiley, one of the last to climb out of the tunnel (he was the 72nd, just ahead of Tom Leigh[27]) had been killed alongside Albert Hake and Leigh. After liberation, Righetti displayed 'an intimate chivalry' by taking the long way home via America and Canada to fulfil his promise to his young friend.[28] 'That was a very hard thing to do,' he recalled, as he encountered uncomprehending grief. 'They were so distressed.' The Wiley family's fears for George's safety had subsided when they learned of his capture. They had been 'so relieved to hear that he was safe in prison camp, only then to have the news that he was murdered.' Their anguish was so profound they had not realised that Righetti had delayed his return to Australia and driven to Ontario from Washington DC (a trip which would take over 13 hours today) to deliver his friend's belongings. They had not recognised that Righetti had been fulfilling Wiley's final, personal request.[29]

*****

Weeks passed with no further news of what had happened to the escapers. On 25 May, Group Captain Douglas Wilson, who had assumed the role of Senior British Officer, was advised by the *kommandant* that the cremated remains of twenty-nine airmen had arrived,[30] including those of Albert Hake and Tom Leigh.[31] The urns were placed on a trestle table in the sick quarters. The shock the airmen had felt on first hearing of the deaths was again acute.[32] They could not have imagined such an ending to their grand enterprise. More remains were sent to the camp over time, including those of Reg Kierath, John Williams, and Jimmy Catanach, until, on 14 July, fifty urns sat on the table.[33] Though cremation as a means of disposing of the dead in Britain and Australia was not unusual by the 1930s, the Geneva Convention only prescribed honourable burial. Indeed, Gabriel Naville, a Swiss Legation inspector who had officially enquired into the Great Escape deaths, observed that 'this is the first time, to our knowledge, that the bodies of deceased prisoners have been cremated.'[34] While Stalag Luft III's kriegies knew that belligerents were obliged to bury prisoners of war and had attended many funerals behind barbed wire, they did not appear to remark on this rarity or its breach of the Geneva Convention. As Paul Brickhill and Conrad Norton revealed, the receptacles marked with a variety of locations 'testified'

---

27   Walters, *The Real Great Escape*, appendix 'The Escapers', 308–12.
28   Alexander, 'Australian Knights of the Air and their Little Touches of Chivalry', 12.
29   AAWFA: Righetti 0984, 16 September 2003; AR: Alan Righetti, email 3 February 2014.
30   AWM 54 1010/6/132: SLIII War Crimes Trial Part 1: Group Captain D.E.L Wilson to Swiss Legation, 27 May 1944; Gabriel Naville, Report on the Visit Made to Stalag Luft III on 5th June 1944.
31   AWM 54 1010/6/132: SLIII War Crimes Trial Part 1: Group Captain D.E.L Wilson to Swiss Legation, 27 May 1944; Gabriel Naville, Report on the Visit Made to Stalag Luft III on 5th June 1944.
32   Walters, *The Real Great Escape*, 260; NLA O'Byrne, 'Reminiscential conversations', Tape 51.
33   Andrews, *Exemplary Justice*, 223. We do not know when the ashes of Kierath, Williams, and Catanach arrived.
34   AWM 54 1010/6/132: SLIII War Crimes Trial Part 1: Naville, 5th June 1944.

to 'the widespread net that the Nazis had put out to trace the escapees', and the resources expended to recapture them.[35] The airmen were proud of the disruptive efforts of their fellows.[36]

With 'vengeful grief',[37] the dead kriegies' friends constructed a memorial vault to both commemorate the dead and house their ashes.[38] Designed by Australian-born architect Wemyss Wylton Todd, and with material supplied by the Germans,[39] the vault and nearby stone cairn were situated in the well-cared for camp cemetery about 450 metres from West compound, close to the burial plots of other POWs who had died in captivity. 'The only time I was outside the barbed wire for 45 months', Justin O'Byrne recalled, 'was to assist in the erection of the memorial' as well as the cairn a few metres in front of it which honoured those who had died in a 'noble but ill-fated attempt to regain their freedom'.[40] Others also took their turn over the next six months, though they found the work physically debilitating. Rations had been cut as German logistics became ever more strained after D-Day. Red Cross parcels were not enough to maintain work fitness. As such, rosters had to be implemented so the builders could conserve their energy.[41]

Surrounded on two sides by fir trees, the vault's setting was attractive and, even in the depths of winter, the kriegies planted as many flowering shrubs as they could obtain.[42] Built from light-grey granite with white terrazzo, the memorial resembled an altar. Fifty names were carved on three scrolls, their bases formed water-tight removable lids which gave access to the vault's interior. An epigraph highlighted that the kriegies viewed their friends' deaths as sacrifices: 'In memory of the officers who gave their lives. Sagan March 1944'. An eagle, evoking their wings insignia and continuing membership of the brotherhood of airmen and their kriegie family, was affixed below the inscription.[43]

The ashes were ceremoniously interred on 4 December 1944 at what Ronald Baines termed a 'burial service'. Not all of the escapers' friends could attend as it was 'censored'.[44] Attended by members of the Swiss Legation, the *kommandant*'s adjutant, and thirty British airmen, the service lasted about 15 minutes. While

---

35 Brickhill and Norton, *Escape to Danger*, 336.
36 Edlington, 'The Great Escape Recalled: 60 years on, survivors tell of famous breakout', 15; NLA O'Byrne, 'Reminiscential conversations', Tape 50.
37 Brickhill and Norton, *Escape to Danger*, 337.
38 AWM 54 1010/6/132: SLIII War Crimes Trial Part 1: Group Captain D.E.L Wilson to Swiss Legation, 27 May 1944; NAUK WO 208/3283: SL.III Camp History, Part III North (Officers') Compound, 78.
39 Preen FA: 'A Prison Camp Memorial'.
40 O'Byrne FA: O'Byrne, '*Mercury* Radio Roundsman'.
41 Walton, and Eberhardt, *From Interrogation to Liberation*, 421–422.
42 MOJ: Group Captain A.S.W Dore DSC, Directorate of Allied Air Co-operation and Foreign Liaison, Air Ministry, to Air Commodore S. Karpinski, Headquarters Polish Air Force 4 January 1945, quoting Stalag Luft III prisoner, Grenfell Godden.
43 Preen FA: 'A Prison Camp Memorial', annotation on back of sketch of the memorial vault by Ley Kenyon that accompanied photos of the vault sent to Noela Hake
44 Baines FA: Baines, wartime log book, 37.

no address was allowed, both the Roman Catholic and Protestant chaplains blessed the memorial and prayed over the urns as they were placed on wooden shelves in the heart of the vault. A trumpeter sounded the 'Last Post' and three airmen, along with a representative of the legation, placed wreathes on the vault's surface.[45]

*****

Although envious of George Wiley and those who had been selected to escape, Alan Righetti did not begrudge missing out. He recalled that 'we were bitterly disappointed' that all had not escaped 'but at the same time, very proud of the fact that we had the whole of the area and the German Army rushing all over the place looking for our fellas.'[46] The Great Escape, however, failed to achieve its aim of creating great havoc. It had little effect on the allied war effort.[47] Because of decades of lionisation of the participants, there are very few latter day criticisms of either the escape organisation or its main proponents, particularly Roger Bushell.[48] Indeed, most of Stalag Luft III's prisoners forgot or ignored Bushell's escape autocracy; some acclaimed him a hero.[49] Sixteen months after Bushell's death, Mac Jones, who had worked in the carpentry department with Reg Kierath and John Williams, claimed that 'the escape was brilliantly planned' by Bushell.[50] Sixty years after Bushell's death, Geoff Cornish, who was active in the 'X' organisation until he transferred to the Belaria compound to work in the sick quarters, still considered the South African to be 'a very great friend'. He 'was brave and he was cunning. He was the ideal type.'[51] Justin O'Byrne's assessment is also typical: 'he was an inspiration for morale building and determination, a very great man.'[52] There were only a handful of dissenters, such as Len Netherway, who thought Bushell was 'mad. Crazy.'[53]

Fifty had been shot, only three had made it back to England, yet the kriegies refused to see their grand enterprise as a failure. At the time, they had seen the deaths as both an 'admirable sacrifice and lamentable atrocity'.[54] Later, they made sense of their friends' deaths by framing them as arising from the highest motives: their duty to escape.[55] After all, that duty had been outlined in *Air Publication 1548*; it was fully endorsed by Wings Day, Roger Bushell,

---

45 'Grim Mystery of Prison Camp', *The Sydney Morning Herald* (NSW), 28 April 1945, 8.
46 AAWFA: Righetti 0984, 16 September 2003; AR: Alan Righetti, email 21 January 2014.
47 Walzer, 'Prisoners of War: Does the Fight Continue after the Battle?', 785.
48 Vance, 'The War Behind the Wire', 690; Meale, 'Leadership of Australian POWs in the Second World War', PhD thesis, 143–144.
49 Meale, 'Leadership of Australian POWs in the Second World War', PhD thesis, 145.
50 'Thousand Prisoners Reach Home. R.A.A.F. Men Tell of Prison Break', *The Sydney Morning Herald*, 25 July 1945, 4.
51 AAWFA: Cornish 1388, 2 July 2004.
52 NLA O'Byrne, 'Reminiscential conversations', Tape 51.
53 AR: Mike Netherway, interview 28 September 2016.
54 Alexander and Ariotti, 'Mourning the Dead of the Great Escape: POWs, Grief, and the Memorial Vault of Stalag Luft III'.
55 NLA O'Byrne, 'Reminiscential conversations', Tape 50.

and 'X'. Reinforcing that they remained active participants in the war behind barbed wire, many highlighted the 'nuisance value' of escape.⁵⁶ It was all part of their commitment to active disruption. Despite the tragic results, Bill Fordyce considered the breakout successful. 'There were tens of thousands of German troops whose sole job was to look for those that escaped.'⁵⁷ Even before the end of the war, the audacity of the 'spectacular' break-out began to overshadow the tragedy.⁵⁸ The glee with which former kriegies such as O'Byrne later told stories 'of prisoners under a big handicap but often coming out on top' highlights their believed success in winning the 'battle of wits' against the Germans, despite the great cost of lost lives.⁵⁹

The Stalag Luft III vault 'In memory of the officers who gave their lives. Sagan March 1944' c. 1945. Courtesy of the Preen family.

---

56 *Air Publication 1548*, 2nd Edition, June 1941.
57 Edlington, 'The Great Escape Recalled: 60 years on, survivors tell of famous breakout', 15.
58 'Thousand Prisoners Reach Home. R.A.A.F Men Tell of Prison Break', *Sydney Morning Herald*, 25 July 1945, 4.
59 O'Byrne FA: O'Byrne, '*Mercury* Radio Roundsman'.

The Australians wore black mourning patches for those killed in the post-Great Escape reprisals, as can be seen on the sleeves of Alan Righetti (front row, second from left), Ronald Baines (centre front) and Paul Brickhill (on Baines' right). Anzac Day 1944. Courtesy of Drew Gordon.

> MARCH 24-25 1944   37
>
> | | | | | | |
> |---|---|---|---|---|---|
> | S/Ldr. | J. Catanach | R.A.A.F | F/Lt | E. Brettell | R.A.F. |
> | F/Lt | A. Hake | R.A.A.F | F/Lt | L. Bull | R.A.F |
> | F/Lt | R. Kierath | R.A.A.F | S/Ldr | R. Bushell | R.A.F.A |
> | S/Ldr | J. Williams | R.A.A.F | F/Lt | M. Casey | R.A.F |
> | F/O | A. Christensen | R.N.Z.A.F | F/O | D. Cochran | R.A.F |
> | F/O | P.P. Pohe | R.N.Z.A.F | S/Ldr | I. Cross | R.A.F |
> | F/Lt | H. Birkland | R.C.A.F | F/O | H. Espelid | R.A.F |
> | F/Lt | G. Kidder | R.C.A.F | F/Lt | B. Evans | R.A.F |
> | F/Lt | P. Langford | R.C.A.F | F/Lt | A. Gunn | R.A.F |
> | F/Lt | G. McGill | R.C.A.F | F/Lt | W. Gruman | R.A.F |
> | F/Lt | J.C. Wernham | R.C.A.F | F/Lt | C. Hall | R.A.F |
> | F/Lt | G. Wiley | R.C.A.F | F/Lt | A. Hayter | R.A.F |
> | Lt | J. Gouws | S.A.A.F | F/Lt | E. Humphries | R.A.F |
> | Lt | H. McGarr | S.A.A.F | S/Ldr | T.G. Kirby-Green | R.A.F |
> | Lt | J. Stevens | S.A.A.F | F/Lt | T. Leigh | R.A.F |
> | F/O | N.J. Fugelsang | Norway | F/Lt | H. Milford | R.A.F |
> | F/Lt | R. Marcinkus | Latvia | F/Lt | C. Swain | R.A.F |
> | F/Lt | H. Picard | Belgium | F/O | R. Stewart | R.A.F |
> | F/Lt | E. Valenta | Czechoslovakia | F/O | D. Street | R.A.F |
> | F/O | S. Krol | Poland A.F. | F/O | J. Stower | R.A.F |
> | F/Lt | A. Kiewnarski | Poland | F/Lt | G. Wallen | R.A.F |
> | F/O | W. Kolanowski | Poland | F/Lt | J. Williams | R.A.F |
> | F/O | J. Mondschein | Poland | F/Lt | J. Long | R.A.F |
> | F/O | K. Pawluk | Poland | Lt | B. Scheidhauer | French Navy (A) |
> | F/O | P. Tobolski | Poland | F/O | S. Skanziklas | Greece |
>
> Shot while attempting to escape.
> Burial Service 4ᵗʰ Dec 1944. Stalag Luft III R.A.F Cemetery
> Services censored.

Shocked at the murder of their fellows, many kriegies, like Ronald Baines, compiled lists of those 'shot while attempting to escape'. Baines, as did others, considered the shootings a war crime. Ronald Baines, wartime log book. Courtesy of the Baines family.

Chapter Fourteen:

BEREAVEMENT

'This is not an easy letter to write', Thelma Anderson told Noela Hake on the day she read in the paper that Albert had been one of the Australian airmen shot after a mass escape from a German POW camp.[1] The story had broken in local papers on 20 May, following an announcement about the shootings by British Foreign Secretary, Anthony Eden, in the British House of Commons on the 19th.[2] 'There are times when words seem very inadequate.' Three days earlier, Noela had opened the telegram containing the devastating news that her husband had 'lost his life ... while attempting to escape' and Thelma knew how distressed her friend would be.[3] 'I don't know just how to express my sympathy without causing you any further pain.' Yet Thelma knew her condolences were needed. She attempted to lift Noela's spirits by telling her to 'try to keep smiling' because she believed 'Albert would wish you to be brave & face it with your chin up'. Society, too, expected Noela to be stoic despite her tragic widowhood.[4] Drawing on their shared faith, Thelma reminded Noela that she did not have to bear her grief alone. 'Fear thou not; for I am with thee: be not dismayed; for I am thy God: I will strengthen thee; yea I will help thee ...'[5] Noela, too, could rely on Thelma. 'Though I'm not very useful at times like these, if there should be anything that I can do to help please let me know, & I will endeavour to do my best.'

Fewer than 300 Australians died in European captivity. Some died of natural causes, others from wounds, or illness. Only a handful were killed other than as a result of escapes. From a statistical perspective, twenty-three RAAF POW deaths in Europe is barely comparable to the 7,412 Australians from all services who died in Japanese captivity.[6] But each death brought immeasurable pain and grief to loved ones. Hope of a safe return was never fulfilled for Noela and the other families of the Australians killed in the post-Great Escape reprisals. Like the thousands who lost sons, husbands, brothers, and nephews, their grief

---

1   Unless otherwise cited, all quotes in this paragraph are from Preen FA: Thelma Anderson to Noela Hake 20 May 1944. See for example 'Allied Airmen Shot after Mass Escape', *The Daily Telegraph* (Sydney), 20 May 1944, 1.
2   Because of time differences, it is difficult to determine exactly when the Australian Government were made aware of the killings. A cablegram detailing Eden's statement to the House dated 19 May sent by the Secretary of State for Dominion Affairs to the Prime Minister's Department was received 20 May 1944. NAA MP729/8 44/431/104 Shooting of Air Force POWs at Stalag Luft III.
3   Preen FA: telegram 17 May 1944.
4   Noakes, *Dying for the Nation*, 11.
5   Isaiah 41: 10.
6   Totals vary. DVA states 265. Rosalind Hearder records 234. Hearder in Beaumont et al., *The Australian Centenary History of Defence Volume VI*, 344–345.

was real, not anticipatory. They, like Mildred Williams, were 'dazed by loss' and 'profoundly affected'.[7] Historian Bruce Scates notes 'the private world of loss and bereavement'[8] yet the Great Escape families had little privacy in their mourning. Initially front page news, details of 'murder' and 'executions', dominated the papers for days.[9] Families' bewilderment over how these deaths could have occurred was perhaps exacerbated by newspapers around the country quoting the aeronautical correspondent of London's *Daily Express* who stated that 'reprisals or severe punishments for trying to escape were not permitted under the Geneva Convention'.[10]

The same day Noela saw her husband's name in the paper as one of '47 Airmen Shot',[11] she received a letter from him.[12] It was a cruel irony: the joy of reading his words, feeling close to him again, experiencing the sense that he still lived was obliterated by the finality of the public announcement followed by the many condolence letters like Thelma's. Noela's family and friends, as did those of the other Great Escape kin, offered sympathy and prayers for God's comfort. But they could not hide how appalled they felt at the circumstances. 'We were all so horrified when the news came through', Ella Fraser told Noela.[13] 'Everyone is distressed at this dreadful act', wrote Malcolm and Hazel McEachern to William Catanach.[14] Some tried to make sense of the escapes which lead to their deaths. 'I suppose he was impatient to get home to you', the Crofts suggested to Noela.[15] Condolers' emotions were strong. Some, however, were unable to articulate them. 'Words are useless at present', wrote the father of one of Jimmy Catanach's crew members and fellow prisoner of war, 'but I do want you to know how deeply we too feel his loss'.[16]

Suffering the second wartime death of a son (and following the loss of her husband and a daughter in 1938), Ada Kierath drew strength from her church and priest.[17] Her family gathered around her; Bert, her eldest son, almost immediately resigned his appointment with the Volunteer Defence Corps.[18] Mildred Williams

---

7   Quote: Williams, *A True Story of the Great Escape*, 245.
8   Bruce Scates et al., *Anzac Journeys: Returning to the Battlefields of World War II* (Port Melbourne: Cambridge University Press, 2013), 11.
9   Front page news, see for example: 'Allied Airmen Shot after Mass Escape', *The Daily Telegraph* (Sydney), 20 May 1944, 1; 'Shootings at Prison Camp. Germans Kill 47 Allied Airmen', *The Advertiser* (Adelaide), 20 May 1944, 1. 'cold-blooded murder': 'Sensational Mass Escape. Airmen Burrowed Out of Stalag', *The Advertiser* (Adelaide), 30 May 1944, 4. See also 'Mass Escape Attempt. Tunnel Dug From Stalagluft III', *Sydney Morning Herald*, 30 May 1944, 3; 'Airmen War Prisoners Killed by Nazis: Two Shore Boys Among Australians Shot Dead', *The Sun* (Sydney) 21 May 1944, 3.
10 'Gestapo Hunted 47 Escaped Allied Fliers', *News* (Adelaide, SA), 20 May 1944, 1; 'Gestapo Shot Air Force Men?, *The Daily News* (Perth, WA), 20 May 1944, 1; 'Shooting of 47 Airmen. Urgent Inquiry by Switzerland', *The Herald* (Melbourne, Vic), 20 May 1944, 2.
11 '47 Airmen Shot. Fate of Allied Escapees', *Sydney Morning Herald* (NSW), 21 May 1944, 1.
12 '4 R.A.A.F. Prisoners Shot in Germany', *Sunday Mail* (Brisbane, QLD), 21 May 1944, 3.
13 Preen FA: Ella Fraser to Noela Hake, 9 August 1944.
14 SOR JCC: 2013.CAT030, Scrapbook Two, Malcolm McEachern to William Catanach, 21 June 1944.
15 Preen FA: Mr and Mrs Crofts to Noela Hake, 19 May 1944.
16 SOR JCC: 2013.CAT030, Scrapbook Two, Ralph B. Anderson to William Catanach, 18 May 1944.
17 AR: Peter Kierath, interview 2 May 2016.
18 NAA B884: record of service, Herbert William Kierath, N353343.

attended séances, hoping to contact John.[19] For Noela, who had had only a brief courtship and marriage before her husband embarked, gleaning details of Albert's past, service, and captive lives from those who knew him became a lifetime endeavour. Isabel Amos shared extracts from her son Bill's letters from Stalag Luft III and, in an altruistic gesture – she would be potentially forsaking news of Bill because of German restrictions on number and length of POW letter forms – told Noela she would 'be only too pleased to ask my son, when next I write, if he can give me any news at all of your husband.'[20] Noela also wrote to Ella Fraser, with whom Albert had spent his leave. Later she read and reread the poetry of Robert Kay Hallam, sent to her in 1962 by the author, a former orderly who was in North Compound during the construction of the escape tunnel; three of his poems honoured the dead escapers.[21] She also corresponded with one of Albert's childhood friends who told her about his early life.[22] Knowing so little about her husband, losing him before their union was tested by marital pressures and everyday stresses, reading and re-reading his letters (despite the pain she felt, even decades later[23]) and treasuring the few records which delineated his short life, did Noela idealise Albert? Did she forever remember him through rose-tinted glasses, overlooking the epistolary indications that they were not always in accord? I think she did – but it is understandable. He was 'most precious to me', she wrote forty-two years after his death. 'He was such an idealist and had so many plans for after the war and I'm so very sure had he come back we would have had a very good and happy life together.'[24] If she viewed their lives nostalgically, and maintained visions of a blissful post-war existence if only things had been different, she was not the only one.[25]

*****

The British public had long embraced the idea that the Great War's POWs were heroic victims. Two months after the armistice, a commemorative service had been held at St Margaret's Westminster publicly valorising the sacrifice of those who had died in captivity.[26] A similar service for the Great Escapers was conducted at the Church of St Martin-in-the-Fields, London on 20 June 1944.[27] Located in Trafalgar Square and long associated with military commemoration, it had become a 'Soldiers' Church' for servicemen throughout Britain and her

---

19   Williams, *A True Story of the Great Escape*, 245.
20   Preen FA: Isabel Amos to Noela Hake, 7 September 1944.
21   AR: Max Preen, email 4 September 2015; Hallam, *The Scarecrow Said and other poems*, 38–41 and 46.
22   Preen FA: Correspondence between Noela Hake and Jean Heckendorf, 1987.
23   Preen FA: Noela Hake, letter to Jonathan Vance, 30 September 1986.
24   Preen FA: Noela Hake, letter to Jonathan Vance, 12 December 1986.
25   Damousi, *Living with the Aftermath*, 64–69.
26   Wilkinson, 'Fate Worse Than Death?', 31.
27   A copy of the service program was kept by Noela Hake, Ada Kierath, and the Catanach Family. Refer SOR JCC as well as Preen and Kierath FAs.

empire.[28] Like that earlier ceremony, the 20 June service articulated a narrative of sacrifice. 'Their indomitable courage, unquenchable hope, and supreme sacrifice had about it, even in these days of many patterns of heroism, something that was unique', the RAF Chaplain-in-Chief declared. He validated the airmen's disruptive efforts, highlighting that they had been carrying out their air force duty in attempting to escape: 'Their freedom in a measure lost, they still fought on, doing their duty twice over.'[29] The men would become exemplars. In 'the years to come, we will not forget the example which your son and the others with him have set', Squadron Leader William Melville of the RAAF's Overseas Casualty Section, who attended the ceremony on her behalf, told Ada Kierath.[30] Counterpointing the narrative of sacrifice, however, was that of atrocity. The horror of their deaths was alluded to in the lesson read by Sir Charles Portal, RAF Chief of the Air Staff: 'In the sight of the unwise they seemed to die: and their departure is taken for misery, and their going to be utter destruction: but they are in peace.'[31]

*****

Letters became talismans of remembrance for the next of kin of those shot by the Germans. Acknowledging the emotive contents and demonstrating their own sentimental attachment to them, Noela and Ada Kierath kept those written by Albert and Reg, as well as condolence letters and telegrams. William Catanach arranged those he received in a scrapbook, preserving his private sorrow for Jimmy between its covers; his list of those who had expressed sympathy fills almost ten double-columned pages.[32] Sometimes stilted and trite, condolers' formulaic responses – 'I am very sorry you are called upon to bear so much sorrow … do try and bear up' – were genuine.[33] They were attempts to convey emotion and empathy even as they reflected a societal expectation of stoic self-control. Regardless of their deficiencies, recipients cherished them as records of love, sympathy, and communal recognition of emotional pain. Families treasured programs from and descriptions of the Great Escape's official memorial service sent by those who had attended in their stead. 'You would, I know, have deeply appreciated the tribute which was paid today had you been present and I only hope that, in what I fear has been a very inadequate way, I have been able to give you something of the scene', William Melville told Ada Kierath.[34]

---

28   SOR JCC: 2013.CAT030, Scrapbook Two, unattributed clipping 'St. Martin-in-the-Fields'.
29   'Honour to Shot Airmen', *The Times* (London), 21 June 1944, 2.
30   Kierath FA: Squadron Leader W.M. Melville, letter to Ada Kierath, 20 June 1944.
31   'Honour to Shot Airmen. Memorial Service in London', *The Times* (London), 21 June 1944, 2.
32   SOR JCC: 2013.CAT030, Scrapbook Two; Alexander, '"How deeply we feel his loss": Condolences to William Mercer Catanach, on the death of his son, Jimmy'.
33   Preen FA: Mr and Mrs Crofts to Noela Hake, 19 May 1944.
34   Kierath FA: Squadron Leader WM Melville to Ada Kierath, 20 June 1944.

Ella Fraser informed Noela that, 'it was really a beautiful service & all the hymns & service seemed to have more meaning'. Highlighting that the Great Escapers had been publicly acknowledged as carrying out their air force duty in attempting to escape, Ella stressed to Noela that the 'Chaplain said they had done more than their duty – they had done it twice over'.[35]

Drawings, photographs, and descriptions of graves consoled. The Great Escapers' next of kin treasured pictures of the prisoners' memorial, where the ashes of their dead had been interred. As we have seen, escapers' personal possessions were auctioned off to raise funds for their families. Most dear to the bereaved, then, were personal effects left behind at operational postings and either kept in storage or in the caring custody of friends. These were the last tangible connections to their loved ones. Precious objects once owned or touched were ultimate proof of death, even as they conveyed a sense of a continuing presence.[36] William Catanach pasted into his scrapbook the letters from the McEacherns referring to the despatch of his son's possessions.[37] Margaret Bligh, sister of Tom Leigh, kept his medals, his Mentioned in Despatches clasp, his air gunner wings, and the few photographs and family letters recording her siblings' childhood before their separation immediately after the death of their mother.[38] (Tom and their brother David stayed in Britain and Margaret was sent to relatives in Australia; David, a member of the Special Air Service Regiment, died of wounds in France on 23 August 1944.) Margaret's uncle later sent her what is now Tom's only extant letter written during captivity.[39]

Grief has conventions which decree how one must mourn. Just as Stalag Luft III's airmen donned their black patches, widows put their emotions on public view in socially acceptable and decreed ways. Noela Hake, who already proudly wore her Female Relatives' Badge in recognition of her husband's wartime contribution, applied for and pinned on the Mothers' and Widows' Badge. Mildred Williams requested the 'bereaved Mother's Badge' but, as her son had served with the RAF, she was not eligible for it.[40] Her granddaughter, Louise, suggests that Mildred saw this not as a matter of bureaucracy, but because her country failed to acknowledge her loss.[41] Perhaps also, in Mildred's eyes, it diminished her Great Escaper son's status and perceived sacrifice.

Memorial notices publicly commemorated loved ones and reminded society

---

35 Preen FA: Ella Fraser to Noela Hake, 9 August 1944.
36 Roberts, *Sheer Misery: Soldiers in Battle in WWII*, 131, 133.
37 Refer SOR JCC: 2013.CAT030, Scrapbook Two.
38 Bligh FA.
39 AR: Bligh family, interview 26 April 2017.
40 Williams, *A True Story of the Great Escape*, 17. Refer NAA A705 163/64/183 for 'bereaved Mother's Badge' and concern about Williams' standing.
41 Williams, *A True Story of the Great Escape*, 233.

of bereavement. Those placed by Noela spanned the decades; her sorrow was evident in *The Sydney Morning Herald*'s 'On Active Service' notices until at least 1969. 'Loved and remembered', she wrote.[42] Jimmy Catanach's parents, Heather Ebbott, family, and nanny, Winifred Munt, inserted loving remembrances into the *Argus*'s Family Notice section.[43] Winifred had pasted news clippings into a scrapbook as she followed her former charge's sterling career. Unsure of her former charge's actual date of death, her last entry in the handwritten service chronology at the back of the book was: 'March 29th ? 1944 Shot after escaping from Stalag Luft III'. In 1969, the elderly woman attended the escape's twenty-fifth anniversary commemoration in London.[44]

*****

Sealed inside the prisoners' memorial vault, the escapers' ashes remained undisturbed for some months. The kriegies did not remove them when they evacuated the camp in late January 1945.[45] Later, the vault was ransacked by Russians apparently in search of gold.[46] Two of the cement covers were broken. The urns were taken out and opened. Some, along with their lids were shattered; many were unidentifiable. Scattered ashes intermingled on the floor, including those of Jimmy Catanach.[47] The eagle emblem was removed.

In 1944, the Royal Air Force had established the Missing Research and Enquiry Service (MRES) to trace those under RAF command from the RAF, Dominion air forces, including the RAAF, and Allied air forces, including the Polish and Norwegian air forces, who were missing believed killed.[48] Located remains were, as much as possible, identified and reburied in Imperial War Graves Commission (IWGC) graves and cemeteries. While the remains of Stalag Luft III's dead airmen were not missing, their continuing safety was uncertain.[49] Major John Da Silva who had visited Sagan in February 1946 and discovered the disturbed vault, recommended the urns be relocated 'to a more secure resting place'.[50] By November 1948, MRES had retrieved the remaining

---

42 As indicated in Trove's on-line newspaper search, and the *Sydney Morning Herald* Archive. Preen FA: Albert Hake to Noela Hake, 20 March 1944.
43 Argus (Melbourne) 25 March 1947, 2. See also Alexander, 'Jimmy Catanach and Heather Ebbott', <https://australiansinsliii.blogspot.com/2016/10/jimmy-and-heather.html>.
44 SOR JCC: 2013.CAT029, Scrapbook One; 2013.CAT055.
45 CWGC ADD 3/1/9 Prisoners of War, Treatment. Sagan: Squadron Leader Joseph Barker, Liaison Officer, DADGRE (Eastern Germany) to RAF Missing Research & Enquiry Service, [undated] August 1947.
46 CWGC Commission ADD 3/1/9 Prisoners of War, Treatment. Sagan: Squadron Leader E.C. Rideal, Officer in Charge Polish Detachment, MRES to Air Ministry, 30 November 1948.
47 CWGC ADD 3/1/9 Prisoners of War, Treatment. Sagan: Major J da Silva, Intelligence Group, Report on Graves of R.A.F. Officers at P.W. Camp, Sagan, 15 February 1946; Squadron Leader E.C. Rideal, Officer in Charge Polish Detachment, MRES to Air Ministry, 30 November 1948.
48 Hadaway, 'Identification methods of the Royal Air Force Missing Research and Enquiry Service, 1944–52', 1.
49 CWGC ADD 3/1/9 Prisoners of War, Treatment. Sagan: Major J. da Silva, Intelligence Group, Report on Graves of R.A.F. Officers at P.W. Camp, Sagan, 15 February 1946.
50 CWGC ADD 3/1/9 Prisoners of War, Treatment. Sagan: Major J. da Silva, Intelligence Group, Report on Graves of R.A.F. Officers at P.W. Camp, Sagan, 15 February 1946.

urns, fragments, and scattered ashes. Under the auspices of the IWGC, they were reinterred in the British Military Cemetery (now Old Garrison Cemetery), Poznań.[51] The ashes of those whose urns were in tact were placed in separate plots. Ashes which had been strewn on the memorial vault's floor – like those of Jimmy Catanach – were scattered in a collective grave; individual headstones gave the illusion of separate burial.

Bereaved families were invited to include personal inscriptions on the headstones. Jimmy Catanach's epitaph positioned his death as both a sacrifice and duty: 'His duty fearlessly and nobly done. Ever remembered'. Margaret Bligh selected a meaningful verse from Rudyard Kipling (which was abridged by the Commission to accord with the sixty-six letter limit) and asked that Tom Leigh's Australian birth and mustering of air gunner be acknowledged.[52] Mildred Williams chose no inscription for John's headstone. She did, however, elect to include reference to the land of her son's birth ('of New Zealand') and that he was a pilot. Ada Kierath did not select an epitaph or provide additional details. Albert Hake's spoke of Noela's abiding love and grief: 'Dearly loved and sadly missed by loving wife Noela'.

Noela joined the War Widows' Guild in 1979, thirty-five years after the death of her husband. The Guild provides mutual, sustaining support, as well as a shared sense of belonging to those who live with loss. While Noela drew emotional strength from her sisters in grief, there is no evidence to suggest that either she or the next of kin of the other Australians killed in the post-Great Escape reprisals gained solace from a mutual bereavement. Tom Leigh was not recognised as an Australian so no-one other than her immediate family and intimate circle knew that Margaret mourned. Nor was she listed officially as her brother's next of kin so she was denied RAF and squadron condolence. The Kierath family archive contains no note from Mildred Williams to Ada, and no Hakes, Kieraths or Williams are recorded as condolers in William Catanach's scrapbook. The Great Escape next of kin, however, were not entirely separate from those who shared a similar grief. Sir Arthur Street, Permanent Undersecretary of the British Air Ministry, whose son, Denys, was one of those killed, sent reproductions of a drawing of the prisoners' memorial to the Australian next of kin. Jadwiga Tobolska, widow of Paweł Tobolski who had also been shot in the reprisals, wrote to Noela 'as one sore heart to another to try to help you in

---

51 CWGC ADD 3/1/9 Prisoners of War, Treatment. Sagan: A.P. Sinkinson, Air Ministry to Squadron Leader E.C. Rideal, Officer in Charge Polish Detachment, MRES, 25 October 1948; Rideal to Air Ministry, 5 November 1948 and 30 November 1948. Two intact urns were not reinterred at Poznan. Those containing the ashes of Denys Street and Nils Fugelsang had earlier been removed from Sagan. Fugelsang's ashes were repatriated to Norway and Street's were interred in the Berlin 1939–1945 War Cemetery. Commonwealth War Graves Commission ADD 3/1/9 Prisoners of War, Treatment. Sagan.
52 Bligh FA: letters, Imperial War Graves Commission to Margaret Bligh, 21 July 1953 and 3 November 1953.

your sorrow ... & to offer my sympathy & friendship.'[53] Harry 'Wings' Day, who was 'on the same escape' as Reg Kierath, offered Ada sympathy and, despite no factual basis, assurance that 'your son knew nothing of the fate in store for him after capture until the actual act was carried out.'[54]

Safely back in Australia, former Stalag Luft III kriegie Charles Lark wrote to the Prisoner of War Relatives' Association. 'The recent escape and ruthless shooting ... left me deeply shocked.' Knowing his letter would be published, Lark wanted to assure as many people as possible that their loved ones were safe, despite the killings. 'I feel sure that the escape was confined to the North Compound. ... To other relatives with airmen in the North Compound I would like to suggest that the Germans will probably be loath to extend the atrocity because of the wide publicity given to it and their fear of reprisals.' Lark's heartfelt words of condolence indicated that he believed his friends had sacrificed their lives in the course of carrying out their air force duty. 'I should like to offer my deepest sympathy to the families of those who were shot whilst in the gallant and courageous performance of their duty.'[55]

Lark's endeavours appear altruistic, emanating from genuine friendship and concern, but his daughter, reflecting on the post-war anxiety he experienced as a consequence of captivity, identifies another potential motivating factor: 'Dad felt guilty that, first of all, he survived the plane crash, then he felt guilty leaving all his friends in prison camp because he was one of the first repatriations.'[56] 'I must admit there were some occasions when I found this very difficult', Lark conceded.[57] It was, however, an important undertaking. Lark, like other supportive family, friends and members of the community, had attempted to soothe troubled hearts and allay sorrow.

Those on the home front also composed the Great Escape deaths as sacrifices or acts of gallantry. It allowed them to both express and assuage their grief.[58] It also elevated the deaths to something above the ordinary. Group Captain Thomas White, former prisoner of the Ottomans and Jimmy Catanach's commanding officer at 1 Initial Training School, Somers, felt, with Catanach's death, 'almost as if I had lost a son myself'. White had been so impressed by Catanach when he met up with him again in England that he 'chose him as an outstanding type' and wrote about him in *Sky Saga*, his epic poem of Australian airmen, which had been published the year before Catanach's death.[59] White believed the young

---

53 Preen FA: Jadwiga Tobolska to Noela Hake, 3 June 1947.
54 Kierath FA: Wing Commander HMA Day to Ada Kierath, 6 July 1945.
55 NLA FERG/4550: *P.O.W.*, No. 29, 15 June 1944, C.R. Lark, 2 June 1944, 5.
56 AR: Jennifer Walsh, interview 29 April 2017.
57 Lark, *A Lark on the Wing*, 80.
58 *The Cost of War*, 72.
59 White, *Sky Saga: A Story of Empire Airmen*.

man's 'name and memory will long endure as among the noblest of those who gave their all.'[60] Friends of the Catanach family wrote of Jimmy's sacrifice in condolence letters and in memoriam notices. William Melville admitted to Ada Kierath that 'I cannot express how much the sacrifice which they have made has meant to me personally.'[61] Wings Day considered that Reg 'would face death as he had already faced [it] before – fearlessly and gallantly.'[62] The escapers' deaths were also publicly construed within the noble tradition of Christian sacrifice.[63] Alluding to the final line in John Gillespie Magee's 'High Flight' where the author-pilot 'Put out my hand, and touched the face of God', the RAF chaplain-in-chief at the Church of St Martin-in-the-Fields commemorative service, stated that, 'their sacrifice was touched by the finger of God.'[64]

Acknowledging that escape derived from air force duty, the Great Escapers were Mentioned in Despatches for 'distinguished service'. The official recognition validated their commitment to and fulfilment of duty as well as the kriegies' program of active disruption. Demonstrating that the British nation valued the 'sacrifice of the dead', Great Escape families – like every other war-bereaved family within the Commonwealth – were sent commemorative scrolls lauding a 'sacrifice' which had 'help[ed] to bring the peace and freedom for which he died.'[65] They also received letters from the King and Queen offering 'heartfelt sympathy' and praying 'that your country's gratitude for a life so nobly given in its service may bring you some measure of consolation'. William and Sybil Catanach framed their formal condolence from the King and Queen, Jimmy's Mentioned in Despatches certificate, and his squadron's next-of-kin letter. Those national, military, and regal expressions of sympathy publicly acknowledged duty and sacrifice. Those on display in the Catanach home ensured that no family member or visitor would ever forget what his father and stepmother saw as Jimmy's ultimate contribution. The Catanach tributes have been donated to the Shrine of Remembrance's archive so future generations can also acknowledge Jimmy's sacrifice in a place which publicly honours sacrifice.

*****

Family, friends, and community helped assuage grief, but they could not obliterate it. In 1986, when historian Jonathan Vance asked Noela Hake for assistance with his account of the Great Escape,[66] she still found thinking about Albert's death and rereading his letters, 'most upsetting even after all these

---

60 Quotes here and above from SOR JCC: 2013.CAT030, Scrapbook Two, Thomas W. White to Mr Catanach. 22 May 1944.
61 Kierath FA: Squadron Leader WM Melville to Ada Kierath, 20 June 1944.
62 Wing Commander HMA Day to Ada Kierath, 6 July 1945.
63 Alexander and Ariotti, 'Mourning the Dead of the Great Escape: POWs, Grief, and the Memorial Vault of Stalag Luft III'.
64 'Honour to Shot Airmen. Memorial Service in London', *The Times* (London), 21 June 1944, 2.
65 'sacrifice of the dead': Noakes, *Dying for the Nation*, 9; 'peace and freedom' from commemorative scroll.
66 Vance, *A Gallant Company*.

years.'⁶⁷ Noela never remarried; her love for her husband was unwavering. Yet he had wanted her to remarry. Shortly after embarking from Australia – 'on the road over' – Hake wrote to his brother-in-law, Ray Preen (Noela's sister's husband). 'If I don't come back, I want Noel' – his nickname for her – 'to marry again.' He charged Preen with 'quietly' making Noela understand that 'it was my wish. ... Noel is still young and a type that should be married. ... for such a girl to live out her life unmarried, would be a crime'. If Hake did not believe Preen could convince Noela to remarry, 'I would "turn on my heel" now and retrace every step. Hang the consequences. I'm prepared to sacrifice a lot, but not that much. One life is enough, not two.'⁶⁸

We can only assume that, because of his friendship for Hake, Preen told Noela of her husband's desire for her future. We do not know if Noela saw her life as a sacrifice to match Albert's, but she stayed true to him, and they were symbolically reunited on her death. Like her husband, she was cremated. Her ashes were interred in a garden setting at Canobolas Gardens Crematorium, Orange, reminiscent of the attractive landscape of the Great Escape graves at Old Garrison Cemetery, Poznań. Twin plaques commemorate the couple: Noela 'wife of Albert' and '"The Compass Maker"'. The inscription on Hake's plaque – 'loved husband of Noela' – echoes the words she chose for his headstone: 'Dearly loved ... loving wife Noela'. 'Lest we forget' responds to Hake's final plea in his last letter to her, written four days before the mass breakout, 'I hope I can justify your faith in me dearest one of these days. Remember me.'⁶⁹

---

67   Preen FA: Noela Hake, letter to Jonathan Vance, 30 September 1986.
68   Preen FA: Albert Hake to Ray [Preen], [undated c. September 1941].
69   Preen FA: Albert Hake to Noela Hake, 20 March 1944.

Headstones of the Australian Great Escapers: James Catanach, Albert Hake, John Williams, Reg Kierath, and Tom Leigh. Old Garrison Cemetery, Poznań, 27 March 2018. Courtesy of Marek Łazarz, director, Muzeum Obozów Jenieckich / POW Camps Museum.

The graves of those killed in the Great Escape reprisals, 23 September 2013. The collective grave, which includes Jimmy Catanach's headstone is at the rear. Albert Hake's headstone is in the centre of the back row, left. Courtesy of Max Preen.

Noela Hake is proudly wearing her Female Relatives' Badge in recognition of her husband's wartime contribution. After his death, she pinned on the Mothers' and Widows' Badge. Courtesy of the Preen family.

Noela's and Albert's commemorative plaques, Canobolas Gardens Crematorium, Orange. Courtesy of the Preen Family.

Chapter Fifteen:

RETRIBUTION

Three days after the memorial service at the Church of St Martin-in-the-Fields, the British Foreign Secretary, Anthony Eden, again spoke to the House. The narrative firmly shifted from sacrifice to atrocity.[1] Condemning the Stalag Luft III killings as 'an odious crime against the laws and conventions of war', Eden recorded the government's 'solemn protest against these cold-blooded acts of butchery'.[2] There was no justification for the 'Nazi Executions' of the airmen prisoners, Adelaide's *Advertiser* reported. The fact that the dead had been cremated led to only one conclusion: the airmen had been murdered.[3] Eden committed to collecting evidence against the perpetrators and tracking the 'foul criminals' down. 'When the war is over', he declared, 'they will be brought to exemplary justice'.[4] Echoing his words, William Catanach sent Eden a telegram expressing his appreciation 'of the serious consideration by the British Government to this odious crime'.[5] William, who had been collecting articles about the deaths to paste into a scrapbook which followed his son's life and death, had included one reporting Eden's speech to the House. Suggesting that he fully supported Eden's commitment to justice, William glued in another sub-captioned 'Mr Eden promises retribution'.[6]

RAF police personnel and members of the War Crimes Interrogation Unit did indeed track down perpetrators and gathered evidence for war crimes trials.[7] Three dealt with the Stalag Luft III crimes. Some aspects were covered in the 1945 Nuremberg trials where senior Nazi men, including Keitel and Göring, were tried. A secondary case dealing with the Stalag Luft III murders was conducted in Hamburg 28 August–6 November 1948. Arguably the most infamous of the Great Escape trials was that of July–September 1947 where eighteen members of the Gestapo and *Kriminalpolizei* were tried for their involvement. Though Australians had been killed, Australia did not participate. Britain prosecuted the cases on behalf of the allied airmen (and, in the Nuremberg trials, civilians).[8]

---

1 Alexander and Ariotti, 'Mourning the Dead of the Great Escape: POWs, Grief, and the Memorial Vault of Stalag Luft III'.
2 Jones, 'Nazi Atrocities against Allied Airmen', 545–46
3 'Nazi Execution of R.A.F. Prisoners. Mr Eden Brands Shooting as Murder', *Advertiser* (Adelaide, SA), 24 June 1944, 1.
4 'Shot Air Force Officers. An "Odious Crime". Mr Eden's Warming of Punishment', *The Times* (London), 24 June 1944, 4.
5 Cited in Walters, *The Real Great Escape*, 270
6 SOR JCC: 2013.CAT030, Scrapbook Two, unattributed clippings: 'Nazi Shooting of Prisoners. "Confession of an Odious Crime"', [*Age*, 24 June 1944, 1]; 'Gestapo murdered captive airmen. Mr Eden promises retribution'. [Not on Trove.]
7 AWM54 1010/6/132: Parts 1 and 2.
8 Jones, 'Nazi Atrocities against Allied Airmen', 543–565.

Australia sent one observer to the 1947 trial.⁹ While no Australian representative was present in 1948,¹⁰ the trials and their outcomes were well covered by the newspapers.¹¹ (One article linking Jimmy Catanach to the war crimes trial – 'Melbourne Pilot Victim. Big Escape: Nazi for Trial' was loosely inserted into his father's scrapbook.¹²)

Details of who killed who were not revealed: testimony relating to Catanach was presented to the court but there was nothing about the deaths of Hake, Williams, Kierath, or Leigh because investigators had failed to unearth specifics.¹³ Accordingly none of the Reichenberg Gestapo involved in the killings of Reg Kierath and John Williams were brought to account.¹⁴ Most of those involved in the deaths of Albert Hake and Tom Leigh and others held at Görlitz were not tried: many from Breslau Gestapo, including Walter Lux, were killed in action in the later stages of the war. The fates of some perpetrators are unknown, one died of natural causes, another perhaps committed suicide, and Wilhelm Scharpwinkel, still in Russian custody, is believed to have died shortly after the conclusion of the Hamburg trial. Richard Hänsel, the only one from Breslau to be tried, was acquitted.¹⁵

Most of those implicated in the death of Jimmy Catanach faced justice with the exception of Franz Schmidt who committed suicide beforehand. At Nuremberg, the International Military Tribunal's judgements confirmed that perpetrators could not turn to a defence based on 'following orders'.¹⁶ Despite this, that defence was used by the accused at the 1947 Stalag Luft III Trial. Again it failed.¹⁷ Accordingly, Johannes Post, Hans Kaehler, Oskar Schmidt, and Walter Jacobs were found guilty of murder and executed. Their drivers were sentenced to ten years imprisonment and Kiel Gestapo chief, Fritz Schmidt, was sentenced to two years.¹⁸ Jimmy's father, William, however, had died in April 1947 of a coronary thrombosis. Before his death by hanging, Hans Kaehler's sister, Elly, wrote to Sybil Catanach asking, 'is it your wish that my brother – who is honestly innocent – now must die?'¹⁹ The English translation is bad but the

---

9   NAA A2217 1401/83/P4 Part 2 Casualties – Shooting of Air Force Personnel at Stalag Luft III: Squadron Leader Keith M. Giles, RAAF Liaison Officer, No 3. MREU to RAAF Overseas Headquarters, 16 October 1947.
10 NAA A2908 C64A Stalag Luft III Case.
11 'Deaths of Airmen. Statement by Accused', *Sydney Morning Herald*, 8 July 1947, 3.'Killing of Airmen. Fourteen Nazis to be Hanged', *West Australian* (Perth), 5 September 1947, 14.
12 SOR JCC: 2013.CAT030, Scrapbook Two, unattributed clipping. [Not on Trove.]
13 NAA A2217 1401/83/P4 Part 2 [RAAF Overseas Headquarters, London] Casualties – Shooting of Air Force Personnel at Stalag Luft III, Judge Advocate General Press Handout to Air Ministry, 20 June 1947; letter, Air Ministry to RAAF Overseas Headquarters, 26 June 1947.
14 Walters, appendix 'The Murderers', 316–20.
15 Walters, appendix 'The Murderers', 316–20.
16 Baker, *Key Concepts in Military Ethics*, 88.
17 NAA A2217 1401/83/P4 Part 2 Casualties – Shooting of Air Force Personnel at Stalag Luft III: Squadron Leader Keith M. Miles, RAAF Liaison Officer, No 3. MREU to RAAF Overseas Headquarters, 16 October 1947.
18 Walters, appendix 'The Murderers', 316–20.
19 SOR JCC: SOR-SHR021, letter to Mrs Catanach from Elly Koester, 14 October 1947.

implication is that Elly hoped Sybil, who had married William Catanach just before Jimmy's eleventh birthday, would offer mercy to the man charged with her stepson's murder. But Sybil dearly loved the young man she had treated as a son.[20] She declined to intervene.

Despite so few individual determinations of guilt and punishment, Australian families were given the impression that those specifically involved in the deaths of their loved ones had been brought to justice. Six months after the guilty were hanged, Melville Langslow, the secretary of the Department of Air's Casualty Section, wrote to Noela advising that members of the Gestapo who had been tried 'for the unfortunate shooting of your husband and his comrades' had been found guilty. Fourteen were sentenced to death, she was told, and three to long terms of imprisonment. Langslow also informed Noela that the trial disclosed that Albert had died on 30 March 1944, not 25 March as she had been told originally. The Commonwealth War Graves Commission (formerly the IWGC), however, records it as 31 March 1944, the date of his cremation.[21] Jimmy Catanach's brother, Bill, received a similar letter; Jimmy's date of death was now 29 March.[22]

Even where fates of the perpetrators were known, no specific details were provided in official communications to Australian families. As such, it is possible that they had no real knowledge of what happened to their loved ones until the 1976 publication of Allen Andrews' *Exemplary Justice*, or when the younger generation dug through British and European archives searching for answers.[23] Andrews' account was too late for some: William Catanach, Ada Kierath, and Len and Mildred Williams had all died. A newspaper cutting of a book review by Tim Bowden is present in the Catanach papers but there is no evidence as to whether it was placed there by Sybil before her death in 1978 or by another family member. Whoever read it, however, discovered that Jimmy had been shot in the back in a field, with Johannes Post describing 'how he had taken pride in announcing to his victims', who he considered 'inhuman', what 'he was going to do' to them. Jimmy's name was underlined.[24]

Louise Williams, in her biography of her uncle John Williams, reveals nothing of her grandparents' reactions to the war crimes trial or verdict.[25] Sybil Catanach did not speak on the public record about her feelings about her stepson's death.

---

20 Refer 'In Memoriam' notices *Argus* (Melbourne), 25 March 1947, 2; 25 March 1948, 2; 29 March 1949, 9.
21 Preen FA: letter, Langslow to M.A [sic] Hake, 4 August 1948; <https://www.cwgc.org/find-records/find-war-dead/casualty-details/2194276/albert-horace-hake/>.
22 Referred to in SOR JCC: 2013.CAT0526, letter Vowell & A'Beckett Solicitors to W.A. Catanach, 10 August 1948.
23 Andrews, *Exemplary Justice*. John Williams' niece, Louise, and Reg Kierath's nephew, Peter, both conducted intensive archival research.
24 SOR JCC: Unattributed clipping, Bowden, 'Book of the Day. 'Reasons for being inhuman'.
25 Williams, *A True Story of the Great Escape*,

Perhaps, like her recently dead husband, she supported Anthony Eden's hunt for the perpetrators of such an 'odious crime'[26] and considered the hangings to be just retribution. Justice may have been patchy for the Australians but, even decades later, Jimmy Catanach's friend Alan Righetti was still 'delighted to know of the execution of all [the] Gestapo they could find.'[27]

---

26 Cited in Walters, *The Real Great Escape*, 270.
27 AR: Alan Righetti to Martin Jackson, email 6 November 2009.

PART FIVE: THE STRAINS OF CAPTIVITY

Chapter Sixteen:

FAITH

*S*imon McGrath faced death. Struggling to escape a plummeting, burning aircraft, 'my life, as we have heard many times before, passed before me. People and events of years gone by were graphically depicted. It was so real. My darling mother, father and family, all flashing before me. I knew my number was up.' A practising Methodist, *McGrath* recalled the engulfing flames, his terror, and 'my despairing call to <u>God</u> who, I hoped, would do something for me.'[1] Citing the old aphorism that there are no atheists in the trenches or in foxholes, it is often assumed that, during combat, men turn to God.[2] Specifically referring to Second World War airmen, S.P. MacKenzie notes that, given the odds of death in combat, 'it would be no surprise if there were as few atheists in cockpits as there were in foxholes.'[3] *McGrath*'s call to God, however, was not just a desperate act. He and others of genuine faith sought succour during their near-death combat experiences and in captivity. They were fortunate they could do so. 'Feeling closer to God' was an important coping mechanism for many prisoners of war.[4]

Religious practice was enshrined in air force law and, thus, firmly entrenched in air force culture.[5] An airman's religion was stamped on his identification disk. Airmen were required to attend church parade, and funerals were conducted in accordance with military protocol and traditional religious rites. Of course, culture or not, faith did not figure deeply in every kriegie's life. Commenting on the mundaneness of captivity, some wit 'pointed out that "Hebrews 13:8" admirably summed up this Kriegy life'[6] – i.e. 'Jesus Christ the same yesterday and today and forever.'[7] Fine paper from bibles was appropriated by the camp forgers. Map-makers used the transparent covers of hymn books for tracing paper. Richard Winn devoured the Bible and Koran from cover to cover: 'these books were so good', not because of their spiritual content, but 'because they took so long to read.'[8] 'God botherer' – a prisoner 'with a religious tendency' –

---

1 DVA NMX280688-01: personal statement, [undated, received 6 August 1993]. Original emphasis.
2 Keegan and Holmes, *Soldiers: A History of Men in Battle*, cited in Robinson, Chaplains at War, 3.
3 MacKenzie, *Flying Against Fate*, dust wrapper blurb.
4 Ursano and Rundell, 'The Prisoner of War', in Jones et al., *War Psychiatry*, 436;
5 *The King's Regulations* clauses 833–842, 332–337. The RAAF had adopted the RAF's *King's Regulations and Air Council Instructions* and former RAAF trainees in RAF squadrons were bound by them.
6 Arnel archive: Train, 'A Barbed-Wire World', 9 October 1942, 37.
7 Arnel archive: Train, 'A Barbed-Wire World', Appendix 23.
8 AAWFA: Winn 1508, 4 March 2004.

was considered an insult in Belaria Compound[9] and some men equated religion with mental instability.[10] Church services in camp other than at Christmas time were sparsely attended, frequented by some looking only to relieve boredom. Yet, many of the Australian airmen found that faith as well as religious practice helped alleviate the strains of wartime imprisonment. Perhaps those killed in the Great Escape reprisals turned to God in the moments before death. Albert Hake had 'great faith', his wife recalled.[11] Even those who did not believe in God, or thought little of religion, or whose faith was sorely tested, enjoyed the comfort and conviviality of religious-based events.

There were no air force chaplains in Stalag Luft III and chaplaincy roles were carried out by Army priests and ministers. Of the 754 Australian Army chaplains serving in the Second World War, thirty-seven were captured; three were in German captivity, including Reverend Douglas McConchie, the only Australian chaplain in Stalag Luft III.[12] According to John Dack, the 'padre', along with the doctor, was one of the two 'most important posts in the camp', and a number administered to the barbed-wire flock.[13] ('Chaplain' was the formal title for ministers of religion; 'padre' was the colloquial term. Both were used by the Australian airmen.) The chaplains catered to the faithful, conducting regular church services which provided comfort and maintained a connection to the shared faith of their loved ones. Services were performed on Sundays, special religious occasions, Armistice Day and, for the Australians and New Zealanders, on Anzac Day. Chaplains offered pastoral care, spiritual aid, and conducted funeral rites for prisoners who died in camp. Reverend Douglas Thompson, a Scottish Methodist army chaplain captured in North Africa, was 'greatly admired'.[14] Working with McConchie before the latter's repatriation, he established a 'church in camp' in East Compound, and recalled ministering to those who 'carried intolerable burdens' such as grief, despair, and challenges to their faith.[15] Jack Morschel recalled Thompson counselling those with psychological problems.[16]

The airmen demonstrated their faith in many ways. 'We are very lucky to be able to attend church services', wrote Anglican William Kloster, 'and I was especially grateful today, for this time a year ago I had the narrowest escape I ever want. ... I realise I have a great deal for which to thank God.'[17] George

---

9   Todd FA: Ken Todd, wartime log book, 12.
10 Arnel archive: Train, 'A Barbed-Wire World', 20 July 1944, 59.
11 Preen FA: Noela Hake, letter to Jonathan Vance, 12 December 1986.
12 Gladwin, *Captains of the Soul*, 101, 129, 160.
13 Dack, *So you Wanted Wings, Hey!*, 93.
14 Morschel, *A Lancaster's Participation in Normandy Invasion 1944*, 71.
15 Thompson, *Captives to Freedom*. 'Church in camp', 160, 'intolerable burden's', 162.
16 Morschel, *A Lancaster's Participation in Normandy Invasion 1944*, 71.
17 NLA FERG/4550: *P.O.W.*, No. 17, 15 June 1942, unattributed letter [William Kloster], 22 November 1942, 5.

Archer, an Anglican who was East Compound's church steward, often told his family about his attendance at church and friendly relationships with the chaplains. He also devoted many pages in his wartime log book to a series of religious studies. Much of Roy Nightingale's wartime poetry indicated a strong connection with God, as did Max Dunn's.[18] Alec Arnel, a member of the Churches of Christ who, at thirteen, 'gave my life to Christ' regularly prayed and called upon God's blessings.[19] He, and others, recalled memorised lines of scripture, hymns and psalms. Errol Green, who was deeply committed to a traditional form of Presbyterianism which particularly valued the psalms, carried his 'little book' – his Bible.[20] He gained strength from his favourite verse: 'My flesh and my heart may fail, but God is the Rock of my heart and my portion forever.'[21] Bruce Lumsden's strong belief and dedicated religious practice enabled him to cope with the trials of captivity, even from the earliest moments. Shortly after capture, while in the local holding cell with his crew, 'I had found an inner support in prayer … committing my case trustingly to a God whom I believed would see me through this ordeal.'[22] Lumsden's faith rarely wavered from that time and he shared its comfort with fellow prisoners. Not all were Christians, or as devout, yet many accepted the solace Lumsden's faith offered and the fellow-feeling it evoked.[23]

Guy Grey-Smith believed there was 'something spiritual about flying … You are alone in the sky, and you face your problems alone.'[24] While Grey-Smith acknowledged the transcendence of flight, he also demonstrated a traditional recognition of God, his blessings, and the expectation that he should give thanks in a prayer-like manner: 'God has been so good to me in giving me Helen as a wife. I beg of God that I may always appreciate the love that so dear a woman has borne to me.'[25] Two decades later, Grey-Smith asserted that captivity was the starting point of his reflection on Christianity and spirituality.[26] He read extensively in the camps, including *Memory Hold-the-Door* by religious philosopher and author John Buchan, and *The Screwtape Letters* by Christian convert and lay theologian C.S. Lewis. He copied inspirational passages which emphasised to him a sense of the divine, particularly in art. Through this, Grey-Smith gained a deep understanding of God-in-nature.[27] Inspired by Helen, a designer who sent him art books and

---

18 Nightingale FA: Nightingale, wartime log book, 48–49, 51; Dunn, *Poems of Norman Maxwell Dunn*.
19 Quote: AR: Arnel, interview 2 March 2017.
20 Green FA: Eva Green, letters to Errol Green, 9 December 1942.
21 Psalm 73:26 as cited by his daughter.
22 Lumsden FA: Bradbeer and Lumsden, 'The Complete Tour', Lumsden, letter 11 July 1988.
23 Lumsden FA: Bradbeer and Lumsden, 'The Complete Tour', Lumsden, letter 5 November 1988.
24 Hetherington, *Australian Painters*, 149.
25 AWM PR05675: Grey-Smith, diary, 19 July 1941.
26 Hetherington, *Australian Painters*, 149.
27 Gaynor, *Guy Grey-Smith*, 2.

supplies, Grey-Smith took up drawing and painting during his imprisonment and his spiritual sensibility infused his later artworks.[28]

Writing home about their religious practice assured loved ones that the airmen had not abandoned their faith. The kriegies, in turn, took comfort in knowing that their families were praying for them. Errol Green was heartened by the unwavering faith of his mother, Eva. Drawing on the language and imagery of their shared Presbyterianism, Eva included in her letters extracts from hymns and prayers. She frequently asked God to 'bless and keep' her son 'always'; recalled to Errol the 23rd psalm; and entreated him to 'keep on Trusting [God] and the time will pass.'[29] In her last letter before her sudden death, Eva promised that, 'We will pray for you always.'[30] Mildred Williams also signed off her letters with love and prayers for her son, John. In her final letter to him (which he did not receive), she requested that 'angels guard thee.'[31]

Not all men, however, enjoyed a deep, sustaining, consoling faith. While Alec Arnel outwardly continued to practise the religion of his youth, drew comfort from it during interrogation, and regularly prayed throughout captivity, he felt alienated from God.[32] Because he had enlisted in the air force despite his Christian-based pacifism, he believed he was not worthy of God's love and compassion. Arnel's correspondence with Margery, however, reveals little of this. In writing of a continuing religious practice, it seems he was assuring her of his faith as much as denying to himself the extent of his crisis. It was only in hindsight, as he grappled to regain his relationship with God after the war, that he fully understood the magnitude of the spiritual chasm.[33]

Alex Kerr more readily conceded his religious doubts. He admitted never being much of a churchgoer. Yet, as he struggled with pain after he had been shot down and wounded, and sure he 'had not very much longer to live', Kerr 'attempted to say the Lord's Prayer.'[34] He still believed in God but, as the years of captivity passed, he grew dissatisfied with orthodox Christianity. His tenuous hold on faith grew weaker. He decided to put religion 'on trial for a year or so' before giving up on it totally. Finally, he gave the chaplain 'a chance to defend his faith' to someone who was approaching disbelief. That defence of Christian tenets was 'not very spirited', and, at the conclusion of the interview, Kerr was left only with 'the padre's recommendation to follow whatever creed appealed to me.'[35] After five months as

---

28 Gaynor, *Guy Grey-Smith*, 14–15.
29 Green FA: Eva Green, letters to Errol Green 31 May 1942, 18 November and undated letter received 14 May 1943.
30 Green FA: Eva Green, letters to Errol Green, 9 December 1942. Eva died on 3 January 1943.
31 Williams, *A True Story of the Great Escape*, 4, 6.
32 AR: Arnel, interviews, 9 October 2014 and 29 October 2015.
33 AR: Arnel, interview, 2 March 2017.
34 Kerr, *Shot Down*, 51.
35 Kerr, *Shot Down* , 162.

a prisoner of war, Harry Train's faith was tested. Although he still attended church, he 'did not derive much comfort from the service I am afraid'. For some time he had felt 'very much a hypocrite in Church these days. Modern war and the part we play in it is hard to reconcile with the Christian spirit and since leaving Canada [where he trained] I have seen many "trespasses" impossible for me to forget or forgive in my heart'. Unlike Kerr, Train appears not to have sought counsel. Nor does his diary indicate any resurgence of faith.[36]

Paul Brickhill's faith waxed and waned over a lifetime. He had attended church as a boy and, while he told the German clerk he was an Anglican when his personal details were recorded on arriving at Stalag Luft III, he had already lost his faith in the wake of terrible events witnessed at war. He moved from atheism to agnosticism during captivity. Suffering great psychological, emotional, and marital turmoil during the post-war years, he attended lectures conducted by the Church Army in hopes of restoring his faith.[37] Subsequently, he embraced a form of non-Christian spirituality where he turned to a higher power during times of financial, marital, and psychological crises.[38] Although 'reared in the Church of England', an infrequent church goer, and bigoted against Catholics in his youth, *Oliver Henderson* converted to Catholicism during captivity. *Henderson*'s dramatic conversion may have offered solace as, after the war, he was anxious for his family to accept his new faith. While they did not discourage it, however, they failed to comprehend his radical turnabout. Indeed, his mother thought he must have been 'a bit mad'. By 1950, in the wake of escalating psychological disturbance arising from captivity, and lacking genuine familial support, he abandoned his faith.[39]

Eric Johnston faced great challenges. Nominally an Anglican, he was not an overly religious person. Indeed, Johnston's wife Evelyn recalled that he was inclined to lay an each way bet on God's existence. After he was betrayed to the Gestapo and thought he would be shot, Johnston, like so many others before and after, prayed that if God released him from his dire circumstance he would live a good life in return.[40] Johnston's retelling of the moment at Buchenwald concentration camp when he was struck by the utter hopelessness of his situation was almost a lament. 'When I got in that shower room, after we'd been stripped … and that guy got to work with those shears' hacking off their hair, 'oh my God … all the other blokes outside all stripped of everything … what the hell

---

36 Arnel archive: Train, 'A Barbed-Wire World', 18 and 25 October 1942, 31, 32.
37 NSW SA: NRS-13495-26-127-514/1962 Divorce papers Margaret Olive Brickhill – Paul Chester Jerome Brickhill 21-02-1962 to 20-07-1964, Margaret Olive Brickhill, maintenance petition, 4 May 1962.
38 Langsam, 'After the Crackup', *The Age*, 1 May 1982; Dando-Collins, *The Hero Maker*, 87 and 315; Wilcox, 'Paul Brickhill's War of Nerves', *State Library of New South Wales Magazine*, Winter 2012, 31.
39 DVA QMX034497-02: report from medical social worker, 3 November 1950.
40 AR: Evelyn Johnston, interview 18 October 2016.

have we got ourselves into here.'[41] Johnston's fellow crew member Keith Mills, an Anglican, 'was praying earnestly' in the concentration camp.[42] After their release, both Johnston and Mills recorded in their wartime log books the unattributed poem, 'Meditation', where the author mourned the loss of friends in combat. 'How many more are yet to fall beneath the reeking, smoking pall of war? I hate it.' By including the poem in their log books, Mills and Johnston imply that they identified with the poet who called out, 'Oh defend and help us, Lord, to speed [war's] end.'[43] They suggest that they had called on God to end their suffering at the hands of the Gestapo and in Buchenwald. Yet despite implying that he too had called on God, Johnston lost what little sense of religion he had, and placed his faith in the strong relationship with his crew. Their emotional bond sustained him throughout captivity.[44] Perhaps Keith Mills, too, lost his pre-war faith. His son suspects it may have been affected by his wartime experiences and his daughter recalls little if any of her father's religious practice. Either their mother or a friend took the children to church, not Mills.[45]

Others also lost their faith in the face of such terrible circumstances. Brought up as a high church Anglican, worship for Charles Lark was, according to his daughter, a family thing.[46] As a cub, scout, and rover throughout childhood and young adulthood, Lark was drawn more to the tenets of scout law than religion.[47] Even so, he maintained a connection with the faith of his childhood and youth, carrying a copy of the New Testament with him when he joined an operational squadron.[48] He left it behind when he flew and the physical separation from it when he was captured was symbolic of his separation in captivity from God and his childhood faith. While the testament was sent back to him after the war, his faith did not return. He could not reconcile himself to a God who would allow the devastation of a world conflict. Like Johnston, he put his faith in humanity.[49] By the end of the war, Cy Borsht, who had drifted from the Judaism of his childhood, had also 'experienced a complete loss of religion'. According to his daughter, he 'came back an atheist'. As with Johnston, the strong bonds of fraternity formed within Borsht's room, rather than God, supported him.[50]

*****

41 Johnston, in documentary, *Lost Airmen of Buchenwald*, 2011.
42 Keith Mills FA: Keith Mills to Phyllis Mills, 22 July 1945; AR: Jan Smith, email 26 March 2018.
43 Burgess RC: Keith Mills, wartime log book, 9; Johnston FA: Johnston, wartime log book, 33.
44 AR: Colin Johnston, email 9 September 2016; AR: Evelyn and Colin Johnston, interview 18 October 2016.
45 AR: Jan Smith, email 3 October 2019.
46 AR: Jennifer Walsh interview, 29 April 2017.
47 Lark, *A Lark on the Wing*, 13–18.
48 NAA A705, 166/24/597, Charles Lark.
49 AR: Jennifer Walsh interview, 29 April 2017.
50 AR: Jennifer Long, interview 28 January 2016.

Christmas is one of the central religious festivals in Christian liturgical calendars. It is firmly entrenched in western Christian-influenced societies and is at the heart of family life. Despite its liturgical importance, Christmas is a hybrid religious and social festival where Christian values are celebrated as much as (if not more than) the birth of Christ. Regardless of their degree of faith, the social rituals of Christmas brought solace, reinforced the strong fraternal ties of captivity, and reminded the kriegies of home and shared family traditions.[51] The Australian airmen sent Christmas cards to loved ones and strung up decorations. Bill Fordyce created annual Christmas menu cards for his friends.[52] James McCleery recorded Christmas recipes in his wartime log book and kept his 1944 Christmas menu – 'What a bash.'[53] When Bruce Lumsden had finished blending the mixture for his room's Christmas pudding, each man stirred the pudding and made a wish. None revealed his wish but, as Lumsden recalled decades later, 'you may be sure that the same wish came from every heart.'[54]

The Australian airmen revelled in the nostalgia, emotion and festivity of the occasion. They planned for it well in advance. 'Now preparing Xmas raisin wine. It's good stuff', Paul Brickhill told a friend in November 1943.[55] Concert programs such as Handel's *Messiah* and their own version of King's College, Cambridge's Festival of Nine Lessons and Carols were popular. Service sheets were printed and distributed to attendees; some kept them as mementoes. Church services held in each compound were well-attended by devout and once-a-year Christians alike. After participating in 'a very nice Carol Service' on Christmas Eve 1942, one group of friends 'drank our "home brew raisin wine", just enough to get pleasantly mellow'. 'Communion on Xmas morning' preceded 'a good breakfast – porridge, sausages, coffee, toast and marmalade'. A hearty dinner was followed by a nap, a supper buffet, some restorative ales and an evening visiting friends in other rooms, and entertaining guests in theirs.[56] Alec Arnel attended a special Christmas eve church service 'and sang again the old carols'. He described to his sweetheart, Margery Gray, how 'our minds wandered far away and nostalgia caused this Xmas to be the quietest most reflective I have ever known. Midnight found me thinking again of that other time four years ago.'[57] Keith Carmody's experience of his first and only Christmas in captivity had nothing of the spiritual about it. It offered a means to distract himself from depression after his June 1944 capture. Suffering mood swings which saw him

---

51 Rosenthal and Marshall, 'Generational Transmission of Family Ritual', 669 and 672.
52 Fordyce FA: Fordyce, wartime log book, 77, 79, 81, 83.
53 AWM PR88/160: McCleery, wartime log book, 70–71.
54 Lumsden FA: Bradbeer and Lumsden, 'The Complete Tour', Lumsden, letter 5 November 1988.
55 AWM PR03099: Brickhill to Del Fox, 27 November 1943.
56 All quotes: NLA FERG/4550: P.O.W., No. 16, 15 May 1943, unattributed letter, 31 December 1942, 14.
57 Arnel archive: Arnel to Margery Gray, [undated, c. Christmas 1944].

spend much time in his bunk, the forthcoming festivity provided genuine cheer. Enthused by the arrival of a Red Cross parcel, Carmody stayed up most of the night making '4 dozen cookies and two cakes'.[58]

Even some of the less devout maintained connections to religious traditions. The letters of Justin O'Byrne, who was raised and schooled as a Catholic, indicate that he only attended mass on special occasions, yet he prayed for the day he and his family would be reunited. He was also a member of the choir rehearsing the *Messiah*.[59] In a late-life interview, Graham Berry, who identified as Methodist, revealed that he believed God had been looking after him during operational service and captivity. While his faith was both a strength and a comfort, he did not always attend church in camp – it was optional – but 'I went several times, even just to sing the hymns'.[60]

*****

There were many agnostics and atheists in Stalag Luft III. For others, however, the rituals of faith, either as overt religious practice or appropriated as part of more secular celebrations, helped mitigate the challenges of captivity and maintain morale. More than that, collective enjoyment of religious-based events and rituals reinforced the airmen's fraternal cohesion and helped sustain them emotionally and psychologically. But in some cases, religion and rituals were not enough to stave off the 'kriegie blues'.[61]

---

58   Barker, *Keith Carmody*, 62.
59   O'Byrne FA: Justin O'Byrne to family, 10 January 1943, 6 February 1944.
60   AR: Berry, interview 7 June 2016.
61   Baines FA: Baines, wartime log book, 'Those Kriegie Blues', 95.

Chapter Seventeen:

ROUND THE BEND

Twenty-four-year-old Alec Arnel missed his sweetheart terribly. His spirits tumbled whenever mail call left him empty handed. One day, he returned to his room and picked up a pencil. Although he knew months would pass before Margery Gray would receive his letter, he poured out his heart. 'My darling. It is so long since I had any mail from you. I hope it starts coming through soon for it would be the thing to fight the "blues".'[1] Even penning a letter to the woman he hoped to marry helped alleviate his depression. 'I cannot imagine a more likely antidote' for the increasingly more 'frequent attacks of the "blues"' that had assailed him since arriving in Stalag Luft III.[2] When his first bundle of mail finally arrived six months after capture, Arnel was elated. 'I had the amazing good fortune of receiving nine letters – and what is more important five of them were from the girl with the laughing eyes.'[3]

Arnel was not the only one affected by the vagaries of mail delivery and captivity in general. Jock Bryce recognised a collective 'indefinable abnormality.'[4] Calton Younger likened his dispiritedness to 'melancholy.'[5] Huie Bowden referred to the "45 Blues' as he entered another year of imprisonment.[6] That prisoners of war suffered emotional and psychological disturbance was well-established. Swiss physician and official prison camp visitor, Adolf Vischer, had identified a 'neurosis' among Great War captives which he termed 'barbed-wire disease'. The syndrome was exacerbated by their captors' rules and restrictions, overcrowding, bland food of little variety, monotony, and segregation from women.[7] Such an abnormal existence influenced the 'mental processes' of the prisoner and was characterised by 'irritability, difficulty in concentrating, restlessness, failure of memory, moodiness, depression, and unpleasant dreams.'[8]

In Charles Lark's view, the effects of segregation from the 'outside world' for an indefinite time, 'surrounded by grim reminders that for some years they cannot live but must merely exist', had an 'inevitable mental effect'. In the months after his medical repatriation, while the memories of his experience

---

1 Arnel archive: Alec Arnel to Margery Gray, 15 September 1944.
2 Arnel archive: Alec Arnel to Margery Gray, 10 October 1944.
3 Arnel archive: Alec Arnel to Margery Gray, [undated, c. Christmas 1944].
4 Bryce FA: 'Jock Bryce's POW Diary 1942–1945', 86.
5 Younger, *No Flight From the Cage*, 67.
6 Bowden FA: 'Diary of Huie Bowden July 1944–May 1945', 'Bod after supper – '45 Blues', 2 January 1945, 58.
7 Vischer, *Barbed-Wire Disease*.
8 Vischer, *Barbed-Wire Disease*, introductory essay by Kinnier Wilson, 3.

were relatively fresh, Lark wrote of the 'many hardships, inconveniences and humiliations' the kriegies had to endure, making it difficult to attune themselves to their new life.[9] Despite bright letters to his family, George Archer's diary reveals that even after six weeks of captivity he still had not acclimatised.[10] 'I can't settle down. Hope to shortly', he asserted positively in his diary.[11] As they adjusted, the airmen were assailed by a variety of moods. Homesickness was prevalent. While they, perhaps, did not admit it at the time, some, like *Barry Bridges*, worried about 'ever seeing the war through', their 'ultimate fate', and that they were 'living on borrowed time'.[12] The result, as Alec Arnel recalled, was a constant state of tension.[13] They were 'filled with anxiety'.[14] Provoked by circumstances, they were on occasion 'cheesed off', 'browned off', or 'brassed off'.[15] Some had 'had it'.[16] Ill-treatment such as hours-long roll calls in snow or rain could bring on a 'harshness' of mood in even the most placid-tempered.[17] More often than not, *everything* about captivity impinged on their state of mind. 'There's always bloody something.'[18]

The kriegies' rich, ironic humour inspired colloquialisms for their off-kilter mental states. In their post-war recollections, Richard Winn and Doug Hutchinson spoke of men who had 'gone off their heads'.[19] Geoff Cornish recalled those who were 'a bit stir happy, a bit crazy'.[20] Paul Brickhill considered that '"wire-happy" was the polite name for it'[21] and 'Stalag Happy'[22] was another popular designation for their psychological state. The phrase the airmen favoured, however, used widely throughout German POW camps, was 'round the bend', an old British naval term with no precise or consistent meaning used equally to describe someone who was simply eccentric, or another poor chap who had gone mad.[23] Despite broad use, 'round the bend' also encompassed a range of prison-camp mental conditions. For Ken Todd it meant 'mental, flak happy'.[24] Earle Nelson defined it as 'mentally

---

9   NAA A705, 166/24/597 Lark: 'Special Leave for Returned Prisoners of War', 15 January 1944.
10 Archer FA: Archer, 1942 Diary, 11 September 1942.
11 Archer FA: Archer, 1942 Diary, 16 September 1942.
12 'seeing the war through': DVA MX167147-01: statement in support of a claim for medical treatment and pension, 29 June 1975. 'ultimate fate': DVA MX076290-01: appellant's letter, 5 October 1953. 'borrowed time': DVA NMX293081-01: lifestyle questionnaire, 27 April 1994.
13 AR: Arnel, interview 29 October 2015.
14 Lumsden FA: Bradbeer and Lumsden, 'The Complete Tour', Lumsden, letter 5 March 1987.
15 'cheesed off': Younger, *Get a Load of this*, [30]; 'browned off': AWM PR03099: Brickhill to Del Fox, 27 November 1943; 'brassed off': Barker, *Keith Carmody*, 60.
16 Preen FA: Albert Hake to Noela Hake, 28 March 1943; Archer FA: Archer, wartime log book, 119.
17 Lumsden FA: Bradbeer and Lumsden, 'The Complete Tour', Lumsden, letter 23 March 1989.
18 Johnston FA: Johnston, wartime log book, 42–43; Kerr archive: Alex Kerr, wartime log book, 12; AWM PR88/160: McCleery, wartime log book, 44–45.
19 AAWFA: Winn 1508, 4 March 2004; AAWFA: Hutchinson 0540, 17 June 2003.
20 AAWFA: Cornish 1388, 2 July 2004.
21 Brickhill, T*he Great Escape*, 127.
22 Makepeace, *Captives of War*, 160 and 'The Sharp End', '*Repatter*', No. 10, 27 August 1945.
23 Makepeace also indicates widespread popularity of 'round the bend': *Captives of War*, 160.
24 Todd FA: Ken Todd, wartime log book, 12.

unstable'.[25] Alex Kerr noted the term was used for those who 'talked to themselves', as well as others who had lost their mind, or hope.[26]

The preference for colloquialisms to describe their conditions is understandable given the social stigma attached to mental illness. Airmen, perhaps, had a more compelling reason. The fine line between legitimate flying fatigue and accompanying nervous strain, and the air force's disciplinary designation 'lack of moral fibre' – with its associated stain of cowardice, implication of failure to fulfil service duty, and sense of letting down their fellow crew members – perhaps saw some operational airmen and prisoners of war equating mental disturbances with LMF.[27] In their eyes, psychological imbalance was something to fear. It also ran counter to the perception of the air force's status as a physical and mental elite. The taint of mental illness also threatened their own conception of themselves as airmen. Not only was mental frailty seen as a feminised condition,[28] the Great War's shell-shocked veterans – those of their fathers' and uncles' generation – were humiliated, 'failed Anzacs'.[29]

There is some disagreement about when POWs started to demonstrate captivity-related psychological symptoms. While Adolf Vischer found that any man imprisoned for longer than six months could succumb to strain, British neurologist Samuel Kinnier Wilson stated that, after two or three years of captivity, some men 'sank into a settled melancholy which took the place of hope and cheerfulness'.[30] Before his medical repatriation, Stalag Luft III's Senior British Officer, Martin Massey, found that mental strain was particularly apparent in those who had been confined for more than two years.[31] In referring to the 'escape fever' of those who had been behind barbed wire for up to five years, Paul Brickhill alludes to the extreme distress and desire for freedom at all costs suffered by the long-term prisoners.[32]

In reality, however, anyone could succumb at any time, particularly those who had experienced battle wounds or bad treatment. Following two months of inhumane treatment at Buchenwald concentration camp, Robert Mills was treated for undernourishment and nervous strain within two months of arriving at Stalag Luft III.[33] No matter how busy they had kept themselves, they could still fall victim. A little over two years after his September 1940 capture,

---

25 Nelson, *If Winter Comes*, 56.
26 IWMSA: Kerr: 24826, 18 March 2003.
27 Borsht Archive: Borsht, 'A Life Well Lived', 16.
28 Karageorgos, 'The Bushman at War', 32.
29 Larsson, *Shattered Anzacs*, 159.
30 Vischer, *Barbed-Wire Disease*, 16 and 53. Quote: introductory essay by Kinnier Wilson, 9.
31 NAUK WO 32/10757: Matthews' report, 17 February 1944; Group Captain H.M. Massey to Swiss Legation, 23 February 1944, (Massey's covering letter to Matthews' report).
32 Brickhill, *The Great Escape*, 178.
33 Burgess RC: Robert Mills, wartime log book, 20.

Harold Bjelke-Petersen, who had worked on escape tunnels and provided physiotherapy services to his fellows, was confined to the sick quarters at Oflag XXI-B, Schubin with a nervous condition, and then in Stalag Luft III's lazaret with *asthénie* (general fatigue, depressive or feeble state) for almost three weeks in November–December 1944.[34]

Letters from home provided 'a perceptible lift in the atmosphere', both for the individual and the entire camp, Huie Bowden noted.[35] The mail gods did not always smile, but the airmen maintained high hopes. 'Had no news this month but should receive bundle any day', John Osborne told his family.[36] George Archer expected his third clothing parcel 'any time now', and, six weeks later, 'any day now', and 'any day now' a month after that.[37] Ronald Baines' moods were often linked to whether or not he had heard from his wife, Irene. They swung from elation at receiving a letter to desolation on days when he returned empty-handed from mail call.

Moods had other triggers. Huie Bowden and his friend Philip 'Snowy' Fussey from Yorkshire felt 'very low today' in April 1945 as 'the end of our imprisonment seems a long way off'. In such a situation, 'we find ourselves unable to maintain high spirits'.[38] Time started to lose meaning for Colin Phelps. It 'seems to drag in some ways, but in others I find it hard to realize that I've been down for over three months'.[39] Moods often fell as significant dates approached. 'TWO YEAR KRIEGIE and still here for some time by the look of things', wrote Baines.[40] Justin O'Byrne conceded that his hope to be with family at Christmas 'will have to be postponed'.[41] Guy Grey-Smith's pangs of homesickness became more acute as Helen's birthday drew near.[42] He experienced a prolonged low period over the summer of 1943 during which he variously 'felt very depressed and not so hot in any direction' as he fretted over his health and worried about Helen.[43] Grief was also a trigger. 'I hear of my dear brother's death – Now Keith has gone', wrote Grey-Smith. 'Words fail me when I try & describe this irrepairable loss.'[44]

As Ronald Baines implied when he described varying moods as the 'wavering graph of optimism and depression', emotional states were not fixed.[45] They altered

---

34 NAA A13950 POW identification card.
35 Bowden FA: 'Diary of Huie Bowden July 1944–May 1945', 15 October 1944, 20.
36 NAM JOC: John Osborne to family, 11 July 1943.
37 Archer FA: Archer, letters to family, 26 May, 11 July, and 12 August 1943.
38 Bowden FA: 'Diary of Huie Bowden July 1944–May 1945', 20 April 1945, 98.
39 MHRC CPA: Colin Phelps to parents, 7 May 1944.
40 Baines FA: Baines, wartime log book, 18 November 1944, 20. Original emphasis.
41 O'Byrne FA: Justin O'Byrne to family, 1 November 1942.
42 AWM PR05675: Grey-Smith, diary, 24 May 1941, 26 May 1943.
43 AWM PR05675: Grey-Smith, diary, 14 May 1943.
44 AWM PR05675: Grey-Smith, diary, 24 December 1942.
45 Baines FA: Baines, wartime log book, 5 July 1944, 15.

over time. Bill Fordyce's drawing of his deteriorating condition shows a decline from the smilingly confident high optimism of July 1942 – 'Yes! Will be home for Xmas' – to the total abject misery of March 1945 – 'I give up. They can do any damned thing.'[46] Moods could also be communal. 'Everybody feeling a bit depressed lately', Grey-Smith recorded in June 1943.[47] When optimism 'is dashed to the ground', particularly when tied to the course of the war, 'there remains a horrid atmosphere of depression', Doug Hutchinson confided to Lola.[48] 'I'm sure a lot of the chaps won't be able to stand the strain of another winter here', Baines wrote in September 1944. As well as 'the usual conditions, we are overcrowded & underfed, very little mail comes in [there are] no cigarette or personal parcels'. On top of all that, 'the fierce mental strain of studying and thinking of the war situation, which seems so good, but still so vague & indecisive', was wearing the kriegies down.[49]

Baines was writing about two types of strain: that arising from having to continually endure an untenable situation, and the gut-wrenching anxiety which derived from an anticipated threat. Both fear – a visceral response to an immediate hazard – and anxiety were accepted facts of operational flying. Rather than labelling the generalised state 'anxiety', it was at the time designated as persistent 'nervous strain'.[50] Such a condition, regardless of label, was also a fact of captivity but, while accepted, it was, as Baines indicated, no less difficult to bear.

As we have already seen, captive airmen experienced many assaults to their personal security. They never felt entirely safe, Alec Arnel recalled; fear was constant.[51] Albert Comber was threatened with shooting for resisting questioning in Italian camps.[52] Justin O'Byrne thought they would starve to death.[53] Some were caught in tunnel collapses, including *Marcus Myatt*. 'Two of us had to be dug out' of one, he recalled. While acknowledging 'our very debilitated state' the accident 'did not apparently cause additional physical injury'. Underplaying the psychological effect of the event (which had occurred at Oflag VI-B, Warburg), *Myatt* explained that it 'was a terribly depressing experience as one man had already died of asphyxiation'.[54] For some, the constant undercurrent of fear proved a factor in temporary or long-term mental distress.[55] The 'privations suffered' by the airmen led to a 'mental instability in the camp' which 'continuously occupied' Senior British Medical Officer George Matthews

---

46　Fordyce FA: Fordyce, wartime log book, title page.
47　AWM PR05675: Grey-Smith, diary, 12 June 1943.
48　Hutchinson FA: Doug Hutchinson to Lola Hutchinson, 7 October 1944.
49　Baines FA: Baines, wartime log book, 24 September 1944, 19.
50　Jones and Wessely, 'British Prisoners-of-War: From Resilience to Psychological Vulnerability', 172; Cochrane, 'Notes on the Psychology of Prisoners of War', 282–284. 'Nervous strain': Burgess RC: Robert Mills, wartime log book, 20.
51　AR: Arnel, interview 27 November 2014.
52　DVA MX078596-01: report from G.S.S. Consultant Psychiatrist to Dr E.A.K., 31 March 1989.
53　O'Byrne FA: O'Byrne, 'Nine o'clock above!'
54　DVA NCPX25587-01: supplementary letter of explanation to injuries, 18 July 1970 [1978].
55　DVA QMX148794-01; DVA MX078596-01; DVA MX247300-01; DVA NMSS04454-01; DVA NMX272113-01.

and his staff which included Roger Playoust of the Australian Army Medical Corps, and medical orderlies Geoff Cornish and Englishman Eric Stephenson.[56]

Poor food took its toll on mental health. So poor were their semi-starvation diets on occasion that many kriegies suffered malnutrition and deprivation-related symptoms, particularly in the latter stages of the war in prison camps, on the forced marches, and in the final months before liberation. (Later, many, including Paul Brickhill, suffered serious dental problems because of prolonged nutritional deprivation while in captivity.) While not recognised at the time, poor nutrition and lack of essential vitamins and minerals – especially Vitamin D – can aggravate depression and negative moods.[57] Lack of thiamine (Vitamin B1) results in neurological symptoms which include poor memory, irritability, sleep disturbance – all of which were considered symptomatic of confinement 'psychosis'.[58] Morale was high and airmen were buoyant during summer when they could play sport, spend time out-of-doors, or carry out escape work, but spirits fell as the cold snowy months set in. During the winter of 1943–44, George Matthews, reported that the camp was afflicted by 'a melancholic irritation for which there is no palliative', and, indeed, one man attributed Germany's 'extreme weather conditions' to his 'mental stress'.[59] As winter deepened, Keith Carmody spent more and more time 'in the pit' (his bunk) and, at the end of his sixth month in captivity, pencilled in his wartime log: '**UTTER PITS!!**'. By January 1945, he had diagnosed himself as suffering depression.[60]

Constant anxiety has physiological consequences. The relationship between gastrointestinal symptoms and anxiety has been long established, with both German and British researchers recognising the link.[61] 'Gastric neurosis' – a nervous upset involving the digestive system – was a common term at the time.[62] RAAF medical staff also clearly understood the connection as they reported on the presence or absence of 'dyspepsia' and 'nervous sequelae' in recently liberated airmen. While some gastrointestinal upsets such as indigestion and diarrhoea were related to infection, hunger, poor quality food, binge eating in times of Red Cross parcel glut (such as at Christmas time), and 'incorrect diet

---

56 NAUK WO 32/10757: Matthews' report, 17 February 1944. 'privations suffered': DVA QMX058112-02: medical history sheet, 29 September 1967. Both Cornish and Stephenson became doctors after the war.
57 Cuomo et al., 'Depression and Vitamin D Deficiency: Causality, Assessment, and Clinical Practice Implications', 606–614.
58 Gibbens, 'The Psychology and Psychopathology of the Prisoner-of-War', MD thesis, 4; Vischer, *Barbed-Wire Disease*, introductory essay by Kinnier Wilson, 3.
59 'melancholic irritation': NAUK WO 32/10757: Matthews' report, 17 February 1944; 'mental stress': DVA QMX076796-01: statement in support of a claim for medical treatment and pension, 18 July 1984.
60 Barker, *Keith Carmody*, 61–62. Original emphasis.
61 Farber and Micon, 'Gastric Neurosis in a Military Service', 343–361; Ackerknecht, 'The History of Psychosomatic Medicine', 17–24; Werden, 'Is it All in Your Mind? Gastrointestinal Problems, Anxiety and Depression', 113–118; Wang et al., 'Gastrointestinal problems in modern wars: clinical features and possible mechanisms'.
62 'Nerves of the Stomach', in 'Service Bureau: Health' column, *The Sun* (Sydney), 17 January 1937, 15; Farber and Micon, 'Gastric Neurosis in a Military Service', 343–361.

while a POW in Germany', some manifestations were, in fact, psychosomatic: they were caused or exacerbated by anxiety.[63]

Reports of Red Cross and Protecting Powers camp visits indicate that gastrointestinal symptoms were common.[64] The Australian airmen rarely admitted them in immediate post-war medical testimony yet Eric Stephenson recalled that, during his tenure as medical assistant in the Belaria sick quarters, 'vomiting diarrhoea' was one of the most common ailments.[65] Harold Bjelke-Petersen and Clive Hall each spent approximately a week in the sick quarters for gastric upsets.[66] Some like *Hubert Hunnicutt* did not recognise the significance of such symptoms at the time. He 'had diarrhoea immediately following capture and which continued for some time. I attributed this to drinking contaminated water'. Hindsight, however, provided clarity. 'In the light of my present knowledge', he wrote in 1986, 'I feel it could have been caused or contributed to by the "emotional stress" of capture'.[67]

'Have felt a bit queer in the stomach, after meals, during the last ten days', wrote Huie Bowden. 'Have vomited all my food three times before going to bed. Not sure of cause as onset appears rather sudden and not traceable to any particular food'.[68] Bowden's unexplained illness coincided with German successes in the Netherlands which he and his fellows had been following closely through *Wehrmacht* reports. Any strong German defence would seriously delay the end of the war and quash their dreams of 'home by Christmas'. Alec Arnel recalled the communal depression during the Battle of the Bulge.[69] It was an anxious time for Bowden and his fellows when 'now there seems no immediate prospect of the confounded war ever ending'. Compounding that, Bowden, whose family was living in Britain, was also disturbed to hear reports of V1 and V2 attacks.[70] Albert Comber, who suffered persistent indigestion throughout captivity, was diagnosed with 'anxiety state' in January 1946.[71] Given the general anxiety many airmen felt regarding their personal security, as well as widespread concerns that the escape organisation might be discovered, it would be no surprise if the majority of kriegie stomach complaints – including Bowden's and Comber's – had been brought on by worry. 'Round the bend', anxiety, and depression may have been constant factors in kriegie life, but the airmen did not simply put up with them. As best they could, they tried to manage their moods and psychological states.

---

63 Quote: DVA MX008152-01: final medical board, 26 February 1946.
64 NAUK WO 224/63A: Red Cross and Protecting Powers reports, 24–25 November 1944, General remarks, 12.
65 Stephenson, 'Experiences of a Prisoner of War', 32.
66 NAA A13950 POW identification cards: Harold 'Pete' Bjelke-Petersen, 73021; Clive Mayor Hall, 402002.
67 DVA MX045167-01: appeal against recognition of condition, [undated, c. June 1986].
68 Bowden FA: 'Diary of Huie Bowden July 1944–May 1945', 10 November 1944, 10.
69 AR: Arnel, interview 9 October 2014.
70 Bowden FA: 'Diary of Huie Bowden July 1944–May 1945', 11 November 1944, 28–29.
71 DVA MX078596-01. Tension: report from G.S.S. Consultant Psychiatrist to Dr E.A.K., 31 March 1989; 'anxiety state': diagnosis on admission to RAAF Convalescent Depot, 28 January 1946; persistent indigestion: final medical board, 26 June 1946.

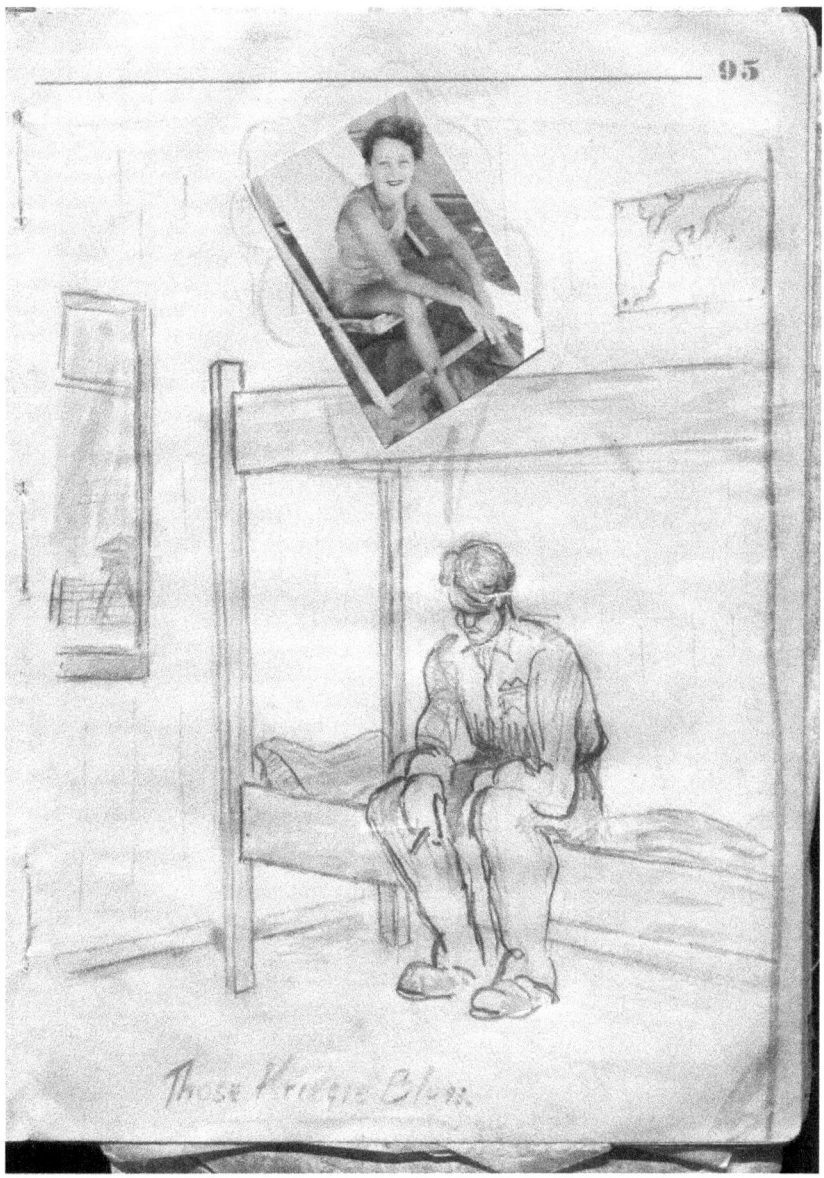

Separated from family and loved ones, kriegies often felt low, or even depressed. Some, like Ronald Baines, found a cure for 'Those Kriegie Blues,' by thinking of home and looking at photographs – rekindling memories of better times. Pencil, watercolour and photograph collage by Ronald Baines in his wartime log book. Courtesy of the Baines family.

Chapter Eighteen:

KEEPING MENTALLY STRONG

John Osborne was feeling fractious. One moment he had been ranging across desert skies as a Kittyhawk fighter pilot. The next he was a prisoner of war. 'Bad luck to finish up in such a place but it could be worse', he wrote to his family. 'The camp is fair, with Red Cross help the food should keep one alive.' Even after a few weeks, Osborne had not 'really settled down yet'. He was 'still quite restless' but was determined to make the most of his new situation. 'Am going to a lecture on "Horse Training" by the cove who trained Windsor Lad, it should be interesting', he declared. Osborne, like all of his fellows, soon realised he had to manage his kriegie life, low moods, and mental health. He also planned to study 'accountancy to fill in time'. Eight days later, he had 'almost settled down but it's no heaven'. He had 'read a few books but mainly walk all day round and round the compound'. Three months after his downing, Osborne appeared to have adjusted well. 'Now I feel almost permanent. ... Still attending economic lectures and find these instructive.' He played cards and devoured books on philosophy, science and religion. 'Three of us are interested in these subjects and have many lengthy discussions.' A former vocalist with 'The Harmoniques', a pre-war musical act, Osborne also joined East Compound's theatre crowd. Proving he had not lost his sense of humour, he told his family about his new roommate who was 'quite a decent cove but typically American – obligingly winning the war for us'.[1]

'One settles down' to captivity eventually, Alec Arnel observed,[2] but, as John Osborne discovered, it took time. Bereft of mail, Colin Phelps initially exhibited little interest in his new life. 'There are plenty of things to do, lots of opportunities to study almost any subject. But I'm afraid I haven't been able to settle down to do anything.'[3] The melancholic tone of Phelps' letters improved little over the months and he shunned all communal activity. With the welcome receipt of long-awaited mail almost seven months after capture, however, he immediately cheered up, looked to the future, and started involving himself in camp life:

> Hopes of the war being over by Christmas are very high. We had some new potatoes and a marrow out of our garden for supper tonight and made a

---

1   Narrative constructed from NAM JOC: John Osborne to family, 7 August 1942, 15 August 1942, and 13 October 1942, and photographs.
2   Arnel archive: Arnel to Mrs M. Gray 30 October 1944.
3   MHRC CPA: Colin Phelps to parents, 7 May 1944.

really marvellous meal. The 50 lap inter-block relay race was a great success, even if our block did finish a bad last. Weather is still warm and I do a lot of sunbathing.[4]

Adapting to kriegie life was not simply a matter of waiting for mail to arrive or time to pass. It required a concerted 'adjustment of mind'.[5] As such, like John Osborne, most airmen found ways to keep mentally strong. 'During my training, I was of a cheerful & happy disposition', *Martin Quinlan* attested. 'Later in POW camp in Germany', he did everything he could to 'maintain that attitude'.[6] Just recording his feelings allowed Huie Bowden to let off steam.[7] Smoking helped. 'My pipe (did I hear you exclaim in horror?) is very comforting these days when everything but tobacco is very scarce', Alec Arnel confessed to his sweetheart's mother.[8] *Arnold Hibbert* recalled of his time in Buchenwald concentration camp that cigarettes not only 'seemed to kill the hunger pains' but 'deaden[ed] the feeling of utter hopelessness and despair'.[9] Work of some sort dispelled even the blackest mood.[10] As we have seen, belief in God, the pastoral care of POW chaplains, and participation in the camp's spiritual communities also helped. So, too, as had eventually been the case for Colin Phelps, did close ties to loved ones, kriegie fraternity, and an appreciation of the lighter side of life, like the obliging American who regaled Osborne with his tales of martial success.

As they had often done, the kriegies turned to humour to ameliorate the worst effects of 'round the bend' or to stave it off. They produced comedic events on stage and off to raise spirits. For his first Christmas in captivity Alex Kerr and his fellows were transported by Stalag III-E, Kirchhain's festive entertainment. 'As every item was more or less humorous, even the most morbid of us soon forgot his troubles and worries and entered into the spirit of it with many a laugh and hearty handclap', Kerr recalled.[11] While at Stalag Luft I, Barth, Tony Gordon told his Aunt Mag that they 'had a big inter-compound boxing tournament last week'. 'One of our batmen, who has done some catch as catch can wrestling and I put on a burlesque of all-in wrestling. A great success. Had everyone in fits of laughter'.[12]

Humour (and an unknown wit) enshrined 'round the bend' in their poetry: 'Now I'm near the bloody end / Almost round the bloody bend / That's the general

---

4   MHRC CPA: Colin Phelps to parents, 13 August 1944.
5   Arnel archive: Arnel to Mrs M. Gray 30 October 1944.
6   DVA NMX188716-01: supporting statement, 25 January 1984.
7   Bowden FA: 'Diary of Huie Bowden July 1944–May 1945', 11 November 1944, 29.
8   Arnel archive: Arnel to Mrs M. Gray 30 October 1944.
9   DVA VMX118518-01: statement relating to smoking, 12 May 1997.
10 Bowden FA: 'Diary of Huie Bowden July 1944–May 1945', 5 April 1945, 90.
11 Kerr, *Shot Down*, 84.
12 Gordon FA: Gordon to Aunt Mag, 20 March 1942.

bloody trend / Bloody, Bloody, Bloody'. It enabled many to cock a snook at the 'Bloody times', the 'Bloody wire', the 'Bloody sawdust in the bread', the 'Bloody tea', and even the 'bloody mail'.[13] Underneath the kriegies' wry humour, however, was recognition that they could manage their own psychological health. Calton Younger reframed 'round the bend' into a less fearful, almost desirable 'blissful state, that kriegie nirvana' of mental escape in a series of captioned drawings entitled 'Stages in the life of a P.O.W'.[14] Laughter cheered even during the worst times, such as when those who had been imprisoned in Italy were crammed into cattle trucks with no water or sanitary facilities for the journey to Germany after the Italian armistice. Jock Bryce recalled the inspirational 'Yorkshireman who with the aid of two or three others made us almost sick with laughter ... we all began to enjoy ourselves and our spirits were soon high. The worst possible catastrophe had befallen us and life held only one thing – the enjoyment of humour'.[15]

Nostalgia soothed. 'At once the harshness of my mood was softened and the bitterness of my mind sweetened', recalled Bruce Lumsden, by thinking about his mother. 'The recollection of all her goodness and love through the years of my life ... gave me inexpressible comfort and relief.'[16] Lumsden also looked on the bright side. 'I had no shoes and I murmured. Then I saw a man who had no feet.'[17] Others valued the small things of their existence such as good, innovative meals prepared with care. Natural beauty brought joy. 'There is a tame yellowhammer that comes and eats seed we put out by the window', wrote Huie Bowden. 'Sometimes chaffinches come too, an occasional redstart and pied wagtail.'[18]

Speculation regarding release stirred the blood. Some hoped they would be 'Home for Christmas'.[19] Others, however, tempered optimism with a dose of clear-sighted reality. James McCleery's cynicism was unrestrained in his cartoon of a German censor scoffing at one kriegie's hopes for an imminent home-coming, 'This one says it won't be long now!'[20] Naturally ebullient Doug Hutchinson acknowledged to Lola that it was 'good to be positive, but need to exercise a little caution ... I rather think that most people are too optimistic.'[21]

The airmen learned to control their moods for their own sakes but also for collective harmony. Self-discipline when living in such close propinquity was

---

13 Unattributed poem, 'There's Always Bloody Something', Johnston FA: Johnston, wartime log book, 42–43; Kerr archive: Alex Kerr, wartime log book, 12; AWM PR88/160: McCleery, wartime log book, 44–45.
14 Younger, *Get a Load of this*, [30–31].
15 Bryce FA: 'Jock Bryce's POW Diary 1942–1945', 120.
16 Lumsden FA: Bradbeer and Lumsden, 'The Complete Tour', Lumsden, letter, 23 March 1989.
17 Lumsden FA: Lumsden, wartime notebook, unpaginated.
18 Bowden FA: 'Diary of Huie Bowden July 1944–May 1945', 15 October 1944, 5.
19 Johnston FA: Johnston, wartime log book, 19.
20 AWM PR88/160: McCleery, wartime log book, 31.
21 Hutchinson FA: Doug Hutchinson to Lola Hutchinson, 28 May 1944.

paramount.[22] Some did not allow themselves to become homesick or dispirited. 'No, I never got depressed', Hutchinson claimed. 'No, you learnt to accept things as they are.'[23] Although he was 'impatient, unreasonable', Huie Bowden knew he could 'get over that'.[24] As 1944 drew to a close, the 'main thought of most POWs these days is to keep a level head', Ronald Baines asserted.[25] The effects of this positive attitude were obvious. Alec Arnel's room was 'well-balanced even though some of them had been there a pretty long time, like Tony Gordon … He held it in, I think'. The fraternal bonds of roommates and close friends, more than anything, kept the 'kriegie blues' in check. 'Laughter came as a result of the people we were with, who jollied you out of' low moods, recalled Arnel. 'If I started talking in a depressed way amongst the group, I'd be quickly pulled into line.'[26]

George Matthews and his medical staff considered that monotony – or 'the atrophying stagnation of a prisoner of war's life', as Paul Brickhill and Conrad Norton referred to it[27] – was among the 'outstanding factors' which contributed to their charges' psychological instability.[28] Certainly, for those like Roy Nightingale who had wanted his war to be 'fast and furious', unrelenting ennui was a trial.[29] Their days were 'diluted by long periods of monotony, occasionally boredom, and once or twice by something approaching despair', wrote Jock Bryce.[30] They all seemed 'alike', Harry Train confided to his diary.[31] According to an unattributed poem entitled 'Prison Camp' which Baines copied into his wartime log book, the days 'stretch[ed] into weeks, the weeks to years', briefly alleviated by dreams, only to face 'hopeless hope' when morning's 'light returns.'[32]

The simplest way to defeat monotony was to do something. Anything. Physical and mental occupation deflected bodily and psychological pain. It also gave the airmen a sense of self-worth and purpose. 'I think it was very clear that those who focused on some activities, or activity, they were the people who stayed on top', Arnel recalled.[33] It was 'a matter of becoming involved', reflected Ron Mackenzie.[34] Accordingly, old stagers urged the new arrivals to keep busy

---

22 Younger, *No Flight From the Cage*, 66.
23 AAWFA: Hutchinson 0540, 17 June 2003.
24 Bowden FA: 'Diary of Huie Bowden July 1944–May 1945', 11 November 1944, 29.
25 Baines FA: Baines, wartime log book, 18 November 1944, 20.
26 AR: Arnel, interview 29 October 2015.
27 Brickhill and Norton, *Escape to Danger*, 113.
28 NAUK WO 32/10757: Matthews' report, 17 February 1944.
29 Nightingale FA: Nightingale, 'Wartime Records of Robert Roy Nightingale' [Prologue], [unpaginated].
30 Bryce FA: 'Jock Bryce's POW Diary 1942–1945', 143–145.
31 Arnel archive: Train, 'A Barbed-Wire World', 28 February 1943, 37.
32 Baines FA: Baines, wartime log book, 27.
33 AR: Arnel, interview 12 November 2015.
34 Mackenzie, *An Ordinary War 1940–1945*, 61.

and airmen threw themselves into camp life.[35] Each compound's 'X' organisation was perhaps the most important mechanism to keep active and engaged but 'there was always something going on to occupy your mind', Doug Hutchinson recalled.[36] 'I don't remember the boredom', Arnel told me. 'I believe that you're only bored if you allow yourself to be bored.' His trick was to 'focus on life' in the camp. 'It might just be noticing an ant and watching its performance or something like that. But certainly focus on life. Even looking up at the posten [sentry] up there and wondering how he's feeling. What he feels about his job.'[37]

Denied flying duties, Tim Mayo almost immediately accepted that, 'now I will have to find something else to do with my time.'[38] Education, particularly to gain qualifications for their future lives, was popular. As Max Dunn suggested in his February 1942 poem 'Let's Grow Up', 'Prepar[ing] ourselves for future years of work' was a clear 'Duty', which would undermine the enemy's belief in a German-won war as much as any overt or covert act of resistance.[39] As such, Dunn resumed his accounting studies.[40] Mayo asked his brother to send textbooks so he could study architecture.[41] Others borrowed educational material from the camp library, well-stocked courtesy of kriegie family and friends, the Red Cross, and other service organisations.

The performing arts such as singing, music, and theatrical pursuits were more than just boredom busters. They brought joy for those acting or participating behind the scenes or watching their fellows on the stage, provided an outlet for creative energy, and were significant contributions to Stalag Luft III's cultural life. They also often doubled as 'X' organisation diversions: concerts, productions and rehearsals covered up noise from digging. Albert Comber joined the theatre crowd designing and painting sets and scenery, produced a number of Australian one-act plays, and was in charge of make-up.[42] Hec Henry played flute in the classical orchestra's recitals, and his participation meant much to him and his camp companions – bringing relief from monotony, and an opportunity for imaginative escape.[43] Concerts, as well as Sunday afternoon musical interludes, where the Germans played classical music records over the loudspeaker system, allowed the airmen to enjoy mental privacy. 'A lot of people found their space there', Alec Arnel recalled.[44] He particularly found music transformative. 'I'd

---

35 Todd FA: Ken Todd, wartime log book, 11; Cousens (ed.), *The Log*, 68; Stephenson, 'Experiences of a Prisoner of War', 29; Winn, *A Fighter Pilot's Diary*,. 44, 47; Borsht Archive: Borsht, 'A Life Well Lived', 20; AR: Borsht, interview 28 January 2016.
36 AAWFA: Hutchinson 0540, 17 June 2003.
37 AR: Arnel, interview, 29 October 2015.
38 Mayo FA: Tim Mayo to parents, 30 May 1942.
39 Dunn, *Poems of Norman Maxwell Dunn*, 'Let's Grow Up', 7–8.
40 'Cheerful and Well', *Mudgee Guardian and North-Western Representative* (NSW), 28 July 1941, 2.
41 Mayo FA: Eric Mayo to parents, 3 June 1942 (quoting his brother Tim's first letter from captivity).
42 AWM: AH Comber, artist, letter 16 December 1990.
43 Details re Henry's flute here and above: AR: Graham Henry, email 6 December 2020.
44 AR: Arnel, interview 27 November 2014.

never listened to heavy music before. I had to get used to it but then I began to allow it to touch parts of me which I don't think had been touched before.' He 'just allowed it to work on me. Just relaxed with it'. He 'absorbed' it. Music became 'a form of release' from his worries, including how much he was missing his sweetheart, Margery. 'You'd sit there and how different you felt when you came out. That was quite a big thing.'[45]

During the long summer days, some gardened or went in for birdwatching. Paul Royle kept himself 'very engaged' by making model aeroplanes and yachts.[46] Guy Grey-Smith delved into art history and also 'found it was relaxing to draw and sketch and mess around with watercolours'.[47] He and other artistically-minded kriegies such as Albert Comber and Howard Taylor developed their art practice, experimenting with media, technique, and perspective.[48] They ran classes and, along with their students, displayed their creations in arts and crafts shows. Reinforcing the importance of creative and intellectual interests, one of the posters in Centre Compound's 1942 show was entitled, 'Keep your mind occupied'.[49] Stimulating pastimes such as debating, bridge, and chess which could take hours to play, were popular. So too was reading, and the camp library was well patronised. 'Books saved minds', recalled Ron Mackenzie, as it offered a chance to mentally range beyond the camp.[50]

Most of the airmen focused on physical fitness. It was good for their mental health and, perhaps, also managed built-up sexual tension. 'Walking around ... with one or more mates was excellent exercise, but also helped relieve frustrated and pent up feelings', Charles Lark wrote.[51] George Archer recalled that sport 'ke[pt] everyone happy'. The Germans encouraged it and the airmen benefited because they could 'enjoy fresh air and exercise. That was one of the things we endeavoured to do'.[52] Many, like Archer, played golf on the 9-hole course they had constructed themselves. Cricket and football were enthusiastically enjoyed but 'any sport you felt like' was on offer, recalled Len Netherway.[53] 'General feeling of pride all round at what we think was a colossal effort for kriegies' after one athletics event, recorded Huie Bowden.[54] An active life enabled the airmen to convince all at home that they were fit and well. Athletic pursuits could also be used to distract guards from escape attempts and the circuit around the

---

45 AR: Arnel, interview, 29 October 2015.
46 IWMSA Royle: 26605, 2 December 2012.
47 Hetherington, *Australian Painters*, 150. Quote: NLA HdBC: Guy Grey-Smith, 29 May 1965.
48 Whitehead, 'World War II Prisoner of War Visual Art', Honours thesis, 9, 11.
49 IBCCDA Hemsworth Collection: 'A15 NCO's Arts & Crafts Exhib. Stalag Luft 3. Aug 42'.
50 Mackenzie, *An Ordinary War 1940–1945*, 61.
51 Lark, *A Lark on the Wing*, 68.
52 George Archer interview, 'Grandstand', ABC Radio, [undated] April 1993.
53 Quote: AWM 54 779/3/129: 11 PDRC post-liberation debrief, Netherway.
54 Bowden FA: 'Diary of Huie Bowden July 1944–May 1945', 15 October 1944, 7.

compound was a safe place to discuss 'X' plans.[55] Importantly, sport ensured they were fit enough to escape or engage in escape-related work such as tunnelling.

The 'X' organisation, however, contributed to some men's psychological problems. A handful discovered they had claustrophobia. Albert Comber found underground work 'terrifying'; he, like others continually battled the 'panicky feeling that accompanied fears of being entrapped by a cave-in in the confined space'.[56] *Robin Sumner* traded-in tunnelling for other tasks because of his claustrophobia. No matter how important they were, he felt ashamed. Returning time and again to captivity in memory and nightmare, he experienced serious late-life anxieties. 'I am back in a POW camp somewhere in Europe', he explained. 'Sometimes I'll be taking part in an escape attempt under enemy fire the circumstances are always hopeless and consequently frightening. In another dream I'm being buried alive in a collapsing escape tunnel (equally hopeless and frightening).'[57] The tension of escape work may also have contributed to a collective mental strain.

Protecting Powers' delegates had visited Stalag Luft III a month before the Great Escape. They reported that George Matthews and his fellow medical staff were concerned about the airmen. 'An increasing number of prisoners and particularly among those who have been in captivity for a long time, (3 or 4 years) are gradually losing their peace of mind, becoming more and more mentally unbalanced.' 'Psychosis cases' were also increasing, perhaps emanating from fear of possible discovery after the '"blitz" campaign' to finish off tunnel 'Harry' began in early 1944.[58] The situation was 'extremely grave' and the 'effect on some of the prisoners may be a lasting one unless some serious steps [are] taken soon'. Rather than transfer the complex cases to a specialist facility, such as at Stalag VIII-B, Lamsdorf, because it 'might do more harm than good', several men were moved to the Belaria compound 'as this would secure a change of surroundings for them'; symptoms abated 'in a very small way'.[59]

The airmen did not know why some of their complement had been relocated. Perhaps reflecting the social stigma of mental illness, their medical and senior officers failed to tell them. The airmen, however, constructed their own narrative which reflected their continuing status as elite airmen on duty behind barbed wire. While some of them, Paul Brickhill recounted, 'were completely harmless types who had nothing to do with "X"', a group of critical operatives in the

---

55 Morschel, *A Lancaster's Participation in Normandy Invasion 1944*, 65.
56 DVA MX078596-01: report from G.S.S. Consultant Psychiatrist to Dr E.A.K., 31 March 1989.
57 DVA NMX272113-01: letter to Deputy Commissioner, DVA, 21 November 1996.
58 'Psychosis cases': NAUK WO 224/63A: Red Cross and Protecting Powers reports, 22–24 February 1944, Medical attention and sickness, 4–5; Brickhill and Norton, *Escape to Danger*, 275.
59 NAUK WO 224/63A: Red Cross and Protecting Powers reports, 22–24 February 1944, Medical attention and sickness, 4–5.

escape organisation and 'fairly important workers' numbered among the Belaria transfers.⁶⁰ Accordingly, the airmen inferred that the Germans were aware that something big was afoot, especially as it followed an upsurge in camp security checks.⁶¹ As time passed, the 'harmless types' were elided from the story to emphasise the purge's connection to escape work. Guy Walters, for example, states that all the Belaria transferees were part of the escape organisation.⁶² Shifting the focus from mental strain reinforced the airmen's wellness and near-universal escape narratives. There was no place for mental disturbance in their expressions of martial masculinity. Brickhill later reinforced this by omitting any reference to depression or psychological disturbance in *The Great Escape*.

Given the increase in escape work in the early months of 1944 and the collective strain of keeping it secret, it is likely that the advancing plans for the mass escape underpinned the medical staff's concerns. But how did the lead-up to the Great Escape affect the mental well-being of those preparing to escape? Reg Kierath's last letter to his mother indicates nothing other than his usual high spirits, tiredness of the domestic regime, and annoyance at the continual blaring of the camp loudspeaker. When he wrote 'I fear I shall be doing the goose step, or else going crazy in the near future', Ada Kierath would have held no doubts about her lively son's sanity. Nor would she have entertained any suspicion that he was planning to escape.⁶³

Albert Hake's correspondence, however, indicates a build-up of emotional turmoil. The tone of his earlier letters had been bright and positive, and despite his separation from Noela, he continued to look to the future: 'tomorrow is another day [where] one's spirit rises with the sun.'⁶⁴ Reading between the lines, Hake's letters indicate he was busy with his work for the 'X' organisation as a compass-maker, as well as his pride in it.⁶⁵ As time passed, Hake became more morose. He continually expressed how much he missed Noela, his desperation to return to her, his fears that she was in love with someone else, his regret about not starting a family, and his sense that he would be too old by the time he returned home.⁶⁶ He was shocked by the news of Mrs Rob's death. His sorrow was acute. Hake's mother, Lilian, had died when he was eighteen. Mrs Rob had stood in as 'a great friend and mother to me. Her kindness and understanding sympathy helped me through many a physical and mental hurt. I have lost my

---

60   Brickhill, *The Great Escape*, 157.
61   Brickhill and Norton, *Escape to Danger*, 280–281.
62   Walters, *The Real Great Escape*, 125.
63   Kierath FA: Reg Kierath to Ada Kierath, 6 March 1944.
64   Preen FA: Albert Hake to Noela Hake, 15 December 1943.
65   Preen FA: Albert Hake to Noela Hake, 31 October 1943.
66   Preen FA: Albert Hake to Noela Hake, 25 December 1943; 28 February 1944 (first letter).

adopted mother'.⁶⁷ Hake's psychological state was exacerbated by the breakup of his close-knit room when two of the members were transferred to Belaria. 'Well after almost two years together our old room (called "Anzac Cove") has finally split'.⁶⁸ These friends had meant much to Hake; he spent little time interacting with others, even fellow Australians, because, as Alan Righetti recalled, he was inside his room all day 'making his brilliant compasses' for the 'X' organisation.⁶⁹ 'The list of names on our door now contains five names under "Anzac Cove"', Hake told Noela, 'with the latters under the heading of "Some Other Cove"'.⁷⁰ By his third wedding anniversary – his second in captivity – Hake's mental state had deteriorated further. 'Living through that happy day of three years ago' appeared to galvanise him towards participation in the ill-fated escape attempt. 'Well damn it all I'll be home for our next anniversary darling', he wrote on 1 March 1944.⁷¹

*****

Protecting Powers' observers detected 'a great nervousness in the whole camp' in the weeks following the Great Escape. Both British and American senior officers were concerned 'about the deplorable effect' on 'the mental state of the prisoners' of the ensuing reprisals on the recaptured escapers.⁷² The situation did not improve. 'The state of mind of the prisoners at this Camp is, naturally, very bad as a result of the death of the 50 officers who were shot', observed the Protecting Powers' representatives after their 22 May 1944 inspection.⁷³ The prevailing feeling of 'insecurity felt by the prisoners of war', lingered.⁷⁴

Hubert Hunnicutt felt he had 'coped well' with all that he had endured: 'the stress of being a member of aircrew, our crash, the post-crash trauma and the P.O.W. Camps'. But 'on reflection', he conceded that he 'may have concealed an "anxiety state" without being conscious of it'.⁷⁵ That *Hunnicutt* could be unaware of his anxiety until decades later highlights Alec Arnel's belief that the Australian airmen 'were fairly tough. Fairly strong emotionally'.⁷⁶ Yet despite his work in the escape organisation and a supportive wife, great escaper Albert Hake was one who failed to cope with confinement and indefinite separation. Most, however, recognised that the blues were a temporary state. Wartime and post-war personal accounts demonstrate that, as well as enjoying the loving support

---

67 Preen FA: Albert Hake to Noela Hake, 30 January 1944.
68 Preen FA: Albert Hake to Noela Hake, 28 February 1944 (second letter).
69 AR: Alan Righetti, email 4 November 2013.
70 Preen FA: Albert Hake to Noela Hake, 28 February 1944 (second letter).
71 Preen FA: Albert Hake to Noela Hake, 1 March 1944.
72 NAUK WO 224/63A: Red Cross and Protecting Powers reports, 17–18 April 1944, General impression, 7.
73 NAUK WO 224/63A: Red Cross and Protecting Powers reports, 22 May 1944, Discipline, 5.
74 NAUK WO 224/63A: Red Cross and Protecting Powers reports, 17 July 1944, General impression, 7.
75 MX045167-01: appeal against determination, 19 August 1985.
76 AR: Arnel, interview 2 March 2017.

of family and kriegie brotherhood, the Australian airmen filled their hours of enforced leisure. Their strength of character, emotional maturity, resilience, and humour enabled the majority to effectively manage their own mental health. Consequently, 'morale was fairly high'.[77] 'We coped', recalled Paul Royle. 'We wouldn't be here if we didn't.'[78] But not all remained mentally strong. Not every airman's 'natural optimism', as Alex Kerr termed it, stopped them from 'going around the bend'.[79]

---

77 Stephenson, 'Experiences of a Prisoner of War', 29
78 IWMSA Royle: 26605, 2 December 2012.
79 IWMSA Kerr: 24826, 18 March 2003.

'I think that in any prison camp I've been in morale was high always', Bill Fordyce stated. The one-time Wellington pilot with 458 Squadron RAAF kept his spirits up by painting, drawing, and working on North Compound's gossipy *Scangriff* scandal sheet. NAA A13950.

Chapter Nineteen:

BARBED-WIRE SUICIDE

The stress of hugger-mugger lives with no end until the much hoped-for allied victory became too much for some. 'Imagine 1,500 young, educated, energetic men cramped up into close barbed wire confinement, repressed physically and mentally', Ronald Baines wrote in his wartime log book. 'Can you wonder that many cannot stand the strain – wire psychosis – complete mental breakdowns – attempted suicides.'[1] Those who suffered the most from confinement required care, and the airmen, as well as the camp medical staff, tried to ensure they received it.

Along with the chaplain, the doctor was the most important post in camp.[2] As well as providing practical medical care, Senior British Medical Officer George Matthews, working with the senior British and American officers, asked the Protecting Powers' delegates to lobby allied governments to repatriate all long-term captives to a neutral country. They also urged Stalag Luft III's first *kommandant*, von Lindeiner, and his successors, Erich Cordes and Werner Braune, for appropriate treatment of airmen who were suffering psychological disturbances. Their interest was not simply professional duty of care. They believed, as did aircrew and the armed services in general, that nervous problems were contagious.[3] On one occasion, Matthews and his medical staff were concerned that two men whom they considered 'mentally absolutely unbalanced' might 'constitute a danger to their comrades and that they might have a bad influence on the mental balance of several prisoners.'[4] Certainly, it was difficult living with those whose condition was serious, and, in some cases forbearance wore thin. Calton Younger recalled that, although 'the melancholic was pitiful, he was 'a burden, and sometimes a menace.'[5] The medicos lobbied for better care and were successful for a time in negotiating parole walks outside the camp.[6] Escorted outings relieved stress and Huie Bowden was one in East Compound who enjoyed a barefooted stroll and swim as well as the 'sense of having "been

---

1 Baines FA: Baines, wartime log book, 5 July 1944, 15.
2 Dack, *So you Wanted Wings, Hey!*, 93.
3 Mackenzie, *An Ordinary War 1940–1945*, 62; NAUK WO 224/63A: Red Cross and Protecting Powers reports, 22 and 23 March 1943. Medical attention and sickness, 4–5; Complaints, 6; Shephard, *A War of Nerves*, 286–287.
4 NAUK WO 224/63A: Red Cross and Protecting Powers reports, 22 and 23 March 1943. Medical attention and sickness, 4–5; Complaints, 6.
5 Younger, *No Flight From the Cage*, 116–117.
6 NAUK WO 224/63A: Red Cross and Protecting Powers reports, 22–24 February 1944, Medical attention and sickness, 4–5.

somewhere".[7] After the Great Escape, however, walks were curtailed in North Compound, as were inter-compound visits, sports, and entertainments.

Matthews also attempted to have severe cases moved to camps specialising in 'mental diseases'.[8] While he had some success later in the war, earlier efforts were often impeded by German suspicion that the medical staff encouraged men to fake symptoms.[9] There was some basis to that belief. Throughout the *Luftwaffe* camp system, airmen simulated physical and mental illness, hoping they would be medically repatriated. Fraser Falkiner, who had genuine wounds to his eyes, rubbed in irritants to make them worse.[10] Some coached others on what symptoms to display, including Digby Young, a medical student before joining the RAF.[11]

Shamming can be viewed in a number of ways. In one reading, would-be repatriates were simply trying to return to flying duties. In another, deceiving the Germans was a vital element of their active disruption. From yet another perspective, fakers were motivated purely by self-interest. Whatever their rationale, the practice was condoned.[12] This had serious consequences. It risked displacing genuine psychiatric cases from repatriation lists and created tension with disbelieving Germans. Certainly, von Lindeiner believed the camp's medical staff played their part in abetting malingerers; he questioned the medical expertise of Matthews and the Australian doctor, Roger Playoust. Two men under their care had been provisionally diagnosed with 'mental disorder', while another, who displayed 'hysteria-like' 'fits' and 'queer' behaviour, was thought to have succumbed to a 'prison psychosis'. As the latter was eventually declared 'mentally normal', the Germans accused the medical staff of inciting him to act in an 'abnormal and striking manner'. Von Lindeiner also suspected the medicos of over-treating their patients.[13] Professional relationships with von Lindeiner soured. 'There seems to be a certain kind of psychologic[al] tension between the British doctors and the Camp Commander', the Protecting Powers visitors reported. Playoust, in particular, bore the brunt of the *kommandant*'s ire and was transferred to another camp.[14]

---

7   Bowden FA: 'Diary of Huie Bowden July 1944–May 1945', 18 August 1944, 8–11.
8   NAUK WO 224/63A: Red Cross and Protecting Powers reports, 22 and 23 March 1943. Medical attention and sickness, 4–5; Complaints, 6.
9   NAUK WO 224/63A: Red Cross and Protecting Powers reports, 22 and 23 March 1943. Medical attention and sickness,. 4–5; Complaints, 5, 6 November 1944. Medical attention and sickness, 5.
10 AAWFA: Falkiner 0661, 17 March 2004.
11 MacKenzie, *The Colditz Myth*, 342; Calnan, Free as a Running Fox, 279.
12 Smith, *Wings Day*, 144–145.
13 NAUK WO 224/63A: Red Cross and Protecting Powers reports, 22 and 23 March 1943. Medical attention and sickness, 4.
14 NAUK WO 224/63A: Red Cross and Protecting Powers reports, 22 and 23 March 1943. Medical attention and sickness, 4, Report from The Senior British Officer [Kellett] Stalag Luft III to Major General Sir Richard Howard-Vyse KCMG, DSO, Chairman, Prisoner of War Department, British Red Cross Society, 25 August 1943. Appendix G: Health Report by Senior British Medical Officer Major G.B. Matthews, RAMC.

At least two men were disadvantaged by German scepticism. 'Both of them are being kept under observation and their condition seems to be improving.' Despite these promising signs, the 'two cases are, however, causing their companions in captivity much concern. They would very much like to see them relocated to a nursing home', the official visitors stated. Despite the medical staff's entreaties, a transfer was denied. 'The German authorities ... refuse to move the men since the attacks they have are neither very serious nor of frequent recurrence.'[15] As a consequence of this failure to recognise the frailty of the airmen's psychological states, one was later killed 'during an attempt – made during a fit of madness – to escape'. As the distressed airman tried 'to fly from the Infirmary' he became entangled in the barbed wire. The sentry, apparently not recognising him as a prisoner, shot him.[16]

As Matthews and his medical staff were unable to protect the serious cases, the airmen ultimately took responsibility for the mental health of their fellows. Old hands warned new arrivals of the dangers of going around the bend. Friends kept alert for symptoms of depression or behavioural changes and reported them to compound leaders. They worried about and cared for those who were not coping. Douglas McConchie, East Compound's Australian chaplain, had difficulty adjusting to the crowded, noisy life and lack of contact from home. He spent much time in his bunk, became more introspective, slept little, and soon required nursing by Reverend Douglas Thompson and a small group of close friends who 'brothered him lovingly'.[17]

Matthews feared 'permanent mental deterioration' in those who had been captive for three or four years.[18] Martin Massey also worried about the increase in 'mental and nervous cases', and recognised that many were reaching 'breaking point'.[19] Two weeks after Matthews and Massey formally stated to the Protecting Powers' visitors their opinions regarding the psychological well-being of their charges, Harry Train wrote in his diary that a kriegie was 'found unconscious in his bed in the East Camp with his wrists cut'. This was not Train's first mention of men who, in his words, failed to 'stick it out'.[20] Yet, contradicting the concern of Matthews, Massey, and Protecting Powers' visitors, as well as the evidence in Harry Train's diary entries, Eric Stephenson recalled that, in his experience as a medical orderly 'the number of those who were so afflicted that they

---

15   NAUK WO 224/63A: Red Cross and Protecting Powers reports, 2 February 1943. Infirmary, 5.
16   NAUK WO 224/63A: Red Cross and Protecting Powers reports, 26 July 1943. Medical attention, 4–5.
17   Thompson, *Captives to Freedom*, 157–158.
18   NAUK WO 32/10757: Matthews' report, 17 February 1944; NAUK WO 224/63A: Red Cross and Protecting Powers reports, 25–26 October 1943, 22–24 February 1944, Medical attention and sickness, 4.
19   Group Captain H.M. Massey to Swiss Legation, 23 February 1944, (Massey's covering letter to Matthews' report).
20   Arnel archive: Train, 'A Barbed-Wire World', 8 March 1944, 50.

stayed in their bunks all day could be counted on the fingers of two hands.'[21] Stephenson remembered only three psychiatric cases in both the Belaria and North Compound sick quarters.[22] Paul Royle recalled, 'one chap ... only one out of thousands.'[23] It seems that in minimising the extent of serious cases, Royle and Stephenson were reinforcing the airmen's carefully constructed narrative of wellness which could not accommodate the psychologically disturbed.

Although troubling for some given their living conditions, suicides – or 'around the bend efforts' as they were dubbed – were not unexpected.[24] What Ronald Baines discovered from witnessing those who could not cope has been well-documented in post-war research: anxiety can precipitate suicide and many who took their own lives had been suffering mental illness.[25] Despite Baines' contemporary recognition that some airmen failed to bear the strain, Sydney 'Syd' Wickham recalled in his memoir that he was 'surprised to learn that ... a Kriegie had committed suicide.'[26] Wickham's astonishment may have arisen from the fact that prisoner suicides throughout the German camp system were rare;[27] even where cases were concentrated in special hospitals their existence appears to have been underplayed.[28] In 'purposely [leaving] a person's name out' of his memoir to 'save them or their relatives undue embarrassment', however, Wickham suggests that his astonishment derives from a still lingering (in 2000) social and religious stigma attached to suicide.[29]

None of the Australian airmen took their own lives during captivity. The survivors honoured as fallen servicemen the few who did – they had lost the barbed-wire battle. Many airmen were empathetic to the plight of those who failed to cope. Reacting against the noise, stench, and almost animalistic behaviour in crowded confinement, Ron Mackenzie for a brief moment had an inkling of why some men took their own lives.[30] Recognising the stigma associated with mental illness, the airmen drew on what author Frederic Manning termed their 'inalienable sympathy of man for man' to protect their fellows' long-term reputations. While Harry Train appeared to lack compassion for those who could not 'stick it out' and included their names in his original camp diary, he omitted them from the copy he distributed to family and friends.[31] Others obscured identities through

---

21 Stephenson, *Three Passions and a Lucky Penny*, 50.
22 Stephenson, 'Experiences of a Prisoner of War', 31.
23 IWMSA Royle: 26605, 2 December 2012.
24 Arnel archive: Train, 'A Barbed-Wire World', 26 September 1942, 29.
25 Barraclough et al., 'A Hundred Cases of Suicide: Clinical Aspects', 355; Rozanov and Carli, 'Suicide Among War Veterans', 2513.
26 Wickham, *We Wore Blue*, 162.
27 Makepeace, *Captives of War*, 3, 178–179.
28 Gibbens, 'The Psychology and Psychopathology of the Prisoner-of-War', MD thesis, 35, 70, 75 (table).
29 Wickham, *We Wore Blue*, 9.
30 Mackenzie, *An Ordinary War 1940–1945*, 47.
31 AWM PR84/139: Train, Henry Roland, diary; Arnel archive: Train, 'A Barbed-Wire World'. Quote from 'A Barbed-Wire World', 8 March 1944, 50.

misspelling, attributing a *nom de guerre*, or by simply not recording their names. Perhaps like Royle and Stephenson and even Wickham, they too were consciously reinforcing the airmen's fit and well narrative.

To those who had learned to cope with the strains of captivity, suicide was calamitous. Although former medical orderly Geoff Cornish recalled encountering only a handful of psychiatric cases, he found the lingering memories of suicide and his powerlessness in the face of them difficult to confront. 'There was, I think, at least two that I know of suicides where the boys just ignored the warning wire, straight up to the main wire and started climbing over it, and of course they were shot, machine gunned', he remembered. 'We weren't allowed to go and help them or anything. They just died there and then. That was horrible to see. I don't want to dwell on that one, it was awful.'[32] Even as they cared for their fellows in extremis the airmen, like Cornish, were unsettled by suicidal intent, their own failure to prevent it, and the sense that, but for 'the grace of God', they could have suffered the same fate. Perhaps because of their discomfiture – and contradicting their narrative of wellness – the few suicides multiplied in some ex-kriegie memories. 'Many prisoners could not stand the strain and "wire fever" was common', *Sean Hanrahan* asserted. 'Many committed virtual suicide by deliberately walking into the wire to be shot.'[33] John Dack, who was captured in late October 1944, three months before Stalag Luft III's evacuation, implied an acute prevalence of mental imbalance when he recalled 'the never-ending occurrence of "Going-round-the-bend".'[34]

For Richard Winn, not committing suicide, no matter how difficult his situation, was a considered choice. Disturbed by one man who was shot running at the wire, he 'decided I would not do this.'[35] Like Winn, the majority of the Australian airmen demonstrated throughout captivity an ingrained personal and collective resilience.[36] They cared as best they could for those of their brothers-in-captivity who had succumbed to the strains. That resilience which made life bearable and 'round the bend' manageable, however, was further tested during one of the most challenging periods of captivity: the forced marches.

---

32 AAWFA: Cornish 1388, 2 July 2004.
33 DVA NCX065122-02: personal statement, 17 January 1980.
34 Dack, *So you Wanted Wings, Hey!*, 93.
35 Winn, *A Fighter Pilot's Diary*, 46.
36 AR: Arnel, interview 2 March 2017.

PART SIX: WAR'S END

Chapter Twenty:

FORCED MARCHES

A 'horrible feeling of suppressed excitement' prevailed as the Red Army pushed forward in late January 1945. Everyone was on edge, wrote Ronald Baines. 'Sagan is only about 100 miles from the Eastern front; we're all wondering what our position may develop into.' Would they be 'dragged into Germany?', he asked. Would they be 'taken over by the Russians?' Would they have to defend themselves? 'We may see a bit of action but I'm afraid a few lives will be lost.' Despite the Klim Klub's clandestine preparations for a last ditch defence, including his own lessons with an ex-paratrooper,[1] Baines knew that 'we're unable to do much for ourselves.'[2]

As the Soviets advanced from the east bringing fear and concern to all prisoners of war, Germany evacuated many of its camps westward, including Stalag Luft III. The NCOs, who had left in mid-1943 for Stalag Luft VI, Heydekrug, were relocated to Thorn briefly in July 1944. They then moved to Stalag 357, Fallingbostel the following month, and were emptied out of that camp in early April 1945. This mass exodus from Germany's camps has been referred to by participants and historians as the 'forced march', the 'long march', or simply, 'the march'. This implies that the entire trek was on foot, but that was not the case for everyone. Some travelled by foot, some were also crammed into cattle trucks; some embarked on multiple marches weeks or months apart. Whether on foot or not, many Australian airmen considered their inhumane treatment – forced to walk in the snow, lack of food, water, and medical facilities, transport in cattle trucks, inadequate shelter, and brutality – to be war crimes.

Stalag Luft III's kriegies were given little notice to exit the camp but made time by 'holding up proceedings as long as we could', Ken Carson proudly declared.[3] Leaving behind most of their personal belongings, some fashioned rucksacks. Others constructed sledges. Carson and his roommates commandeered their communal table, 'turned it upside down and broke up the beds to get timber for the sledge runner. We then tore the room to pieces to get nails and timber which like everything else was verboten to kriegies'. Carson and his friends had no qualms about destroying their room. 'If we damaged any furniture or parts of the buildings the goons could always get us on a sabotage charge', he joked to his

---

1   Unless otherwise cited, all quotes from Baines FA: Baines, 'Shot Down', 12. 100 miles is equivalent to 161 kilometres.
2   Baines, wartime log book, 25 January 1945, 22.
3   Carson FA: Ken Carson to mother and sister, 10 May 1945 (first letter).

family. 'We finished the sledge, tore up sheets and blankets for the harness' and then piled their possessions on to it.[4] 'It was 30 degrees below zero,' Alan Righetti recalled, 'and we were loaded down with everything we could carry for warmth and food.'[5] Huie Bowden did not make a sledge. 'I carried very little and regretted it later when we were hungry.'[6] The kriegies left 'the camp in a terrific shambles'. They also set one block on fire.[7] The airmen continued to make life difficult for their German guards. 'We were a "bolshy" crowd and made our own slow pace, hoping the British army would catch us up,' asserted Carson.[8] 'We were very resistant,' wrote Roy Nightingale.[9] Despite their disruptive efforts, the marches were for some, like Nightingale, the 'worst experiences of the war.'[10] 'It was no picnic trekking through the snow carrying on our backs everything we needed,' Allan Mulligan told his mother, Eulalie.[11] 'Survival was on our mind all the time,' recalled Alec Arnel.[12]

The airmen slogged for days through the snow and, as it thawed, mud and slush. There was 'no march discipline'. Rather, as Huie Bowden recorded, simply 'a long straggling bunch of sledges and men tramping slowly about 3 kilometres to the hour, along frozen roads.'[13] Some of the makeshift contraptions fell apart, or would not run through the thaw. Larger items which could not be carried were left behind. Albert Comber discarded his artworks. 'It was a matter of survival – I dropped the paintings in the snow beside the road, relieved to be rid of some of the load, fearful that even so we'd never make it home alive.'[14] Bill Fordyce's larger drawings, however, were saved. Before the mass exodus, Tony Gordon had fashioned a metal tube out of food tins to protect them.[15] Doug Hutchinson kept safe the packet of letters from Lola. Errol Green's from his mother also survived, and many men, including Fordyce, carefully preserved their wartime log books to ensure a permanent record of their captivity. Hec Henry secured his silver flute in a sledge. He did not retain the instrument that had meant so much to his peace of mind in camp, however. He sold it soon after arriving in Australia so he could send food parcels back to his wife, Edith, in Bournemouth. Selling it was a wrench, but he did not regret his altruistic act for the sake of his wife.[16]

---

4   Carson FA: Ken Carson to mother and sister, 10 May 1945 (first letter).
5   AR: Alan Righetti, email 3 February 2014.
6   Bowden FA: 'Diary of Huie Bowden July 1944–May 1945,' 'The Move from Sagan,' 69
7   Carson FA: Ken Carson to mother and sister, 10 May 1945 (first letter).
8   Carson FA: Ken Carson to mother and sister, 10 May 1945 (first letter) and 24 May 1945 (first letter).
9   Nightingale FA: Nightingale, 'Wartime Records of Robert Roy Nightingale' [Part I], 122.
10 Nightingale FA: Nightingale, 'Wartime Records of Robert Roy Nightingale' [Part I], [Prologue], [unpaginated].
11 'Bride Flew to Meet Freed P.O.W Husband,' *The Sun* (Sydney), 1 July 1945, 10.
12 AR: Arnel, interview, 23 June 2016.
13 Bowden FA: 'Diary of Huie Bowden July 1944–May 1945,' 'The Move from Sagan,' 70.
14 AWM, AH Comber, artist, letter 16 December 1990.
15 AR: Drew Gordon, email 28 March 2020.
16 Details re Henry's flute here and above: AR: Graham Henry, email 6 December 2020.

They dossed down where they could, often in damp fields or 'barns along with the cattle and horses', Wesley Betts recorded.[17] At Halbau, about 20 kilometres from Sagan, George Archer and Huie Bowden were two of the fortunate 'billeted in RC church. Very cold and feet wet. Slept on pew near altar.'[18] It was perhaps one of their more comfortable resting places. The Germans provide no food for the journey. 'We were very hungry but forced to ration ourselves severely', recorded Bowden.[19] To supplement what they carried, they bought, traded, or scrounged supplies from civilians as they passed through farms and villages. But it was never enough; some was even unfit for human consumption. They endured extreme hunger, bouts of dysentery, and lost weight. They became bodily and mentally debilitated. 'During that forced march', Ronald Baines wrote days later, 'I knew what it was like to be physically exhausted and practically down to begging food; bitterly cold, morale zero.'[20] Bowden, however, tried to lift his spirits by looking on the bright side: with 'food and one's feet OK ... marching is a pleasure.'[21]

Some stole. 'Two or three men would go to the front door and make a fuss and half a dozen would go around the back and burgle the house. ... we did it very successfully', recalled Bill Fordyce.[22] Ken Carson willingly admitted to his mother and sister that 'all kriegies are expert thieves and we stole when and where we could'. He could barely contain his pride: 'in fact we were a most unscrupulous crowd.'[23] While theft reflected badly on individuals it sprang, as Justin O'Byrne recognised, from the 'innate thing in every human being to survive.'[24] However, theft was perhaps not always necessary. John Lietke was 'surprised at the decent treatment meted out to us by German civilians (especially women) who all seemed sympathetic and willing to give a little food and invariably a drink to the POWs.'[25] Others also observed the generosity of German civilians and noted the ample opportunities to barter, while Fordyce himself recorded that 'trading flourishes' on the march.[26] Fordyce's and Carson's responses reveal that, for some, there was more than just the survival instinct at play. In explaining their behaviour, they betrayed an element of pride in their ingenuity and ability to live off the land, even at the expense of civilians suffering privation in the dying days of Germany's war.

---

17 NAA A9300, Betts W H, war crimes questionnaire.
18 Archer FA: Archer, wartime log book, 28 January 1945, 124.
19 Bowden FA: 'Diary of Huie Bowden July 1944–May 1945', 'The Move from Sagan', 71.
20 Baines FA: Baines, wartime log book, 8 February 1945, 22.
21 Bowden FA: 'Diary of Huie Bowden July 1944–May 1945', 31 January 1945, 78.
22 AAWFA: Fordyce 0523, 19 June 2003.
23 Carson FA: Ken Carson to mother and sister, 10 May 1945 (third letter).
24 Justin O'Byrne, quoted by Anne O'Byrne, AR: Anne O'Byrne, interview 26 May 2016.
25 AWM 54 779/3/129: 11 PDRC post-liberation debrief, Lietke.
26 Fordyce FA: Fordyce, wartime log book, 132.

Collective altruism suffered because of such individualism; as well as stealing from civilians, some stole from their fellows.[27] Yet, despite the survival instinct provoking bitter, violent, and selfish responses during the forced marches, altruistic fraternity came to the fore. Decades later, one man wrote to Justin O'Byrne's widow, Anne, telling her how O'Byrne never left his side during that time. He told her how O'Byrne 'kept him walking by talking and keeping up his will to continue'. The former kriegie attributed his survival to the force of O'Byrne's personality but his innate compassion is apparent.[28] Alec Arnel was grateful for his roommates' strong bonds. When his strength failed on the march and he could no longer carry his shoulder pack, Hugh Lambie told him to throw it onto the makeshift sledge constructed by his roommates. Arnel had earlier rejected the offer, believing he could fare well enough trekking by himself with a hastily fashioned pack. 'It was a bit of a come down', Arnel admitted, when faced with true altruistic friendship.[29] *Rodney Patton*'s life was saved by his friends. Near to collapse, Eric Johnston and Keith Mills, who, like *Patton*, had survived Buchenwald concentration camp, stood on either side and forced him to walk.[30] Mirroring that act, and the tender ministrations of those caring for comrades near death in Japanese prison camps, Tony Gordon carried and hand-fed a friend in extremis.[31]

The Senior British Officer had issued orders not to escape during the march. Despite this and threats by the German guards to shoot stragglers and escapers, some airmen took their chances and slipped away, hoping to make their way to allied lines. Many were successful. Others were recaptured or, finding the solo trek difficult, returned to their companions.

Marching columns were attacked by allied aircraft.[32] There were many fatalities. William Hawke attested that two naval officers were killed en route to Lübeck.[33] Kenneth Gaulton, Calton Younger and other former Centre Compound NCOs, along with a large group of prisoners including soldiers, were machine-gunned on the road from Stalag 357, Fallingbostel. John Shierlaw and an Australian soldier were 'killed outright'. Two other Australians were wounded.[34]

From Stalag Luft III, the kriegies trekked to Spremberg, about 96 kilometres away.[35] There they were divided up and put in crowded, insanitary cattle trucks to embark on the 'next grim part' of their journey, as Ronald Baines described

---

27 Johnson, 'Resisting Captivity', PhD thesis, 43.
28 AR: Anne O'Byrne, interview 26 May 2016; quote from email 4 December 2020. AR: Arnel, interview 29 January 2015.
29 AR: Arnel, interview 27 November 2014 and additional comments 29 October 2015.
30 AR: Evelyn and Colin Johnston, interview 18 October 2016.
31 AR: Drew Gordon, interview 19 July 2016.
32 Train, 'A Barbed-Wire World', 74; NAA A9301, 403176 [Wright], war crimes questionnaire.
33 NAA A9300 Hawke, W C, war crimes questionnaire.
34 NAA A705 166/37/60, Shierlaw, Statement by Sgt Bobbie Lewis Fenton, 11 May 1945; Younger, *No Flight From the Cage*, 215; AAWFA: Gaulton 1276, 3 February 2004.
35 Much of this section is taken from travel schedule in 3 Squadron RAAFA: 'Tom Wood Diary'.

it.[36] 'Travelling in those boxcars was shocking.'[37] No water was issued for 30 hours, 'any signs of modesty I ever had left went by the board too – calls of nature were obeyed where you could, alongside the tracks; people passing by meant nothing.'[38] Approximately half of East Compound, along with those of North Compound, were sent to *Marlag und Milag Nord*, a naval camp near Tarmstedt, arriving on 4 February. Between 9 and 28 April, they trekked another 149 kilometres to Trenthorst, near Lübeck. The rest of East Compound and those in Belaria arrived at Stalag III-A, Luckenwalde on 4 February. The physical and psychological strains were great. 'When we reached LUBECK on BALTIC SEA many of us were very ill', recalled Hec Henry.[39]

Safety in those final holding camps was not assured. Those at Trenthorst were in earshot of the fighting. 'Heard tremendous barrage midnight. Turned out to be Elbe crossing', wrote Bill Fordyce. The fighting was almost on top of them. 'We believe that we are 7 kilos from front', he wrote the next day. 'Very heavy fire round us. Colossal air cover goon jets all round, too. Suspense terrible.'[40] Ronald Baines, who had been confined to *Marlag und Milag Nord*'s sick quarters when the rest of the camp evacuated to Trenthorst, and had subsequently transferred to a merchant navy camp, was also worried. The fighting was 'too damn close' to him: 'one of our aircraft bombed and strafed the camp … 6 killed, 20 odd wounded.'[41]

Regardless of which camp they were in, and despite fear, anxiety, and deteriorating conditions in the closing weeks of conflict, the POWs settled in as best they could. Kriegie ingenuity, and their innate resilience, did not let them down. 'We made an oven out of empty tins and have fitted it on the stove pipe, it works very well, when we have anything to put in it', Colin Phelps wrote.[42] They met up with old friends and crew members, re-established prayer groups, played sports, wrote letters, hoped for mail, and compiled narratives of their trek in wartime log books. Morale rose and fell. Moods worsened when scarce food was rationed further and in the wake of bad weather. 'The bloody German ration is cut again', Baines recorded. 'I'm really brassed. To hell with everything.'[43] Huie Bowden was also discontented. 'Cold and damp weather. Felt in black mood.'[44] But, as they had time and again before the evacuation, spirits lifted when Red Cross parcels arrived, when they heard good news regarding the course of the war, and at the thought of loved ones and imminent reunions. As usual, work

---

36 Baines FA: Baines, wartime log book, 10 February 1945, 23.
37 Baines FA: Baines, wartime log book, 3 February 1945, 71.
38 Baines FA: Baines, wartime log book, 10 February 1945, 23.
39 Henry FA: Annotation on Henry's copy of Brickhill and Norton, *Escape to Danger*.
40 Fordyce FA: Fordyce, wartime log book, 30 April and 1 May 1945, 137.
41 Baines FA: Baines, wartime log book, Monday, [no date] April 1945, 26.
42 MHRC CPA: Colin Phelps to parents, 23 March 1945.
43 Baines FA: Baines, wartime log book, 5 March 1945, 24.
44 Bowden FA: 'Diary of Huie Bowden July 1944–May 1945', 5 April 1945, 90.

helped. Bowden's mood improved after sitting down 'to make some chips [for the heater] out of some toughish wood [from] my third bed board. Felt better even after hacking off chips for an hour.'[45] The trick, as it had been at Stalag Luft III, was to keep busy. 'Get something to do all day is the answer.'[46]

Those in Stalag III-A, Luckenwalde believed Hitler had gathered the thousands of kriegies to use as a negotiating tool. As such, Bowden thought it more and more unlikely that they would 'move to the safer camps in the west.'[47] For three days before the Red Army arrived, the reverberations from nearby fighting were so bad that 'intermittently … the huts didn't stop shaking', Keith Mills told his sister, Phyllis. 'I think I have seen everything that makes a noise.'[48] When the Red Army arrived in mid-April, they, according to Wesley Betts, were a 'wild lot' and 'we didn't feel at all safe with them.'[49] They made no move to release prisoners and the airmen wondered what would happen. 'Rumour from abwehr says we were bound for Nuremburg as hostages', wrote Ken Todd.[50] Later, the kriegies believed that, when the Russians stopped them from boarding American trucks on VE Day, the allied prisoners were ever more certain they would be 'used as bargaining chips, so that Russian POWs in the allied zones who were reluctant to return to Russia would be forced to return', recalled Cy Borsht.[51] Conditions in Luckenwalde became so bad Ken Todd dubbed it a 'concentration camp.'[52] Ross Breheny recalled starving men 'reached the stage of walking x-rays.'[53] Medical supplies were scarce and dysentery was rife.

Fears for safety intermingled with exasperation and anxiety. Ronald Baines' impatience was clear. 'The Army hasn't arrived yet – drat 'em! … Come on Monty!' 'Still no news of our prospects here', he noted a few days later. '[A]ll the [navy] and RAF boys … are pretty jumpy about things.'[54] Bill Fordyce, at a 'berg called "Trenthorst"', was equally impatient.[55] 'Gosh they can't be long now', he anticipated on 30 April. 'Rumours by the million!', he penned the next day. 'News of drives on Kiel & Lubeck.'[56]

Despite the trials of those final camps, knowing they were close to release made it easier for some to cope, Alec Arnel told me.[57] Others, however, suffered

---

45 Bowden FA: 'Diary of Huie Bowden July 1944–May 1945', 5 April 1945, 90.
46 Bowden FA: 'Diary of Huie Bowden July 1944–May 1945', 20 April 1945, 98.
47 Bowden FA: 'Diary of Huie Bowden July 1944–May 1945', 31 March 1945, 88.
48 Keith Mills FA: Keith Mills to Phyllis Mills, 22 July 1945.
49 SLSA SRG 869 Series 14: Wesley H. Betts, item 92, 23 January 2002.
50 Todd FA: Ken Todd, wartime log book, 15 April 1945, 92.
51 Borsht Archive: Borsht, 'A Life Well Lived', 24.
52 Todd FA: Ken Todd, wartime log book, 4 February 1945, 89.
53 SLSA SRG 869 Series 16: Ross Breheny, item 12 [undated].
54 Baines FA: Baines, wartime log book, Monday, 20 April and [no date] April 1945, 26.
55 Fordyce FA: Fordyce, wartime log book, 29 April, 136.
56 Fordyce FA: Fordyce, wartime log book, 30 April and 1 May 1945, 137.
57 AR: Arnel, interview 12 November 2015.

some degree of psychological distress. 'We lived like animals at [Luckenwalde] for about three months with practically no food and warmth ... the strain was terrific', Mark Derrett recalled. 'Although the physical privations during the last 4–5 months had been hard to bear the nervous strain and anxiety concerning our ultimate fate were even worse and cannot be described.'[58]

When it finally came, liberation was exhilarating. The contrast between the traumatic experiences of the final months of captivity and the joy of release was overwhelming. Paul Royle recorded the exact moment when the Trenthorst camp was liberated on 2 May, and even the name of the British tank. 'Armoured recco. vehicle "Joan-Ann" arrived at camp 1300 hours.'[59] For Colin Phelps also at Trenthorst, it was the 'best thing [to] happen since I've been in this God forsaken country'.[60] But liberation was also unsettling. 'Kriegies wandering round in teeming rain looking dazed', wrote Bill Fordyce. 'I feel like crying.'[61] They were whisked back to Britain by RAF and RAAF crews in Operation *Exodus*, the massive allied POW repatriation effort. 'England again', recalled Albert Comber. 'The sun shining, no more sound of war – heaven on earth!'[62] But their disconcerting emotions did not cease.

Even when space was limited and extra weight was a trial on the forced march, Doug Hutchinson carried his wife's letters. Lola treasured every one of Doug's letters written while on operations as an air gunner with 454 Squadron RAAF and throughout captivity. Later, Doug lovingly preserved their correspondence. It is a rare record of a couple's experience of wartime love and separation. Courtesy of Robert Douglas Hutchinson.

---

58 DVA MX076290-01, appellant's letter, 5 October 1953.
59 Royle archive: Royle, wartime log, Tarmstedt, 41.
60 MHRC CPA: Colin Phelps to parents, 2 May 1945.
61 Fordyce FA: Fordyce, wartime log book, 2 May 1945, 137.
62 AWM: AH Comber, artist, letter 16 December 1990.

'Roadside Rest. The March from Sagan.' Albert Comber discarded his artworks during the forced march, 'relieved to be rid of some of the load, fearful that even so we'd never make it home alive.' Comber recreated some of those images immediately after the war and these are held by the Australian War Memorial. This pen and ink sketch of a weary group of kriegies was done for a friend. Courtesy of Alan Righetti, and with permission of the Comber family.

Tony Gordon was a 'tin basher', an important prison camp position. Using metallic bits and pieces, he constructed and repaired secret radios, fabricated utensils to make domestic life easier, and carried out other assorted metalwork tasks. He also made this 30 cm tube from food tins to protect Bill Fordyce's artwork. Tim Mayo fashioned something similar in which to carry his paintings and drawings. Courtesy of Drew Gordon.

Chapter Twenty-one:

HOMECOMING

Stepping out of their transport aircraft, the 'dishevelled but happy' crowd of ex-kriegies were 'mobbed by the good folk who had come to the aerodrome', Alec Arnel wrote.[1] Their emotions were at fever pitch. 'I am so thrilled at being back in England', Eric Johnston enthused to Evelyn Charles.[2] When a member of the Women's Auxiliary Air Force asked Alan Righetti if she could help him with his kit bag, 'I almost burst into tears'. It was 'the first kind word I had heard in two and a quarter years'. It was an overwhelming moment but practicalities helped put aside emotion. 'Then we were deloused and sent off to barracks to brush up for the VE celebrations in London!'[3] Paul Brickhill was one of many who could not 'grasp' the idea of freedom at first. He could 'only absorb little bits here and there'. Brickhill, however, would not allow himself time to relax into liberty. He and South African war correspondent, Conrad Norton, were going to finish a book, later published as *Escape to Danger*.[4]

The RAAF had established 11 PDRC at Brighton to help the repatriates settle into post-captivity life. (Members of the RAF attended 106 PRC Cosford.) As well as health checks, they were given newspapers, books, and lectures to reacquaint themselves with current affairs. Within hours of arriving at the reception centre, Alec Arnel and his friends 'removed the outward signs of our recent experiences'. In decent clothing, with telegrams despatched to loved ones, they then 'set about doing those things which we had promised ourselves so often.'[5] Ronald Baines lost no time in phoning his wife. Thrilled to be reunited with her husband – assured that he had not abandoned her – Irene caught the train from London the next day and they 'met at the Brighton station – after two and a half years – wonderful.'[6] Others, however, were disorientated; their emotions remained out of kilter. 'These last few days have been hectic ones', Alec Arnel told Margery Gray. 'I have been in a "flat spin"' since setting foot on British soil. 'So much excitement for nerves that have become somewhat frayed.' Within a few days, he was enjoying Brighton's delights. He and others soon 'knew our mistake. We weren't ready for the hustle and bustle of this life.

---

1 Arnel archive: Arnel to Margery Gray, 21 May 1945.
2 Johnston FA: Johnston to Evelyn Charles, 27 May 1945.
3 AR: Alan Righetti, email 8 April 2014.
4 AWM PR03099: Brickhill to Del Fox, 28 May 1945.
5 Arnel archive: Arnel to Margery Gray, 21 May 1945.
6 Baines FA: Baines, wartime log book, [6 May 1945], 34.

We couldn't stand the crowds. Noises irritated.' Freedom was too much. Arnel's nerves snapped. 'I am going away for a rest.'[7] Eric Johnson also found liberty disquieting. 'My thoughts haven't quite adjusted themselves back to normal', he confessed to Evelyn.[8] Even after a few days, Ken Carson was 'still rather dazed as it has been quite a change from Kriegie existence to civilisation.'[9] Ron Mackenzie wept, 'and did not stop for a couple of hours'. He found it difficult to articulate to his sister the confusion he was experiencing: 'One feels curiously defenceless when the need for defence disappears. Anne, I can't talk about this anymore now – I'm still in a mental fog.'[10] They and other former kriegies experienced what might now be called 'culture shock'. Having become largely habituated to captivity, barbed-wire life was 'normal.'[11] Freedom was not.

Speaking for himself and collectively, Arnel admitted that, during those early weeks in Britain the emotionally stunned 'failed dismally to cope.'[12] Yet, despite their disjunction, as they had done in captivity, the former kriegies tried to assume control. Attempting to regain his mental balance, Ron Mackenzie decided to take things slowly. While only 'blurred images are visible' in his confused mental state, they were 'very pleasant' with 'no clear-cut outlines'. Rather than resist them, or try to grasp them and understand them, he told his sister, Anne, he was 'content to sit in the sun, and let them flow past, in, over, around me.'[13]

Other new repatriates assured loved ones they were in fine fettle. As ever, they told their homefolks that they were fit and well. Some, with eyes firmly on their futures, pursued commercial opportunities. 'Now Mum, I might delay a couple of months in England', George Archer explained. 'I want to visit the Liverpool, London etc offices [of the Cunard White Star Line] and pick up some information on the passenger business – a grand opportunity … and I don't want to miss it.'[14] Alan Righetti, who had partially completed an agricultural science degree before the war, went to Bradford 'to have a look at the wool industry'. Subsequently, he took a short course in textiles at Leeds University.[15] Sporty types publicly displayed their fitness. Hugh Lambie and William 'Bill' Trickett were two of the RAAF rowing representatives at the Henley-on-the-Thames regatta.[16] Keith Carmody resumed his place as captain in the RAAF cricket team, and joined the Australian Services XI for the Victory Test series.[17]

---

7   Arnel archive: Arnel to Margery Gray, 21 May 1945.
8   Johnston FA: Johnston to Evelyn Charles, 27 May 1945.
9   Carson FA: Ken Carson to mother and sister, 9 May 1945.
10 Mackenzie, *An Ordinary War 1940–1945*, 106–107.
11 Whiles, 'A Study of Neurosis among Repatriated Prisoners of War', 697–698.
12 Arnel archive: Arnel to Margery Gray, 21 May 1945.
13 Mackenzie, *An Ordinary War 1940–1945*, 106–107.
14 Archer FA: Archer to family, 25 June 1945.
15 AAWFA: Righetti 0984, 16 September 2003.
16 'Swivel', 'Australian Oarsmen on the Thames', *Weekly Times* (Melbourne), 18 July 1945.
17 Barker, *Keith Carmody*, 71–80.

They, and others, demonstrated to all that they had physically recovered from the privations of the last months of war.

A holiday tour courtesy of the Dominion and Allied Services Hospitality Scheme[18] helped the former kriegies become attuned to freedom. The silence of country homes proved a balm after the hubbub of overcrowded camps. 'That was a healing thing', recalled Arnel, who spent hours alone, wandering through his hosts' house and grounds.[19] 'So far on this leave I have been successful in avoiding town life and the crowds', which had unsettled him after his return to Britain. 'I always enjoyed a ramble in the bush – now it is almost an obsession.' As well as allowing them to reacquaint themselves with a more normal life, solitude enabled some to focus on what would come next. 'I find that I can sort out my thoughts', Arnel confided to Margery Gray. 'And I need to think. To get my ideas into their correct perspective.' He desperately wanted 'to examine' himself 'honestly', and to reconcile the past with the present, and future.[20]

Recognising how much some needed care, motherly hostesses provided vital nurturing. Arnel was cossetted by Mrs de Ross who was 'intent on making me fit again, so I am eating like a horse, drinking lots of milk, and sleeping early and later'. Mrs Westray, with whom Geoff Cornish had spent many leaves before his capture and who had sent parcels and letters during his four-year confinement, invited him to her home while he was on 'recoup leave'. 'It was on four hundred acres … the sheer freedom of being able to wander anywhere I wanted to be on my own in those glorious woods … and without somebody saying, "Hoch! Put your hands up"… Your soul felt like it could fly.'[21]

Eric Johnston and *Rodney Patton*, neither of whom had totally recovered from the rigours of Buchenwald concentration camp before suffering the privations of the last few months of captivity, were also well fed. 'My aunt made us eat plenty of good food', Johnston wrote. She 'used to buy seven pints of milk a day and at night time it had all gone'.[22] By the end of his holiday, he had 'put on five pounds so that put me back to nearly normal again'.[23] His 'nerves [were] very much steadier' by the time he returned to Brighton.[24] Arnel, however, did not recover. 'I'm in hospital', he wrote to Margery Gray. He had experienced a complete physical and psychological collapse. But, he assured his sweetheart, 'I am on the mend again and apart from a sore throat (tonsils) I am in fairly good shape. My trouble was probably delayed reaction from the earlier days of excitement after

---

18　Alexander, 'Miss Celia Macdonald of the Isles "who has been a particularly good friend"', 15–25.
19　AR: Arnel interview, 27 November 2014.
20　Arnel archive: Arnel to Margery Gray, 12 June 1945.
21　AAWFA: Cornish 1388, 2 July 2004.
22　Johnston FA: Johnston to Evelyn Charles, 24 June 1945.
23　Johnston FA: Johnston to Evelyn Charles, 6 July 1945.
24　Johnston FA: Johnston to Evelyn Charles, 24 June 1945.

my release from Germany.'[25] Arnel did not admit it to Margery but he had been vomiting constantly. He later attributed his 'collapse' not to the rich, wholesome food he had eaten but relief that his ordeal was over. That emotional release 'did something to my system. I don't know what it was. I think at that time I was finding it hard to believe.'[26] Arnel did not recover quickly. Ten days after discharge from hospital, he was still on sick leave.[27] The next day, however, after proposing marriage to Margery by letter, he felt he was truly recovered. As he explained to his soon-to-be mother-in-law, 'I have settled down now and the madness of the last 4½ years of war + prison life are no longer the masterful phantom which brought me almost to be its servant'.[28]

It was a heady time for many. The unattached went to parties, rekindled platonic friendships, or enjoyed romantic attachments. Some proposed to the women who had waited. Some married them. After so long without the physical presence of women, many simply wanted 'pure sex.'[29] Bill Amos was soon 'chasing around the popsies in Brighton'.[30] Many 'went crazy' as they released sexual tension with willing partners.[31] Some appear to have been less than careful. Nasty discharges and rashes did not necessarily indicate sexually transmitted diseases, but any unusual symptoms in the genitals could be alarming and at least one recently engaged man was so concerned about his that the RAAF medical officer ordered a test (which proved negative).[32] Later, before his March 1946 discharge, Paul Brickhill wanted 'to exclude VD infection' so asked to be tested.[33]

There was perhaps more than 'pure sex' precipitating the post-liberation rush to women. After years without female contact, short rations, malnutrition, and reduced fitness, many had feared they might be impotent. As ever, they hid their anxieties behind the veil of humour. In one cartoon, Calton Younger depicted a pretty girl welcoming a bashful-looking returning airman. 'Bill Smith. I've waited for you since I was 13 and now you say you're too shy to kiss me.'[34] A story told by Bill Fordyce metaphorically reflects their concerns regarding prospective sexual performance. After his welcome on the tarmac by an attractive WAAF, the dishevelled and potentially lice-ridden Fordyce 'grabbed this girl by the arm. I hadn't seen a woman for over three years and I was terribly impressed. And I thought to myself, "I'm going to take this bird out tonight"'. A feast had been

---

25 Arnel archive: Arnel to Margery Gray, 5 July [1945].
26 AR: Arnel, interview, 29 October 2015. 'Collapse' from interview, 2 March 2017.
27 Arnel archive: Alec Arnel to Margery Gray, 24 July 1945.
28 Arnel Archive: Alec Arnel to Mrs Gray, 25 July 1945
29 AR: Arnel, interview, 23 June 2016.
30 Roe (ed.), *The Bill Amos Story*, 71.
31 AR: Arnel, interview 23 June 2016.
32 DVA NMX292929-01.
33 NAA C139 NMX283109-01: Brickhill, Paul Chester – service number 403313 [DVA medical case file; box 59618]: Request for Laboratory Examination, 26 March 1946.
34 Younger, *Get a Load of this*, [47].

laid on for the new arrivals but Fordyce was not interested. 'I thought, "To hell with the meal. Concentrate on the girl"'. Before reaching the hangar, Fordyce's escort diverted the new arrivals to the delousing block where they encountered 'a man with one of these big bicycle pumps' who 'covered me with this powder'. The embarrassed Fordyce brushed himself down and followed the WAAF to the laden table. With his mind on the young woman he had forgotten that, when captured, the Germans had removed the fly buttons from his uniform trousers. As he sat down 'to do a line with this girl', he crossed his legs. 'Out of my gaping fly came a great puff of white powder, and I thought this is a horror of war. First woman and I can't even do more than a puff of white powder.'[35]

The majority of the former kriegies wanted to return home as soon as possible but, with lack of shipping, delays were inevitable. Doug Hutchinson turned his thoughts to Lola. Whenever he had a quiet moment, 'he relapse[d] into pleasant thoughts, thinking of you and the pleasant days to come.'[36] But memories of Lola, the kind attention of his hosts, and renewal of old acquaintances were not enough for Hutchinson. He had waited so long to return to his wife. As younger friends raced around Brighton or London with their 'popsies', his constancy did not falter, but, 'At the moment I feel quite lost, and don't know what to do with myself … somehow I can't settle down'. He had kept himself busy at camp to distract himself from morbid thoughts but, now, there was simply nothing to do. The extended period of inactivity – 'I have just arrived back from my third lot of leave and am off again on Friday for a further fourteen days' – began to pall. 'I am getting sick and tired of all this dashing backwards and forwards.'[37] All Hutchinson wanted to do 'is get home to you and stay with you for a long long time.'[38]

Although homesick and anxious to return to Lola, Hutchinson was physically and mentally well. Others, elated by the prospect of home, calculatedly hid or inadvertently masked physical debility, emotional reactions, or lingering psychological disturbances. They brushed them aside because they wanted 'a quick discharge' once they were cleared to return to Australia.[39]

*****

Many ex-kriegies found homecoming as disconcerting as liberation, particularly those who had dreamed of quiet reunions with family, sweethearts, fiancées, or wives.[40] 'Darling my wish is that I would like to step out of an aircraft … and wait for you to come home in your room with just the two of us, that would be perfect

---

35 AAWFA: Fordyce 0523, 19 June 2003.
36 Hutchinson FA: Doug Hutchinson to Lola Hutchinson, 27 July 1945.
37 Hutchinson FA: Doug Hutchinson to Lola Hutchinson, 11 July 1945.
38 Hutchinson FA: Doug Hutchinson to Lola Hutchinson, 28 June 1945.
39 DVA MX076290-01: statement accompanying DVA Claim for Medical Treatment and Pension, 4 October 1982.
40 See also Alexander, 'The Legacy of Captivity'.

and a wonderful welcome home', wrote Charles Fry who had not seen Beryl Smith since July 1937. He confessed he would be embarrassed to have a public reunion.[41] Rather than an understated return, many disembarking repatriates were greeted with street parades and 'tumultuous' public welcomes in Sydney, Melbourne, and other capitals.[42] The throngs overwhelmed some, like Alec Arnel.[43] Even so, the 'joy of reunion' was the prevailing emotion.[44] Underneath however, was a sense of hollowness as some airmen realised they could not forget the trials of captivity as easily as they had anticipated, and that life would not be as they had imagined. 'Do you think, if we asked nicely, for a passage back', Max Dunn, cynically enquired, 'That the Gov'ment would allow it – or would they still insist / We endure our homeland's "welcome" from that Hell.'[45]

'The new beginning was fraught with difficulties', recalled Ron Mackenzie.[46] The 'tremendous shock' of homecoming was akin to that of capture; the need to adapt to their post-war domestic circumstances was reminiscent of the accommodations they had to make behind barbed wire. John Dack found that 'whilst everything was still the same, somehow everything was different.'[47] Mackenzie felt 'we were strangers at home.'[48] For some there was an awakening grief. Alex Kerr's 'delight' at return was 'tinged with sadness' when he discovered that friends and 'neighbourhood kids' had died during the war.[49] Some, like Errol Green who returned to a home without his supportive mother and grandmother, had to face life without their loving presence.

Acknowledging that the newly returned needed an additional adjustment period before discharge, the RAAF sent them to medical rehabilitation units. 'This two weeks did wonders for our return to normal, both mentally and physically', John Dack recalled.[50] Alec Arnel, however, was one whose emotions were still awry but, as he had recently married Margery, he kept his symptoms to himself because, all he 'wanted to do was get out' and return to his bride. He insisted that he was 'as fit as a fiddle.'[51] As they had done in Britain, Arnel and others pretended all was well. His, and other undeclared nervous conditions, went undetected. They had survived captivity but, despite their hopes of a return to normal life with loved ones, they soon discovered that the war for them was not over.

---

41 Fry FA: Charles Fry to Beryl Smith, 20 June 1945.
42 'Tumultuous': SLSA SRG 869 Series 14: Wesley H. Betts, item 92, 23 January 2002.
43 AR: Arnel, interview 2 March 2017.
44 Johnston FA: 'The joy of reunion', *Sun News Pictorial* (Melbourne), undated news clipping.
45 Dunn, *Poems of Norman Maxwell Dunn*, 'Let's Go Back', 19 September 1945, 23.
46 Mackenzie, *An Ordinary War 1940–1945*, 114.
47 Dack, *So you Wanted Wings, Hey!*, 146–147.
48 Mackenzie, *An Ordinary War 1940–1945*, 114.
49 Kerr, *Shot Down*, 190.
50 Dack, *So you Wanted Wings, Hey!*, 148.
51 AR: Arnel, interview 2 March 2017.

THE JOY OF REUNION is well expressed in this human study of W./O. E. L. Johnson and Miss Evelyn Charles as they hugged each other at the Melbourne Cricket Ground yesterday. The young airman had just returned from Europe, where he was a prisoner of war in Germany.

Eric Johnston, a 78 Squadron RAF wireless operator, had spent sixty days in Buchenwald concentration camp before arriving at Stalag Luft III. His sweetheart, Evelyn Charles, had no news of his fate for some months. Their relief at being together again is evident, and this photograph exemplified the joy experienced by other reuniting couples. 'The Joy of Reunion,' Sun News Pictorial *(Melbourne), undated news clipping. Courtesy of Evelyn Johnston.*

The long waiting for letters from Charles Fry was 'most unbearable' for his fiancée, Beryl Smith. Overseas service with 112 Squadron RAF and captivity had separated them for eight years before they married in September 1945. Courtesy of Pat Martin.

Margery Gray was Alec Arnel's lodestar to home. He dreamed of seeing her smile again. They married within weeks of his repatriation. So too, did many other former kriegies. At least 40 per cent of Stalag Luft III's Australian bachelors tied the knot before the end of 1946. Almost two-thirds of those who had been single at liberation were married by 1950. Courtesy of Alec Arnel.

AFTERWORD

The odds of surviving aerial combat were not high, particularly for bomber crew. Bomber Command's chief, Arthur Harris, knew that his men faced 'the virtual certainty of death'.[1] So, too, did all RAF and RAAF airmen. 'Proven odds', Harry Train asserted, were 'about 10 to 1 against getting away with being shot down'.[2] Captivity saved their lives, but how did airmen ensure they did not succumb to the strains?

Resilience was a fact of life for the Australian airmen's generation. Many had seen the Great War's physical and mental legacy on fathers, family, and community members. They were children and young adults of the Depression. They had experienced hardship. 'Our parents had gone through the previous war, so war wasn't exactly foreign to us', Alec Arnel told me. 'But at the same time, we'd learned from our parents that it wasn't any fun, either. Yes, I think [we were] probably – more self-confident. We'd had to deal with life when it wasn't easy'. His 'generation was pretty tough because we'd been through … the worst part of the twentieth century'.[3] Anne O'Byrne spoke of her husband's 'hard life' before the war which had forged his 'considerable maturity and resilience'. This, along with his age – he was seen as a father or older brother figure in camp – helped Justin O'Byrne to support 'the younger boys'.[4] Life experience as well as a cultural resilience had enabled Arnel, O'Byrne and other kriegies to manage the trials of captivity.

Temperament and personal attributes were important facets of resilience, including 'reflectiveness when confronted with new situations' as Joan Beaumont has noted of the Great War generation.[5] So, too, was optimism, that happy ability to look on the bright side.[6] The Australian airmen had no doubt that the Allies would win the war and they would return to their loved ones. Their 'inbuilt optimism' allowed Alex Kerr and his kriegie compatriots 'to bear the vicissitudes of incarceration with fortitude'.[7] Resilience was a mainstay of coping but it wasn't everything. Keeping busy, faith, and continuing connections to supportive loved ones, family, and the community, including

---

1 Cited in MacKenzie, *Flying Against Fate*, 9.
2 Arnel archive: Train, 'A Barbed-Wire World', 15 May 1942, 8.
3 AR: Arnel, interview 2 March 2017.
4 AR: Anne O'Byrne, interview 26 May 2016.
5 Beaumont, 'Remembering the resilient', in Holbrook and Reeves (eds), *The Great War*, 142.
6 Segovia et al., 'Optimism Predicts Resilience in Repatriated Prisoners of War: A 37-Year Longitudinal Study', 334.
7 Kerr, *Shot Down*, 196.

the extended brotherhood of airmen, were fundamental to emotional survival. More important than anything, though, RAF Station Sagan protected its kriegie community; air force fraternity underpinned successful coping. *Kriegies* shows, as Alec Arnel emphatically claims, that captivity was 'not about me'. '"I" wasn't just "me", "I" was "us"'. And 'we' survived.

All their lives, ex-kriegies vividly recalled their captor's taunt, 'For you the war is over'. For many, the war ended shortly after repatriation. For others, the residue lingered a little longer. Some experienced captivity trauma[8], but not every veteran was traumatised.[9] Indeed, one-third of those whose medical records I examined – a significant minority – did not appear to suffer any degree of psychological disturbance or, if they had, it had not worried them unduly, and did not warrant claims to the Repatriation Department or, it's successor, the Department of Veterans' Affairs. They, like Donald Fraser and Tim Mayo, lived full, happy, and active lives. Mayo in particular looked back on captivity fondly, enjoying the good memories. Despite all the deprivations as a POW, he told his son, Peter, that he would again enlist and fight to keep the war away from his parents.[10] Cy Borsht's daughter, Jennifer Long, believes her father 'was fairly free of a lot of the lasting trauma suffered by many'. Borsht settled into post-war life well, and 'was always a very matter of fact type of man, the type to get in there and do the job to the best of his ability'. His life was full of laughter, conviviality, and family. While 'he may have had nightmares … they weren't overwhelming and he was able to cope with the fearful memories … I never recall him being violent, antagonistic, or showing signs of PTSD'.[11]

But for two-thirds of what I called my medical sample, the war never ended: the war for them was *not* over. 'Have never been able to settle down and get back to a normal way of living', Frank Everton attested in 1971.[12] 'How long did it take you to settle back to civilian life then?', oral historian Janet Billett asked Bill Fordyce on 5 September 2002. 'What's the date today?', Fordyce responded. 'It took until today. I haven't recovered yet.'[13] For *Everton*, Fordyce, and too many others, the traumatic legacies of captivity lasted a lifetime. But that is another story.

---

8 Alexander, 'Emotions of Captivity: Australian Airmen Prisoners of Stalag Luft III and their Families', Chapter Ten.
9 Hunt, *Memory, War and Trauma*, 81; Twomey, *The Battle Within*, 133; Demobbed, 220.
10 AR: Peter Mayo, email 20 September 2021.
11 AR: Jennifer Long, email 4 September 2019.
12 NAA B503 POW Trust Fund application: R873, 29 June 1971.
13 Fordyce in Billett, *Memories of War*, 2004, 206. Fordyce died in February 2008.

ACKNOWLEDGEMENTS

*K*riegies: *The Australian Airmen of Stalag Luft III* arises from my PhD candidature at UNSW Canberra which was funded by the Australian Government Research Training Program Scholarship through its Tuition Fee Offset scholarship. I would not have been able to view interstate research collections or conduct interviews without grants from UNSW's HASS Postgraduate Research Fund and the Andrew Dennis Travel Fund. Thank you UNSW Canberra. During the five years of my candidature and beyond, I benefited immeasurably from the keen insight and gentle critiques of my supervisors, Peter Stanley and Michael McKernan. I also enjoyed many enlightening conversations with Eleanor Hancock which sparked off exciting trains of thought. This book owes much to them. Thank you Peter, Michael, and Eleanor. Some of the sections relating to the Great Escape were drafted during my tenure as research assistant to Kate Ariotti of the University of Queensland. I penned it as background detail for a co-authored article written under the auspices of her Australian Research Council DECRA project (DE200100099) relating to the war corpse. I am grateful for Kate's permission to give that material a new life here.

I have been blessed by kindness. I would like to thank historians and friends who read earlier extracts from or versions of this book, or thesis, or both. Thank you to Kate Ariotti (my thesis examiner who became my supervisor and dear friend), Karl James (who has also commissioned two articles for *Wartime* based on chapters from *Kriegies*), Peter Hobbins, Clare Makepeace, Michael Molkentin, Aaron Pegram, Peter Rees, Alfred Riley, Effie Karageorgos and Anne-Marie Schwirtlich for their comments and suggestions. Extra thanks must go to my husband David and my dear friend Jill who read through the final manuscript looking for the last, stubborn typos. If any remain, well, it's not their fault or mine (I did one final look-over). This, after all, is an air force story and we know how Gremlins are always an annoying part of air force life!

I have enjoyed the warm friendship of the aviation community over the last two decades and I am indebted to James Kightly, Phil Vabre, Mark Lax, Ross Mahoney, Mike Nelmes, Owen Zupp, Geoff Simpson, Andy Wright, James Oglethorpe, a font of wisdom regarding the airmen of 3 Squadron RAAF who shared Tom Wood's diary, and Martin Jackson of the RAAF/Rhodesian association, who shared with me some of his records relating to Alan Righetti.

My particular thanks, however, go to David Fredericks and Martin James of the Directorate of History – Air Force for their longstanding friendship and support, and to Rob Lawson who wrote this book's foreword. I deeply appreciate RAAF endorsement.

I am honoured that many of the extended Stalag Luft III family communicated so openly with me about their former kriegies and opened up intimate archives. Thank you Margie and Jamie Bradbeer, Rex Breheny, John Carson and Toni Hinds, Connie Comber, Cath McNamara, Gerry Smith, Lily Fordyce, Ian Fraser, Drew Gordon and Trudy Brentnall, Robert Douglas Hutchinson, Colin Johnston, Peter Kierath, Jennifer Long, Anne O'Byrne, Ross and Jude Preen, Max Preen, Pat and John Martin, Mike Netherway, Jennifer Walsh, and Louise Williams. Winifred Chevalier hosted two research visits, and also organised a family meeting so I could speak with her siblings Janie Miller, Trish Norman, and Michael Bligh. When I was unable to travel, many brought precious documents and artefacts to me, or entrusted them to post, email, or courier. Richard Baines unwrapped his father's wartime log book at a convenient café, and Lee Baines later sent me a PDF of it. Peter Rees acted on behalf of David Archer to transfer to my care for many months all of George Archer's wartime records. Charles Page in Western Australia liaised with Paul Royle and Alex Kerr and professionally photographed their wartime records. Others spoke to me on the phone or carried out lengthy email conversations. For so willingly overcoming the tyranny of distance (including from one side of Canberra to the other), thank you Stuart Baines, Bruce Bowden, Jane Bryce, Colin Burgess, Lisa Fardy, Barbara Fotheringham, Joan and Jeff Franklin, Helen Green, Charles Green, Kim Griffiths, Drew Harrison, Graham Henry, Peter Mayo, Greg McLeod, Craig Nightingale, Carlene Scifleet, Andrew RB Simpson, Jan Smith, and Peter Todd. I also extend my thanks to Damian Coburn who referred me to Craig Nightingale; Garth O'Connell who asked Stuart Baines to relate his family story; Mike Nelmes who introduced me to Peter Kierath and the Narromine Aviation Museum's collection; Louise Williams who referred me to Drew Gordon and Robert Douglas Hutchinson and for writing her uncle John's story; Frank McCann who put me in touch with Anne O'Byrne; and Les Sullivan who led me to Alec Arnel. I also extend my thanks to Ben van Drogenbroek and members of the Facebook group, Stalag Luft 3 – The Great Escape – Prisoners of War – P.O.W. for sharing their memories and insights into captivity.

Images tell a story that has often not been put into words. I am indebted to the many families who gave permission to use photos and artworks to help illustrate the kriegies' personal experiences but which also revealed the collective narrative. I especially thank Peter Mayo for allowing me to base *Kriegies*' cover on one of his father's watercolours. When he sent me copies of Tim's photos and artworks back in 2015 I was stunned at the clarity of images painted in camp 70-odd years earlier. One in particular struck me: 'Everlasting Vigil – The Goon in His Box'. The limited colour palette, the barbed wire, and the alert German sentry summed up for me the claustrophobia of camp life. That they exist – like Bill Fordyce's artworks – is a small miracle. When the order came to evacuate, Tim rolled up his drawings and slid them into a cylinder made out of Klim tins. He carried them with him during the forced march and kept them save throughout the final, challenging, months of captivity. He brought them home, 'very hard won prizes for us', Peter told me. They are treasured artefacts of Tim's lived experience of captivity and I am honoured that Peter allowed me to bring 'Everlasting Vigil', and two other paintings, to a broader audience. *Kriegies*' brilliant cover, and indeed the entire book, was designed by Diane Bricknell. I am thrilled she took on the project and waved her magic design wand over it. Thank you Diane.

While the majority, by far, of the primary evidence which contributed to the richness of this book came from family archives, I also enjoyed consulting records held by UNSW Canberra's Australians at War Film Archive, the Australian War Memorial, History and Heritage Branch – Air Force, the National Library of Australia, the National Archives of Australia, a variety of state libraries and archives, and British repositories. In addition, I took great delight in examining lesser known public collections. I particularly acknowledge the assistance of: Danielle Trewartha of the Marion Heritage Resource Centre, Adelaide; Peter Kierath and Mike Nelmes of the Narromine Aviation Museum; and Jenna Blyth and Neil Sharkey of the Shrine of Remembrance, Melbourne. My thanks also to Michael Greet, Assistant Archivist, Commonwealth War Graves Commission, who graciously shared documents from the Commission's archive and to Marek Łazarz, director of Muzeum Obozów Jenieckich / P.O.W. Camps Museum, Poland who shared his photographs of the Great Escape headstones and other museum records.

My deepest thanks go to Mark Neal, formerly of the Department of Veterans' Affairs. Neither thesis nor book could have been written without that Department's approval to consult veteran case files under Section 56 (2) of *The Archives Act 1983*. I am so grateful for this rare privilege and especially Mark's assistance in obtaining those records and interpreting them.

This book belongs to the former kriegies and their wives who spoke with me: Cy Borsht, Graham Berry, Alan Righetti, Bill Rudd, not mentioned in the text, but who generously provided encouragement and background briefing on the state of captivity, Evelyn Johnston who shared precious memories of Eric, and Anne O'Byrne who told me much about Justin. This book owes much to Alec

Arnel (who enriched my life so much); without him, much of *Kriegies* could not have been written. I met with Alec on ten occasions (and spoke frequently on the phone). During lengthy interviews, he spoke frankly about many facets of captivity. He openly shared difficult emotions and experiences. Alec also proved an exemplar when life was difficult for me; his resilience was inspiring. I certainly would not have written this book without Peter Stanley and Michael McKernan, so it belongs to them too. It belongs to so many, but it is dedicated to the one who continues to lovingly support, sustain, and feed me (I do not cook), and tolerates lengthy disappearances into my own little research and writing world: **David.**

BIBLIOGRAPHY

Newspaper citations are listed separately in the footnotes. All internet sources were verified on 30 April 2023.

Public archive collections

Australian War Memorial, Canberra, ACT (AWM)

AWM 54 81/4/135: [RAAF Historical Records Section Reports] MI9 Reports-Statements & interviews of RAAF members shot down over Europe. [AWM 54 81/4/135: MI9 reports].

AWM 54 779/3/126 part 1: [Prisoners of War and Internees—Examinations and Interrogations:] Statements by Royal Australian Air Force Personnel from Prisoner of War Camps in Germany and Italy]. [AWM 54 779/3/126 part 1: POW statement].

AWM 54 779/3/129: Prisoners of War and Internees—Examinations and Interrogations: Statements by repatriated or released Prisoners of War (RAAF) taken at No. 11 PDRC, Brighton, England, 1945 [AWM 54 779/3/129: 11 PDRC post-liberation debriefs].

AWM 54 1010/6/132: The Stalag Luft III War Crimes Trial Commencing at Hamburg 1 July 1947 Parts 1 and 2. [SLIII War Crimes Trial].

AWM: AH. Comber, artist, letter, 16 December 1990.

AWM PR03099: Brickhill, Paul Chester Jerome.

AWM PR90/035: Ferres, Torres.

AWM PR05675: Grey-Smith, Guy.

AWM PR00506: Morschel, John Robert Gordon.

AWM PR84/139: Train, Henry Roland.

Keith Murdoch Sound Archive of Australia in the War of 1939–45 (KMSA):

AWM S00551 KMSA: Coombes, Geoffrey Bernard, 23 March 1989.

Australians at War Film Archive, UNSW Canberra (AAWFA)

Austin, Rex: 0382, 5 June 2003.

Cornish, Geoff: 1388, 2 July 2004.

Falkiner, Fraser 'Jum': 0661, 17 March 2004.

Fordyce, Horace (Bill): 0523, 19 June 2003.

Gaulton, Kenneth: 1276, 3 February 2004.

Hutchinson, Douglas: 0540, 17 June 2003.

Kerr, Alexander: 1489, 3 March 2004.

Righetti, Alan: 0984, 16 September 2003.

Winn, Richard: 1508, 4 March 2004.

Department of Veterans' Affairs (DVA)

Second World War repatriation case files consulted under Special Access provisions of Section 56 (2) of the *Archives Act 1983*.

Commonwealth War Graves Commission (United Kingdom) (CWGC)

ADD 3/1/9 Prisoners of War, Treatment. Sagan:

Imperial War Museum Sound Archive (United Kingdom) (IWMSA)

Bernard, Dave, 26561, June 2004 [no date].

Kerr, Alexander, 24826, 18 March 2003.

Royle, Paul, 26605, 2 December 2012.

International Bomber Command Centre Digital Archive (IBCC Digital Archive):

Hemsworth Collection: 'A15 NCO's Arts & Crafts Exhib. Stalag Luft 3. Aug 42'.

Marion Heritage Research Centre, Adelaide, SA (MHRC CPA)

Colin Phelps' Archive, courtesy of the family of the late C.G. Phelps and the Marion Heritage Research Centre.

Narromine Aviation Museum, Narromine, NSW (NAM JOC)

John Osborne Collection.

National Archives of Australia, Canberra, ACT (NAA)

NAA A705: Correspondence files [RAAF casualty files].

NAA A1608 AT20/1/1: 'War Records—Prisoners of War. Shooting of Air Force Personnel (POW) in Germany'. [Shooting of Air Force Personnel (POW) in Germany].

NAA A2217 1401/83/P4 Part 2: Casualties – Shooting of Air Force Personnel at Stalag Luft III

NAA A9300: RAAF Officers Personnel files, 1921–1948 [service records].

NAA A9301: RAAF Personnel files of Non-Commissioned Officers (NCOs) and other ranks, 1921–1948 [service records].

NAA A12372: RAAF Personnel files—All Ranks [service files].

NAA A13950: German Prisoner of War [POW] identification cards for captured RAAF officers.

NAA B503: [Prisoners of War Trust Fund] Application forms for grants and associated documents [POW Trust fund applications].

NAA B884: Citizen Military Forces Personnel Dossiers, 1939–1947 [service records].

NAA C139 NMX283109-01: Brickhill, Paul Chester – service number 403313 [DVA medical case file; box 59618].

National Library of Australia, Canberra, ACT (NLA)

NLA FERG/4552: *The Red Cross Prisoner of War Official Monthly Bulletin*, Melbourne: Australian Red Cross Society.

NLA FERG/4550: 'P.O.W. the Monthly Newsletter of the Australian Prisoners of War Relatives' Association', Sydney: The Association. (POWRA).

NLA Oral TRC 1/97 Guy Grey-Smith, interviewed by Hazel de Berg, for the Hazel de Berg Collection [sound recording], 29 May 1965, Bib ID 1755104. [NLA HdBC].

NLA Justin O'Byrne interviewed by John Meredith for the John Meredith folklore collection, BiB ID 2783443, recorded at Launceston, Tasmania on 31 October 1986. [NLA JMFC].

NLA 'Reminiscential conversations between the Hon. Justin O'Byrne and the Hon. Clyde Cameron' [sound recording], BiB 1244653, recorded 29 August 1983–28 July 1984. [NLA O'Byrne, 'Reminiscential conversations'].

NSW State Archives (NSW SA)

Divorce and matrimonial cause case papers.

Shrine of Remembrance, Melbourne, VIC (SOR JCC)

James Catanach Collection.

State Library of South Australia, Adelaide, SA (SLSA)

Records of Ex-Prisoner of War Association of South Australia, SRG 869 Special List, Series 14. [SLSA SRG 869 Series 14].

Records of Ex-Prisoner of War Association of South Australia, SRG 869 Special List, Series 16. [SLSA SRG 869 Series 16].

State Library of Western Australia, Perth, WA (SLWA)

Paul Royle, interview with John Bannister, 4 March 2014 and continued on 19 March 2014 (for the Nedlands and South Perth oral history project).

National Archives, United Kingdom (NAUK)

AIR 40/269: Milag–Marlag Nord–Oflag L (Ex Stalag Luft III): reports on forced evacuation and finance, submissions to protecting power and nominal roll. [NAUK AIR 40/269: Stalag Luft III reports and nominal roll.]

AIR 40/285: Stalag Luft III (Sagan): report 'X' compiled by members of escape organisations. [NAUK AIR 40/285: 'X' report.]

WO 32/10757: Prisoners of War Repatriation (Code 91(F)) Re-habilitation of repatriated prisoners of war, Major G.B. Matthews RAMC, Report on the Mental Health of Prisoners of War by Senior British Medical Officer, Stalag Luft III, 17 February 1944. [NAUK WO 32/10757: Matthews' report, 17 February 1944.]

——, The Repatriate Prisoner of War from the Medical Aspect, Australian military Forces [Undated, c. mid 1944]. [NAUK WO 32/10757: Repatriate POW report.]

WO 208/3328 to 3335: MI9/SPG/LIB Liberation reports.

WO 208/3283: Camp History of Stalag Luft III (Sagan) Air Force Personnel, April 1942– January 1945, Part I East (Officers') Compound, Part II Centre (NCO's) Compound, Part III North (Officers') Compound, Part V Belaria (Officers') Compound [no date]. [NAUK WO 208/3283: SLIII Camp History.]

WO 224/63A: International Red Cross and Protecting Powers (Geneva): Reports concerning Prisoner of War Camps in Europe and the Far East. Unnumbered Reports. Stalag Luft III. [NAUK WO 224/63A: Red Cross and Protecting Powers reports.]

Muzeum Obozów Jenieckich / P.O.W. Camps Museum (Poland) (MOJ)

Photographs and records relating to Stalag Luft III.

Private archive collections

Sources of unpublished manuscripts, recordings, photos, letters and other documents cited from private collections are recorded in the endnotes.

3 Squadron RAAF Association, NSW (3 Squadron RAAFA)

Arnel Archive (Arnel archive)

Archer Family Archive (Archer FA)

Baines Family Archive (Baines FA)

Bligh Family Archive (Bligh FA)

Borsht Archive (Borsht Archive)

Bowden Family Archive (Bowden FA)

Bryce Family Archive (Bryce FA)

Colin Burgess Research Collection (Burgess RC)

Carson Family Archive (Carson FA)

Comber Family Archive (Comber FA)

Fordyce Family Archive (Fordyce FA)

Fraser Family Archive (Fraser FA)

Fry Family Archive (Fry FA)

Gordon Family Archive (Gordon FA)

Green Family Archive (Green FA)

Harrison research collection (Harrison RC)

Henry Family Archive (Henry FA)

Hutchinson Family Archive (Hutchinson FA)
Johnston Family Archive (Johnston FA)
Kerr Archive (Kerr archive)
Kierath Family Archive (Kierath FA)
Lark Family Archive (Lark FA)
Long Family Archive (Long FA)
Lumsden Family Archive (Lumsden FA)
Mayo Family Archive (Mayo FA)
Keith Mills Family Archive (Keith Mills FA)
Netherway Family Archive (Netherway FA)
Nightingale Family Archive (Nightingale FA)
O'Byrne Family Archive, (O'Byrne FA)
Preen Family Archive (Preen FA)
Paul Royle Archive (Royle Archive)
Andrew R.B. Simpson Research Collection (Simpson RC)
Todd Family Archive (Todd FA)

Author's records – interviews and email correspondence (AR)

Arnel, Alec, interviews 9 October 2014, 27 November 2014, 29 January 2015, 29 October 2015, 12 November 2015, 23 June 2016, 2 March 2017, 21 February 2018.

Baines, Stuart, interview 9 July 2015.

Bligh family (Winifred Chevalier, Janie Miller, Trish Norman and Michael Bligh), interview 26 April 2017.

Berry, Graham, interview 7 June 2016.

Borsht, Cyril, interview 28 January 2016.

Bradbeer, Jamie, email 9 September 2016.

Carson, John, interview 28 January 2016.

Winifred Chevalier, interviews 5 April 2014; 2 September 2015.

Fraser, Ian, interview 25 May 2016.

Fotheringham, Barbara, interview 26 June 2016; undated letter, received 4 July 2016.

Gordon, Drew, interview 19 July 2016; email 28 March 2020.

Henry, Graham, email 6 December 2020.

Hutchinson, Robert Douglas, interview 19 December 2016.

Johnston, Colin, interview 18 October 2016; email 9 September 2016.

Johnston, Evelyn, interview 18 October 2016.

Kierath, Peter, interview 2 May 2016.

Long, Jennifer email 4 September 2019.

Mayo, Peter, emails 13 July 2015, 4 May 2020, 5 May 2020.

McNamara, Cath, interview 18 July 2016.

Netherway, Mike, interview 28 September 2016.

O'Byrne, Anne, interview 26 May 2016.

Preen, Max, email 4 September 2015.

Righetti, Alan, emails 31 October 2008, (to Martin Jackson) 6 November 2009, 27 April 2012, 4 November 2013, 21 January 2014, 3 February 2014, 8 April 2014.

Scifleet, Carlene, interview 9 June 2016.

Simpson, Andrew R.B., email 21 March 2016.

Smith, Jan, emails 26 March 2018, 3 October 2019.

Todd, Peter, interview 13 October 2015.

Walsh, Jennifer, interview 29 April 2017.

Official reports/publications

Air Publication 1548: *Instructions and Guide to all Officers and Airmen of the Royal Air Force regarding Precautions to be taken in the event of falling into the hands of an Enemy*, [no publication details], March 1936.

Air Publication 1548: *Instructions and Guide to All Officers and Airmen of the Royal Air Force regarding Precautions to be taken in the Event of Falling into the Hands of an Enemy*, [no publication details], 2nd Edition, June 1941.

Air Publication 1548: *The Responsibilities of a Prisoner of War*, [no publication details], 3rd Edition, April 1944.

The King's Regulations and Air Council Instructions for the Royal Air Force with Appendices and Index 1942. London: His Majesty's Stationery Office, 1942.

Books

(NOTE: details of chapters cited are included in endnotes.)

Alexander, Kristen, *Jack Davenport Beaufighter Leader*. Crows News: Allen & Unwin, 2009.

Allport, Alan, *Demobbed: Coming Home after the Second World War*. New Haven and London: Yale University Press, 2010.

Anderson, Robert and Westmacott, David, *Handle with Care: A Book of Prison Camp Sketches Drawn and Written in Prison Camps in Germany*. Cookham: privately published, 1946.

Andrews, Allen, *Exemplary Justice*. London: George G. Harrap, 1976.

Auslander, Leora and Zahra, Tara (eds), *The Material Culture of Conflict and Displacement*. Ithaca: Cornell University Press, 2018.

Barker, Tony, *Keith Carmody: Keith Miller's Favourite Captain*. Cardiff: Association of Cricket Statisticians and Historians, 2012.

Beaumont, Joan, with Joshi, Vijaya, Bomford, Janette, Blair, Dale and Pratten, Garth, *The Australian Centenary History of Defence, Volume VI, Australian Defence: Sources and Statistics*. Melbourne: Oxford University Press, 2001.

Beaumont, Joan, Grant, Lachlan, and Pegram, Aaron (eds), *Beyond Surrender: Australian Prisoners of War in the Twentieth Century*. Carlton: Melbourne University Press, 2015.

Billett, Janet Roberts, *Memories of War: Members of the Naval and Military Club recall World War II. Fifty Interviews*. Melbourne: The Naval and Military Club, 2004.

Bongiorno, Frank, *The Sex Lives of Australians: A History*. Collingwood: Black Inc., 2012.

Bourne, Stephen, *Fighting Proud: The Untold Story of the Gay Men who Served in Two World Wars*. London: I.B. Taurus & Co Ltd, 2017.

Brickhill, Paul, *The Great Escape*. London: Faber and Faber, 1951.

Brickhill, Paul and Norton, Conrad, *Escape to Danger*. London: Faber and Faber, 1954.

Brown, Kingsley, *Bonds of Wire: A Memoir*. Toronto: Collins Publishers, 1989.

Calnan, T.D., *Free as a Running Fox*. London: Macdonald & Co. (Publishers) Ltd, 1970.

Cousens, Bryce (ed), *The Log: Stalag Luft III Belaria–Sagan 1939–1945*. Cheltenham: the author, [1947].

[Crawley, Aidan], *Escape from Germany: True Stories of POW Escapes in WWII*. Kew: The National Archives, 2009.

Dack, Irwin John, *So, You Wanted Wings, Hey! An Autobiography. Part One*. Moorabbin: The author, 1993.

Damousi, Joy, *The Labour of Loss: Mourning, Memory and Wartime Bereavement in Australia*. Cambridge: Cambridge University Press, 1999.

——, *Living with the Aftermath: Trauma, Nostalgia and Grief in Post-War Australia*. Cambridge: Cambridge University Press, 2001.

Dando-Collins, Stephen, *The Hero Maker: A Biography of Paul Brickhill*. North Sydney: Penguin Random House Australia, 2016.

Dunn, Norman Maxwell, *Poems of Norman Maxwell Dunn: Composed 1942–1946*. [Privately published; no publication details], 1981.

Foot, M.R.D. and Langley, J.M., *MI 9: The British Secret Service that Fostered Escape and Evasion 1939–1945 and its American Counterpart*. London: Book Club Associates, 1979.

Francis, Martin, *The Flyer: British Culture and the Royal Air Force 1939–1945*. Oxford: Oxford University Press, 2008.

Garton, Stephen, *The Cost of War: War, Return and the Re-shaping of Australian Culture*. Sydney: Sydney University Press, 2020.

Gaynor, Andrew, *Guy Grey-Smith: Life Force*. Crawley: UWA Publishing, 2012.

Gilbert, Adrian, *POW: Allied Prisoners in Europe 1939–1945*. London: John Murray (Publishers), 2007.

Gladwin, Michael, *Captains of the Soul: A History of Australian Army Chaplains*. Newport: Big Sky Publishing, 2013.

Hallam, Robert Kay, *The Scarecrow Said and other poems*. London: Press of Villiers Publications Ltd, 1961.

Harsh, George, *Lonesome Road*. London: Longman Group Limited, 1972.

Hetherington, John, *Australian Painters: Forty Profiles*. Melbourne: F.W. Cheshire, 1967.

Herington, John, *Australia in the War of 1939–1945. Series Three. Air. Volume IV: Air Power Over Europe, 1944–1945*. Canberra: Australian War Memorial, 1963.

Holbrook, Carolyn and Reeves, Keir (eds), *The Great War: Aftermath and Commemoration*. Sydney: NewSouth Publishing, 2019.

Hunt, Nigel C., *Memory, War and Trauma*. Cambridge: Cambridge University Press, 2011.

James, B.A. (Jimmy), *Moonless Night: The World War Two Escape Epic*. Barnsley: Pen & Sword Military, 2008.

Kerr, Alex, *Shot Down: A Secret Diary of one POW's Long March to Freedom*. Newport: Big Sky Publishing, 2015.

Lark, Charles R, *A Lark on the Wing: Memoirs World War II and 460 Squadron*. [No publication details].

Larsson, Marina, *Shattered Anzacs: Living with the Scars of War*. Sydney: University of New South Wales Press, 2009.

Macintyre, Ben, *Colditz: Prisoners of the Castle*. Penguin Random House UK, 2022.

Mackenzie, Ron, *An Ordinary War 1940–1945*. Wangaratta: Shoestring Press, 1995.

MacKenzie, S.P., *The Colditz Myth: British and Commonwealth Prisoners of War in Nazi Germany*. Oxford: Oxford University Press, 2004.

——, *Flying Against Fate: Superstition and Allied Aircrews in World War II*. Lawrence: University Press of Kansas, 2017.

Makepeace, Clare, *Captives of War: British Prisoners of War in Europe in the Second World War*. Cambridge: Cambridge University Press, 2017.

Mason, W. Wynne, *Official History of New Zealand in the Second World War 1939–45*, Uckfield: The Naval & Military Press Ltd, no date.

Matt, Susan J. and Stearns, Peter N., (eds), *Doing Emotions History*. Urbana: University of Illinois Press, 2014.

Morschel, J.R.G. (Jack), *A Lancaster's Participation in Normandy Invasion 1944.* [No imprint details; private publication], 1999.

Nelson, Earle M., *If Winter Comes: RAAF Service 1939–1945.* Lovely Banks: Earle M. Nelson, 1989.

Noakes, Lucy, *Dying for the Nation: Death, Grief and Bereavement in Second World War Britain.* Manchester: Manchester University Press, 2020.

Oppenheimer, Melanie, *The Power of Humanity: 100 Years of Australian Red Cross 1914–2014.* Sydney: HarperCollinsPublishers, 2014.

Osborn, R.B., *Circuits and Bumps.* Berwick: R. Osborn, 1996.

Raphael, Beverley, *The Anatomy of Bereavement.* Lanham: Roman & Littlefield Publishers, Inc., 2001.

Riseman, Noah, Robinson, Shirleene, Willett, Graham, *Serving in Silence? Australian LGBT Servicemen and Women.* Sydney: NewSouth Publishing, 2019.

Roberts, Mary Louise, *Sheer Misery: Soldiers in Battle in WWII.* Chicago: University of Chicago Press, 2021.

Robinson, Alan, *Chaplains at War: The Role of Clergymen During World War II.* London: Tauris Academic Studies, 2008.

Roe, Charles (ed.), *The Bill Amos Story: Being a Brief Account of his Life, Including his Experiences as an RAAF Pilot, with Particular Attention to his Time as a Prisoner of War in Germany in World War II.* [No publication details].

Rolland, Derrick (ed.), *Airmen I have Met: Their Stories.* Bright: The author, 1999.

'Scangriff', (Winston, M.S) (ed.), *Spotlight on Stalag Luft III.* Consett: Ramsden Williams [1946].

Scates, Bruce, with McCosker, Alexandra, Reeves, Keir, Wheatley, Rebecca, and Williams, Damien, *Anzac Journeys: Returning to the Battlefields of World War II.* Port Melbourne: Cambridge University Press, 2013.

Shephard, Ben, *A War of Nerves: Soldiers and Psychiatrists 1914–1994.* London: Pimlico, 2002.

Simpson, Andrew R.B., *'OPS' Victory at all Costs: On Operations over Hitler's Reich with the Crews of Bomber Command. Their War – Their Words.* Pulborough: Tattered Flag Press, 2012.

Sly, Edward 'Ted', *The Luck of the Draw.* Brookvale: the author, 2003.

Smaal, Yorick, *Sex, Soldiers and the South Pacific, 1939–45: Queer Identities in the Second World War.* Houndmills: Palgrave Macmillan, 2015.

Smith, Sydney, *Wings Day: The Man who led the RAF's Epic Battle in German Captivity.* London: Collins, 1968.

Stephenson, Eric, *Three Passions and a Lucky Penny.* Canberra: Air Power Development Centre, 2008.

Sweanor, George, *It's All Pensionable Time: 25 Years in the Royal Canadian Air Force.* Colorado Springs: Adman Publishers, 1981.

Townsend, Nicole, Pandy, Kus, and Pendlebury, Jarrod (eds), *Australian Perspectives on Global Air and Space Power: Past, Present, Future.* Abingdon: Routledge, 2023.

Thompson, Douglas, *Captives to Freedom.* London: The Epworth Press, 1955.

Twomey, Christina, *The Battle Within: POWs in Postwar Australia.* Sydney: NewSouth Publishing, 2018.

Vance, Jonathan F., *A Gallant Company: The Men of the Great Escape.* Pacifica: Pacifica Military History, 2000.

——, (ed.), *Encyclopedia of Prisoners of War and Internment.* Millerton: Grey House Publishing, 2006.

Veitch, Michael, *Heroes of the Skies.* Melbourne: Penguin Group (Australia), 2015.

Vischer, A.L., *Barbed-Wire Disease: A Psychological Study of the Prisoner of War*. London: John Bales, Sons & Danielsson Ltd, 1919.

Walley, Brian, (ed.), *Silk and Barbed Wire*. Perth: The Royal Air Forces ex Prisoners of War Association (Australian Division), 2000.

Walters, Guy, *The Real Great Escape*. London: Bantam Press, 2013.

Walton, Marilyn Jeffers, and Eberhardt, Michael C, *From Interrogation to Liberation: A Photographic Journey. Stalag Luft III—The Road to Freedom*. Bloomington: AuthorHouse, 2014.

——, *From Commandant to Captive: The Memoirs of Stalag Luft III Commandant Col. Friedrich Wilhelm von Lindeiner gennant von Wildau with Postwar Interviews, Letters and Testimony*. Lulu Publishing Services [no other imprint details] 2015.

Ward-Jackson, C.H., *'It's a Piece of Cake': RAF Slang Made Easy*. London: The Sylvan Press, [undated].

While you were Away: A Digest of Happenings in Australia 1940–1945. Melbourne: The Argus, [no date, c. 1945].

White, Andrew, *Extremes of Fortune: From Great War to Great Escape. The Story of Martin Massey CBE DSO MC*. [No place]: Fighting High, 2020.

White, Thomas, *Sky Saga: A Story of Empire Airmen*. Melbourne: Hutchinson & Co (Publishers) Ltd, 1943.

Wickham, Syd, *We Wore Blue: A Diary of RAAF Service*. Castlecrag: S. Wickham, 2000.

Williams, Louise, *A True Story of the Great Escape*. Crows Nest: Allen & Unwin, 2015.

Winn, Richard, *A Fighter Pilot's Diary of World War 2*. Sydney: the author, 2003.

Wotherspoon, Garry, *'City of the Plain': History of a Gay Sub-Culture*. Sydney: Hale & Iremonger, 1991.

Younger, Cal, *Get a Load of this: A Cartoon Record of Active and Inactive Service*. Middle Park: CH Younger, [c. 1947].

Younger, Calton, *No Flight From the Cage: The Compelling Memoir of a Bomber Command Prisoner of War during the Second World War*. [No place]: Fighting High, 2013.

Articles

Absalom, Roger, '"Another crack at Jerry"?: Australian Prisoners of War in Italy 1941–45', *Journal of the Australian War Memorial*, No. 14, April 1989, 24–32.

Ackerknecht, Erwin H., 'The History of Psychosomatic Medicine', *Psychological Medicine*, No. 12, 1982, 17–24.

Alexander, Kristen, 'Australian Knights of the Air and their Little Touches of Chivalry', *Sabretache: the Journal of the Military Historical Society of Australia*, Vol. 53, No. 4, December 2012, 4–14.

——, 'Miss Celia Macdonald of the Isles "who has been a particularly good friend"', *Sabretache: the Journal of the Military Historical Society of Australia*, Vol. LIV, No. 3, September 2013, 15–25.

——, 'The Legacy of Captivity', *Wartime*, No. 95, Winter 2021, 54–58.

——, 'The "Kriegie" Personalkarte', *Iron Cross*, Vol. 15, December 2022, 88–97.

Alexander, Kristen and Ariotti, Kate, 'Mourning the Dead of the Great Escape: POWs, Grief, and the Memorial Vault of Stalag Luft III', *Journal of War and Culture Studies*, 2022, <http://dx.doi.org/10.1080/17526272.2022.2097774>.

Barraclough, B., Bunch, J., Nelson, B., and Sainsbury, P., 'A Hundred Cases of Suicide: Clinical Aspects', *British Journal of Psychiatry*, Vol. 125, 1974, 355–373.

Carson, John, 'Brisbane's Ken Carson: Prisoner of the Axis. Part Two. From Alexandria to Tobruk', *Barbed Wire and Bamboo. Official Organ Ex-Prisoners of War Association of Australia*, Vol. 69, No. 3, June 2017, 19–22.

——, 'Brisbane's Ken Carson: Prisoner of the Axis. Part Four. From Sulmona as an Italian

POW to Ford Bismarck as a German POW", *Barbed Wire and Bamboo. Official Organ Ex-Prisoners of War Association of Australia*, Vol. 69, No. 6, December 2017, 24–29.

——, 'Brisbane's Ken Carson: Prisoner of the Axis. Part Nine. Induction and Orientation, Stalag Luft 3 Style', *Barbed Wire and Bamboo. Official Organ Ex-Prisoners of War Association of Australia*, Vol. 71, No. 3, June 2019, 21–25.

——, 'Brisbane's Ken Carson: Prisoner of the Axis. Part Ten. Kriegies Didn't Live for Food Alone', *Barbed Wire and Bamboo. Official Organ Ex-Prisoners of War Association of Australia*, Vol. 71, No. 4, August 2019, 19–23.

——, 'Brisbane's Ken Carson: Prisoner of the Axis. Part Eleven. The Daily Grind and Ken's Night on the Hooch', *Barbed Wire and Bamboo. Official Organ Ex-Prisoners of War Association of Australia*, Vol. 71, No. 5, October 2019, 15–18.

Cochrane, A.L., 'Notes on the Psychology of Prisoners of War', *The British Medical Journal*, Vol. 1, No. 4442, 23 February 1946, 282–284.

Cuomo, Alessandro, Giordano, Nicola, Goracci, Arianna, and Fagiolini, Andrea, 'Depression and Vitamin D Deficiency: Causality, Assessment, and Clinical Practice Implications', *Neuropsychiatry (London)*, Vol. 7, No. 5, 2017, 606–614.

Drummond, John J., 'Respect as a Moral Emotion: A Phenomenological Approach', *Husserl Studies* 22, 2006, 1–27.

Edlington, David, 'The Great Escape Recalled: 60 years on, survivors tell of famous breakout', *Air Force News: The Official Newspaper of the Royal Australian Air Force*, Vol. 46, No. 4, 25 March 2004.

Farber, Leslie H. and Micon, Leonard, 'Gastric Neurosis in a Military Service', *Psychiatry Interpersonal and Biological Processes*, Vol. 8, No. 3, 1945, 343–361.

Gould, A.H., 'Those Icarian Rustics: Reminiscence of an "Old Boy" AH Gould', *HAC Journal*, December 1998, 10–11.

Gunderson, Brian S., 'Pilot Officer Prune, Royal Air Force: "Dutiful but Dumb"', *Air Power History*, Winter 1990, 23–29.

Hadaway, Stuart 'Identification methods of the Royal Air Force Missing Research and Enquiry Service, 1944–52', *Forensic Science International*, Vol. 318, January 2021, 1–9.

Hall, Kevin T., 'Luftgangster over Germany: The Lynching of American Airmen in the Shadow of the Air War', *Historical Social Research*, Vol. 43, No. 2, 2018, 277–312.

Jones, Edgar, '"LMF": The use of Psychiatric Stigma in the Royal Air Force during the Second World War', *The Journal of Military History*, Vol. 70, April 2006, 439–458.

Jones, Edgar and Wessely, Simon, 'British Prisoners-of-War: From Resilience to Psychological Vulnerability: Reality or Perception', *Twentieth Century British History*, Vol. 21, No. 2, 2010, 163–183.

Jones, Priscilla Dale, 'Nazi Atrocities against Allied Airmen: Stalag Luft III and the End of British War Crimes Trials', *The Historical Journal*, Vol. 41, No. 2, June 1998, 543–565.

Karageorgos, Effie, 'The Bushman at War: Gendered Medical Responses to Combat Breakdown in South Africa, 1899–1902', *Journal of Australian Studies*, Vol. 44, No. 1, 2020, 18–32.

Macleod, A.D., 'The reactivation of post-traumatic stress disorder in later life', *Australian and New Zealand Journal of Psychiatry*, Vol. 28, 1994, 625–634.

Mahoney, Ross, 'Trenchard's Doctrine: Organisational Culture, the "Air Force Spirit" and the Foundation of the Royal Air Force in the Interwar Years', *British Journal for Military History*, Vol. 4, No. 2, February 2018, 143–177.

Main, T.F., 'Clinical Problems of Repatriates', *Journal of Mental Science*, Vol. 93, No. 391 April 1947, 354–363.

McCarthy, John, 'Aircrew and "Lack of Moral Fibre"', *War & Society*, Vol. 2, No. 2, September 1984, 87–101.

Newman, P.H., 'The Prisoner-of-War Mentality: Its Effect After Repatriation', *The British Medical Journal*, Vol. 1, No. 4330, 1 January 1944, 8–10.

Page, Charles, 'Centenarian Great Escaper: Pilot Officer Paul Royle', *Britain at War*, No. 88, August 2014, 33–39.

Paris, Michael, 'The Rise of the Airmen: The Origins of Air Force Elitism, c. 1890–1918', *Journal of Contemporary History*, Vol. 28, 1998, 123–141.

Rachamimov, Alon, 'Disruptive Comforts of Drag: (Trans)Gender Performances among Prisoners of War in Russia, 1914–1920', *The American Historical Review*, Vol. 111, No. 2, 1 April 2006, 362–382.

Rosenthal, Carolyn J. and Marshall, Victor W., 'Generational Transmission of Family Ritual', *The American Behavioural Scientist*, Vol. 31, No. 6, July/August 1988, 669–684.

Rozanov, Vsevolod and Carli, Vladimir, 'Suicide Among War Veterans', *International Journal of Environmental Research and Public Health*, Vol. 9, 2012, 2504–2519.

Segovia, Francine, Moore, Jeffrey L., Linnville, Steven E., Hoyt, Robert E., and Hain, Robert E., 'Optimism Predicts Resilience in Repatriated Prisoners of War: A 37-Year Longitudinal Study', *Journal of Traumatic Stress*, Vol. 25, June 2012, 330–336.

Smith, Barbara, Parsons, Matthew, and Hand, Jennifer, 'War Leaves an Enduring Legacy in Combatants' Lives', *Journal of Gerontological Social Work*, Vol. 58, No. 8, 2014, 790–809.

Stephenson, Eric, 'Experiences of a Prisoner of War: World War 2 in Germany', *Journal of Military and Veterans' Health*, Vol. 18, No. 2, April 2010, 27–34 (reprinted from *Australian Military Medicine*, Vol. 9, No. 1, 2000, 42–50).

Ursano, Robert and Rundell, James, 'The Prisoner of War', *Military Medicine*, Vol. 155, No. 4, April 1990, 176–180.

Vance, Jonathan F., 'The War Behind the Wire: The Battle to Escape from a German Prison Camp', *Journal of Contemporary History*, Vol. 28, No. 4, October 1993, 675–693.

Walzer, Michael, 'Prisoners of War: Does the Fight Continue after the Battle?', *The American Political Science Review*, Vol. 63, 1969, 777–786.

Wang, Wei-Feng, Guo, Xiao-Xu and Yang, Yun-Sheng, 'Gastrointestinal problems in modern wars: clinical features and possible mechanisms', *Military Medical Research*, Vol. 2, No. 15, 2015.

Werden, Meghan Rieu, 'Is it All in Your Mind? Gastrointestinal Problems, Anxiety and Depression', *Undergraduate Review*, Vol. 5, 2009, 113–118.

Whiles, W.H., 'A Study of Neurosis among Repatriated Prisoners of War', *The British Medical Journal*, Vol. 2, No. 4428, 17 November 1945, 697–698.

Whittaker, Mark, 'The Men Marked X', *The Australian Magazine*, 26–27 March 1994, 38–41.

Wilcox, Craig, 'Paul Brickhill's War of Nerves', *State Library of New South Wales Magazine*, Winter 2012, 30–31.

Theses and Unpublished Reports

Alexander, Kristen Margaret, 'Emotions of Captivity: Australian Airmen Prisoners of Stalag Luft III and their Families'. PhD Thesis, University of NSW, 2020.

Bomford, Janette, 'Fractured Lives: Australian Prisoners of War of the Japanese and their Families', PhD thesis, Deakin University, 2001.

Gibbens, Trevor C.N., 'The Psychology and Psychopathology of the Prisoner-of-War', MD thesis, University of Cambridge, 1947.

Johnson, Matthew, 'Resisting Captivity: An Analysis of the New Zealand POW Experience During World War Two', PhD thesis, University of Waikato, 2018.

Meale, Katie, 'Leadership of Australian POWs in the Second World War', PhD thesis, University of Wollongong, 2015.

Whitehead, Eileen, 'World War II Prisoner of War Visual Art: Investigating its Significance in Contemporary Society', Honours thesis, Edith Cowan University, 2009.

Film/TV/Documentary

Enemy Interrogation of Prisoners, 1940, produced by Gee Films Ltd, directed by Aveling Ginever. <https://www.youtube.com/watch?v=KoXQIcgMEhs>.

Lost Airmen of Buchenwald, 2011. Directed by Michael Dorsey.

Internet sources

Alexander, Kristen, 'Australian compass makers and more', <http://australiansinsliii.blogspot.com/2016/08/australian-compass-makers.html>.

——, '"How deeply we feel his loss": Condolences to William Mercer Catanach, on the death of his son, Jimmy', <http://australiansinsliii.blogspot.com.au/2016/11/how-deeply-we-feel-his-loss-condolences.html>.

——, 'Jimmy Catanach and Heather Ebbott', <https://australiansinsliii.blogspot.com/2016/10/jimmy-and-heather.html>.

—— 'Thomas Barker Leigh', <https://kristenalexanderauthor.blogspot.com/2014/10/thomas-barker-leigh.html>.

—— "' For you the war is (not) over": Active disruption in the barbed wire battleground', *From Balloons to Drones*, <https://balloonstodrones.com/2017/12/18/for-you-the-war-is-not-over-active-disruption-in-the-barbed-wire-battleground/>.

Australian Dictionary of Biography (ADB):

Wilcox, Craig, 'Brickhill, Paul Chester (1916–1991)', <http://adb.anu.edu.au/biography/brickhill-paul-chester-14647>.

Johnson, Bob, 'From Choirboy to Dogfighter', <https://www.smh.com.au/national/from-choirboy-to-dogfighter-20070929-gdr816.html>.

The US Militaria Forum, 'Stalag Luft III "I Wanted Wings"', <http://www.usmilitariaforum.com/forums/index.php?/topic/6728-stalag-luft-iii-i-wanted-wings/>.

The Wartime Memories Project – The Second World War Sgt. C. Alf Miners <https://www.wartimememoriesproject.com/ww2/view.php?uid=500963>.

INDEX

11 Personnel Despatch and Receiving Centre, 11 Personnel Despatch and Receiving Centre, Brighton (11 PDRC)   98, 189
106 Personnel Reception Centre, Cosford (106 PRC)   98, 189
Abwehr   5, 108, 186,
Adams, Denis Gordon   53
Adams, Herbert   53
Air Publication 1548   16, 17, 87, 88, 94, 126
Altruism   XIV, XVIII, 19, 20, 36, 59, 132, 137, 182, 184
Amos, Isabel   132
Amos, Norman Newell (Bill)   132, 192
Anderson, George Robert (Bob)   8, 36
Anderson, Thelma   130, 131
Anzac Day   128, 149
Archer, Frederick   55
Archer, George Alfred   44, 46, 59, 70, 71, 76, 77, 83, 102, 157, 159, 169, 186, 190
Archibald, Margaret   59
Armytage, Peter Charles Tustin   37
Arnel, Alexander Francis (Alec)   XV, 1, 6, 9, 10, 14, 24, 28, 34, 35, 39, 44, 62, 65, 68, 69, 72, 76, 86, 99, 150, 151, 154, 156, 157, 160, 162, 164, 165, 167, 168, 172, 182, 184, 186, 189, 190, 191–192, 194, 196, 197, 198
Austin, Rex Alan   10, 17, 18, 26, 35, 36
Baines, Irene   11, 64–65, 66, 67, 82, 159, 163, 189
Baines, Ronald Prior   10–11, 15, 16, 20, 23, 29, 31, 32, 63, 64–65, 66, 67, 68, 75, 76, 77, 82, 87, 125, 128, 129, 159, 160, 163, 167, 175, 178, 181, 183, 184, 185, 186, 189
Berry, Graham Royston   17, 155
Betts, Reverend Walter   51, 53
Betts, Wesley Hirst   10, 183, 186
Bjelke-Petersen, Harold Ridley   101, 159, 162
Bligh, Margaret (née Leigh)   134, 136
Boomerang Club   33–34
Borsht, Cyril (Cy)   5, 10, 12, 17, 18, 27, 35, 59, 88, 89, 95, 153, 186, 198
Bowden, Huie James Westland   156, 159, 162, 165, 166, 167, 169, 175, 182, 183, 185–186

Bradford, Mervyn   24
Brandon, Cedric (pseudonym)   9, 17, 99
Braune, Werner   175
Breheny, Ross Thomas   4, 30, 186
Brickhill, Paul Chester Jerome   XV, 31, 78–79, 80, 83, 99, 100, 105, 124, 128, 152, 154, 157, 158, 161, 167, 170–171, 189, 192
Bridges, Barry (pseudonym)   157
Bristow, John   47
Brown, Kingsley   80
Bryce, John Magarey (Jock)   2, 5, 11–12, 24, 34–35, 38, 70, 71, 92, 93, 103, 156, 166, 167
Buchenwald Concentration Camp   2, 5, 9, 23, 36, 67, 68, 82, 83, 88, 100, 152, 153, 158, 165, 184, 191, 193
Bull, Leslie   114, 115, 120
'Bullet Decree'   88, 89, 112
Bushell, Roger Joyce (Big 'X')   29, 90–91, 92, 102, 105, 112, 126
Calver, Michael   38
Cameron, Cecil William Francis   8
Camp Welfare Fund   37
Carmody, Douglas Keith (Keith)   24, 71, 77, 154–155, 161, 190
Carson, John   60
Carson, Kenneth Francis (Ken)   2, 5, 12–13, 27, 60, 89, 181, 182, 183, 190
Casey, Michael   114
Catanach, James (Jimmy)   XV, XVI, 8, 23, 30, 36, 42, 63, 90, 103, 104, 105, 106, 107, 108, 112, 113, 115–119, 124, 131, 133, 134, 135, 136, 137–138, 141, 142, 144, 146
Catanach, Sybil   63, 138, 144–145
Catanach, William   63, 133, 134, 135, 136, 138, 143, 145
Catanach, William Alan (Bill)   104, 145
Charles, Evelyn   52, 53, 56, 62, 68, 152, 189, 190, 195
Christensen, Arnold   106–107, 108, 113, 115–117
Comber, Albert Henry   14, 72, 89, 98, 100, 107, 160, 162, 168, 169, 170, 182, 187, 188
Committee of Adjustment   123

Cook, Emmet 26
Coombes, Geoffrey Bernard 13, 99
Cordes, Erich 107, 121, 175
Cornish, Geoffrey James (Geoff, Cherub) 10, 29, 35, 92, 126, 157, 161, 179, 191
Crawley, Aiden 91, 97
Cross, Ian 114
Da Silva, John 135–136
Dack, Irwin John (John) 5, 8, 23, 35, 40, 44, 149, 175, 179, 194
Davidson, John 8–9
Day, Harry Melville Arbuthnot (Wings) 29, 58, 90, 92, 96, 97, 126, 137, 138
Deans, James (Dixie) 29
Delousing Escape 92
Denkmann, Artur 113, 116
Department of Veterans' Affairs (DVA) (Repatriation Department) XVII, 198
Derrett, Mark (pseudonym) 187
Dixon, Patrick Leslie (Les) 39, 98, 100
Dominion and Allied Services Hospitality Scheme 59, 191
'Donald Duck' 26, 32
Dulag Luft 15–20, 21, 23, 28
Dunn, Norman Maxwell (Max) 25, 33, 62, 68, 150, 168, 194
Ebbott, Heather 63, 135
Eden, Anthony 130, 143, 146
Enemy Interrogation of Prisoners (training film) 16, 19
Espelid, Halldor 108, 113, 115–117
Everton, Frank (pseudonym) 198
Falkiner, Fraser 176
Ferres, Torres Davey 16, 17, 19, 24, 45, 103
Ferry, Roderick Roland 46
Foodacco 33, 36
Fordyce, Horace Spencer Wills (Bill) 2, 25, 30, 38, 44, 46, 60, 69, 71, 72, 75, 76, 77, 79, 82, 86, 89, 98, 103, 107, 127, 154, 160, 174, 182, 183, 185, 186, 187, 188, 192–193, 198
Fotheringham, Alison 59–60
Fotheringham, Barbara 59–60
Fotheringham, Nellie 59–60
Fox, Del 83, 154
Fraser, Augustus Charles (Gus) 58
Fraser, Donald Ian 23, 51, 52, 53, 198
Fraser, Ella 131, 132, 134

Fraser, Ian 23
Fraser, May 51, 52, 53, 59
Fry, Charles Horace 53, 54, 55, 56, 57, 59, 62, 63, 65, 66, 69, 194, 196
Fugelsang, Nils 108, 113, 115–117, 136
'Führer order' ('Sagan order') 112
Garside, Ted 51, 52
Gaulton, Kenneth James Frederick 18, 30, 71, 80, 94, 184
Geneva Convention (1929) XIV, 4, 9, 12, 16, 17, 19, 23, 24, 37, 45, 109, 111, 121, 124, 131
Gestapo 2, 9, 13, 18, 107, 108, 113, 114, 115, 116, 117, 143, 144, 145, 146, 152, 153
Gibbs, Dot and Harold 59
Giddey, Reginald (Reg) 9, 70, 92, 121,
Glemnitz, Hermann 92
Gordon, James Anthony Cathcart (Tony) 25, 27, 36, 37, 42, 44, 47, 48, 165, 167, 182, 184, 188
Göring, Hermann 108, 143
Gray, Margery 65, 68, 69, 151, 154, 156, 169, 189, 190, 191, 192, 194, 195
Great Escape (March 1944 mass escape) XV–XVI, XVIII, 17, 42, 97, 98, 99, 102–110, 118, 119, 124, 126, 139, 143, 149, 171, 172, 176
Great Escape, The (book) XIII, XV, XVI, 78, 79, 97, 171
Great Escape, The (film) XIII, XVI
Green, Errol Edward 16, 54, 150, 151, 182, 194
Green, Eva 54, 151, 182
Grey-Smith, Guy 63–64, 69, 100, 150–151, 159, 160, 169
Grey-Smith, Helen 63–64, 69, 150, 159
Grossfahndung 108
Hake, Albert Horace XVI, 4, 6, 47, 62, 63, 64, 65, 66, 67, 69, 70, 103, 104, 105, 106, 107, 108, 111, 112, 113–114, 117, 122, 124, 136, 139, 141, 142, 144, 149, 171–172
Hake, Noela 62, 63, 64, 65, 66, 67, 69, 70, 104, 123, 125, 130, 131, 132, 133, 135, 134, 136, 137, 138–139, 142, 145, 149, 171–172
Hall, Clive Mayor 162
Hallam, Robert Kay 132
Handle with Care (by Robert Anderson and David Westmacott) 75
Hanrahan, Sean (pseudonym) 12, 87, 100, 179
Hänsel, Richard 114, 144
Harsh, George 96, 97
Hawke, William Charles 184

Hayes, John   8
Henderson, Oliver (pseudonym)   152
Henry, Edith   182
Henry, Hector Jerese (Hec)   1, 92, 168, 182, 185
Hibbert, Arnold (pseudonym)   165
Hitler, Adolf   XVI, 108, 109, 186
Hohemark Clinic, Frankfurt   12, 18
Homosexuality   XIV, XVII, 71–72, 76, 77, 78–81, 97
Humphreys, Edgar   103, 106, 107, 108, 111
Hunnicutt, Hubert (pseudonym)   162, 172
Hutchinson, Douglas Frank (Doug)   18, 24, 46, 52, 55, 56–57, 58, 59, 62–63, 64, 67, 69, 74, 76–77, 78, 79, 81–82, 83, 94, 101, 157, 160, 166, 167, 168, 182, 187, 193
Hutchinson, Lola   51, 52, 55, 56–57, 58, 59, 61, 62–63, 64, 67, 69, 74, 77, 81, 83, 160, 166, 182, 187, 193
Imperial (later Commonwealth) War Graves Commission   135–136, 145
Jacobs, Walter   113, 116, 117, 144
James, Bertram (Jimmy)   97
Johnston, Eric   51, 52, 56, 62, 68, 88, 89, 152–153, 184, 189, 191, 195
Johnston, Sophie   51, 52
Jones, Malcolm John (Mac)   47, 126
Kaehler, Elly (Koester)   144–145
Kaehler, Hans   113, 116, 144–145
Keitel, Wilhelm   108, 109, 117, 143
Kelly, Vivian   123
Kerr, Alexander McBride (Alex)   11, 37, 39, 81, 82, 93, 100, 151, 152, 158, 165, 173, 197
Kerwin, Basil Virgil   53, 55
Kerwin, Lola   53, 55, 59
Kierath, Ada   43, 123, 131, 133, 136, 137, 138, 145, 171
Kierath, Bert   131
Kierath, Reginald Victor (Reg, Rusty)   XVI, 36, 43, 44, 45, 47, 48, 71, 103, 104, 105, 106, 107, 108, 112, 113, 114–115, 117, 120, 124, 126, 133, 137, 138, 141, 144, 171
Kirby-Green, Tom   112
Klim Klub   87, 181
Kloster, William Gordon   149
Kriegie (origin of nickname)   XVI, 28
Kriegie Ingenuity   43–47, 185
Kriegsgefangener   XVI, 28
Kriminalpolizei (Criminal Police)   108, 112, 113, 115, 117, 143
Lack of Moral Fibre (LMF)   11–12, 158
Lambie, Hugh Tannahill   44, 92, 98, 184, 190
Lane, Gerard (pseudonym)   99
Langslow, Melville   145
Lark, Charles Roland   1, 8, 20, 35, 60–61, 83, 100, 137, 153, 156–157, 169
Leigh, David   134
Leigh, Margaret (Bligh)   134, 136
Leigh, Thomas Barker (Tom)   XVI, 58, 84, 103, 104, 105, 106, 107, 108, 110, 111, 112, 113, 114, 117, 124, 134, 136, 141, 144
Leu, Rudolph Maurice   86, 89
Lietke, John   183
Light, Kevin William   13
Long, Jennifer   198
Longworth, Harold Leonard Edward   54
Luftgangster   12, 27
Lumsden, Bruce Clyde   5, 16, 19, 27–28, 35, 44, 86, 93, 150, 154, 166
Lux, Walter   114, 144
Lynchjustiz   13, 27
McCleery, James   26, 54, 60, 75, 88, 89, 154, 166
McCleery, Laura   54
McConchie, Douglas   149, 177
McEachern, Hazel   131, 134
McEachern, Malcolm   131, 134
McGrath, Simon (pseudonym)   1, 148
McInnes, Alan Fithie   13
McIntosh, Ian Alexander (Digger)   36, 92
McKechnie, John Philip (Jock)   102
Mackenzie, Ronald Charles (Ron)   13, 40, 72, 77, 79, 81, 87, 96, 101, 167, 169, 178, 190, 194
McLeod, Douglas Burton   17
McSweyn, Allan   92
Marshall, Henry   111
Massey, Herbert Martin (Martin)   29, 90, 121, 122, 158, 177
Matthews, George   160, 161, 167, 170, 175, 176, 177
Mayo, Timbury Alan (Tim)   37, 41, 43, 58, 168, 188, 198, 200–201
Melville, William   60, 133, 138
Memorial Vault   125–126, 127, 135–136
Mental health   XVII, 156–179, 198
Merten, Hans   112–113
MI9 (British Directorate of Military Intelligence)

28, 88, 89, 91, 92
Mills, Keith Cyril   67, 153, 184, 186
Mills, Robert Neil   23, 158
Miners, Clarence Alfred (Alf)   92
Mohr, Peter   113
Mondschein, Jerzy   114, 115, 120
Morale   15, 20, 25, 28, 29, 30, 70, 87, 93, 126, 155, 161, 173, 174, 183, 185
Morschel, John (Jack)   3, 11–12, 39, 149
Mosse, Wilfred (pseudonym)   38
Mulligan, Alan Roy   44, 182
Mulligan, Eulalie   44, 55, 61, 182
Munt, Winifred   63, 135
'Murder Inc' / 'Der Mord Verein' / 'the murder club'   27, 28
Myatt, Marcus (pseudonym)   11, 160,
Naville, Gabriel   124
Nebe, Arthur   112–113
Nelson, Earle Milton   157
Netherway, Leonard James (Len)   46, 68, 103, 126, 169
Netherway, Mavis   68, 103
Nightingale, Robert Roy (Roy)   29, 150, 167, 182
Norton, Conrad   124, 167, 189
O'Byrne, Anne   197
O'Byrne, Justin Hilary   39, 40, 45, 54, 79, 80, 81, 87, 90, 93, 98, 100, 102–103, 105, 107, 108, 122, 125, 126, 155, 159, 160, 183, 184, 197
Officer, Terence Leslie William   96, 97, 101
Ogilvie, Keith   111
Osborn, Richard Bentley   79, 81
Osborne, John Carlisle   27, 37, 46, 53, 159, 164, 165
Osborne, Julia   53
Page, Dominic   70
Paton, Barbara   62, 68
Patton, Rodney (pseudonym)   184, 191
Phelps, Colin Gregory   159, 164, 165, 185, 187
Phelps, Walter   53
Playoust, Roger   161, 176
Pohe, Porokoru Patapu (Johnny)   107, 108, 111, 112, 114
Pollard, Freda   53
Portal, Sir Charles   133
Porter, David   71
Post, Johannes   113, 115–116, 119, 144, 145
Poulton, Bill   55
Poulton, Warwick Brian   55
Power, Dorrie   51–52, 53
Preen, Ray   139
Prisoner of War Camps
- *Marlag und Milag Nord*   185
- Oflag VI-B, Warburg   100, 160
- Oflag X-C, Lübeck   39, 90, 100
- Oflag XXI-B, Schubin   90, 159
- PG 19, Bologna   89
- PG 35, Padula   2
- PG 57, Gruppignano   2
- PG 75, Bari   2
- PG 78, Sulmona   2, 89
- Stalag III-A Luckenwalde   185, 186, 187
- Stalag III-E, Kirchhain   100, 165
- Stalag VIII-B, Lamsdorf   92, 170,
- Stalag VIII-C, Sagan   3
- Stalag 357, Fallingbostel   181, 184
- Stalag Luft I, Barth   3, 28, 47, 90, 95, 165
- Stalag Luft III, Sagan   (throughout)
- Stalag Luft VI, Heydekrug (later Thorn)   4, 33, 35, 81, 93, 96, 181
Prisoner of War Relatives' Association (POWRA)   57, 58, 59, 61, 137
Protecting Powers   4, 24, 162, 170, 172, 175, 176, 177
'Prune, Pilot Officer Percy'   26, 76
Quinlan, Martin (pseudonym)   165
Red Cross   2, 4, 17, 20, 36, 39, 47, 53, 54, 58, 59, 60, 70, 75, 87, 125, 168, 155, 161, 162, 164, 185
Resilience   XIV, XVIII, 6, 25, 173, 179, 185, 197
Righetti, Alan   XV, 2, 12, 30, 33, 36, 40, 98, 99, 103, 107, 123–124, 126, 128, 146, 172, 182, 188, 189, 190
Righetti, Ethel   53
Royle, Paul Gordon   XVI, 5, 9, 30, 90, 93, 95, 103, 105, 106–107, 108, 111, 112, 113, 122, 169, 173, 178, 179, 187
Russell, George Gray   47, 105
Sanders, Paul   84
St Martin-in-the-Fields (Church)   132–133, 138, 143
Scangriff (scandal sheet)   86, 174
Scharpwinkel, Wilhelm   113–114, 144
Schmidt, Franz   113, 116, 144
Schmidt, Fritz   115, 116, 144

Schmidt, Oskar   113, 115, 116, 117, 144
Schrock, Arthur Reginald Britton   82
Seamer, Frederick   33, 93, 96
Self-interest   XVII, 91, 93, 176
Sex   XIV, XVII, 56–57, 62, 66, 71–73, 75–83, 169, 192
Shand, Michael   111
Shierlaw, John Gow   184
Simpson, Lorraine Joseph (Laurie)   2, 25, 37, 38, 44, 46, 76, 123
Smith, Alexander Henderson   45, 88
Smith, Beryl   53, 54, 55, 56, 57, 59, 61, 62, 63, 64, 65, 67, 69, 194, 196
Smith, Sydney (POWRA)   57
Spear, Reginald Sydney   34
Stalag Luft III compounds
- Belaria Satellite   5, 33–34, 46, 76, 79, 81, 86, 87, 91, 94, 101, 126, 149, 162, 170–171, 172, 178, 185
- Centre Compound   4, 5, 33, 36, 37, 47, 70, 81, 92, 93, 94, 96, 169, 184
- East Compound   4, 5, 36, 47, 84, 87, 102, 103, 149, 150, 164, 175, 177, 185
- North Compound   5, 29, 33, 37, 47, 86, 87, 91, 92, 96, 97, 98, 102–107, 115, 121, 122–123, 132, 137, 174, 176, 178, 185
Steele, Philip John Rupert   34
Stephenson, Eric   161, 162, 177–178, 179
Street, Sir Arthur   136–137
Street, Denys   136
Struve, Wilhelm   113, 116
Stubbs, Peter   47
Sumner, Robin (pseudonym)   100–101, 170
Sweanor, George   105
Swiss Legation   124, 125
'Tally Ho' organisation   96
Tavistock Clinic   78–79
Terrorflieger   12, 27
Theatre   46, 58, 69–73, 78, 79, 98, 164, 168
Thompson, Douglas   149, 177
Tin basher   46, 47, 188
Tobolska, Jadwiga   137
Tobolski, Paweł   112, 137
Todd, Wemyss Wylton   71, 125
Todd, William Kenneth (Ken)   45, 46–47, 91, 157, 186
Tonder, Ivo   114–115

Train, Henry Roland (Harry)   1, 23–24, 36, 58, 151–152, 167, 177, 178, 197
Trenchard, Air Marshal Sir Hugh   33
Trickett, William Alexander (Bill)   190
Vaughan, James Douglas   44
Vischer, Adolf   156, 158
Volksjustiz   12, 13
von Lindeiner, Friedrich Wilhelm von Lindeiner gennant von Wildau (referred to throughout as von Lindeiner)   3, 94, 107, 121, 175, 176
Walsh, Jennifer   35
War Crimes Interrogation Unit   113, 143
War Crimes Trials (Nuremberg and Hamburg)   113, 117, 143–144, 145
War Widows' Guild   136
White, Thomas   137–138
Wickham, Sydney Thomas (Syd)   178, 179
Wielen, Max   117
Wiley, George   112, 114, 123–124, 126
Williams, John Edwin Ashley (Willy)   XVI, 36, 47, 49, 103, 105, 106, 107, 108, 112, 113, 114–115, 117, 120, 124, 126, 134, 136, 140, 144, 145, 151
Williams, Louise   134, 145
Williams, Mildred   131, 132, 134, 136, 145, 151
Wilson, Douglas Ernest Lancelot (Del)   29, 33, 87, 124
Wilson, Samuel Kinnier   158
Winn, Betty   55
Winn, Richard William   15, 18, 27, 30, 55, 79, 80, 102, 148, 157, 179
Wood, Thomas Goddard (Tom)   10, 29–30, 47
Wood, Victor Thomas Lawrence   102
Wooden Horse Escape   47, 102
Wright, Kenneth Lindsay   53
'X' (or escape) organisation   29, 36, 37, 39, 47, 49, 86, 90, 91, 92, 94, 95, 96, 97, 98, 100, 101, 103, 104, 105, 126, 127, 162, 168, 170, 171, 172
'X' organisation departments:
- carpentry   47, 49, 92, 103, 105, 115, 126
- compass making   47, 103, 105, 171, 172
- forgery   92, 102, 105
- photography   92
- tailoring   47, 118
Yelland, Jean   61
Young, Digby Aretas   25–26, 58, 176
Younger, Calton Hearn (Cal)   25, 65, 71, 72, 75–76, 81, 156, 166, 175, 184, 192

EASTER EGG

After completing the index, we were left with a couple of blank pages. Rather than leave them in all their white glory, I decided to include a few extra words, rather like an 'Easter egg' – a hidden or unlisted track – on a record or CD.

We have read how the kriegies celebrated Christmas, but what about Easter, a suitable topic for an 'Easter egg'? Sadly, I found only a handful of Easter mentions in the personal collections I consulted. It seems as if Easter didn't have the same resonance for the majority as a time of Christian celebration but, for some, it provided a handy point of reference when recalling events.

For Geoff Cornish, it marked the beginning of captivity. He was 'marched off to a car … and taken away up to Amsterdam, and that was Easter Thursday 1941 … I spent Easter Thursday in gaol in Amsterdam'. Then, on Easter Monday, he was taken to Dulag Luft for interrogation. 'There they questioned you, tried to get information about you more than your name, rank and number but it was fairly easy to resist, there was no torture or anything like that. If you didn't answer you didn't answer.'

At PG 78, Sulmona in Italy, Albert Comber sent 'Easter greetings special thoughts' to his loved ones via the Vatican. He had been much cheered by the recent war news and, 'everyone of course wishes that the whole business would end very soon'. But when Easter 1943 came and went, 'one realised how quickly the months slip by – perhaps Christmas will see me home'. (It didn't; by that stage he was in Stalag Luft III.)

As we have seen, prisoners of war relied on humour to help them cope with a seemingly limitless captivity. And chocolate. Just after Easter 1943, Justin O'Byrne wrote to his family and told them how the Easter Monday sports day had been marred by the weather. Life, however, was not *too* bad in Stalag Luft III, he told them. 'I have become quite used to the diet now, but look forward to the chocolate in the clothing parcels … so bung in the chocolate for all you're worth.'

'Once more Easter is with us', George Archer wrote to his family in 1944, 'and I only trust the next service will be at St Marks', his local church. He was to be disappointed. He was still a prisoner of war at Easter 1945. By Easter 1946, however, the war was over and he and his fellows were free men at last.

I couldn't find any drawings relating to Easter in wartime log books but I am quite taken by this rendition of Bugs Bunny by Cy Borsht, poking fun of their kriegie accommodation.

Courtesy of Cy Borsht.

www.ingramcontent.com/pod-product-compliance
Lightning Source LLC
Chambersburg PA
CBHW051536010526
44107CB00064B/2742